The Rinehart ESL Workbook

The Rinehart ESL Workbook

Second Edition

Charles Hall

Memphis State University

Holt, Rinehart and Winston, Inc.

Fort Worth   Chicago   San Francisco   Philadelphia
Montreal   Toronto   London   Sydney   Tokyo

Designed and Typeset by: North 7 Atelier Ltd.

Printed in the United States of America

ISBN 0-03-032758-X

0 1 2 3   095   9 8 7 6 5 4 3 2 1

Holt, Rinehart and Winston, Inc.
The Dryden Press
Saunders College Publishing

Contents

Chapter 3   Adjectives and Adverbs   59

Chapter 4   Verbs and Verb Phrases   108

Chapter 5 Verbals and Verbal Phrases 147

5a. Infinitives and Infinitive Phrases 147

5b. Participles and Participial Phrases 147

5c. Gerunds and Gerund Phrases 148

5d. Absolute Phrases 149

Chapter 6 Function Words 164

6a. Prepositions and Prepositional Phrases 164
(1) The wrong preposition 164
(2) Unnecessary prepositions 166
(3) Forgotten prepositions 166

6b. Conjunctions 167
(1) Coordinating conjunctions 167
(2) Correlative conjunctions 167
(3) Subordinating conjunctions 168
(4) Comparative conjunctions 168

6c. Determiners 169
(1) The article system 169
(2) Possessive pronouns and possessives 174
(3) Demonstrative pronouns 175
(4) Indefinite pronouns 175
(5) Interrogative pronouns 177
(6) Cardinal numbers 178

6d. Expletives 179

Chapter 7 Clauses and Sentences 212

7a. Clause Patterns 212

7b. Independent Clauses 215

7c. Dependent Clauses 215
(1) Adverb clauses 215
(2) Adjective clauses 215
(3) Noun clauses 215

7d. Elliptical clauses 217

7e. Kinds of Sentences 219
(1) Simple sentences 219
(2) Compound sentences 219
(3) Complex sentences 219
(4) Compound-complex sentences 219

Part II   Revising Sentences: Structural and Grammatical Problems   247

Chapter 8   Sentence Fragments   248

Chapter 9   Comma Splices and Fused Sentences   258

Chapter 10   Subject-Verb Agreement   270

Chapter 22   Semicolons   383

Chapter 23   Colons   391

Chapter 24   Dashes, Parentheses, and Brackets   399

To the Instructor

Purpose and Design

The Rinehart ESL Workbook gives instructors and ESL (English as a Second Language) students exercises and explanations in those areas of writing which present challenges to non-native speakers of English. Since this workbook strives to meet the specific needs of ESL students, it expands and explores, in depth, topics which the handbook, designed for native speakers, needs to mention only in passing.

For those concerns which are almost exclusively ESL topics (such as article or preposition usage), the expanded explanatory materials allow the workbook to be used either by ESL specialists or composition instructors who have the occasional one or two international students in their classes. For more traditional topics, better handled by the handbook or instructor, little explanatory material is included.

Although the workbook parallels the organization of the first 39 chapters of the handbook, students can complete most exercises without referring to the handbook. Consequently, this workbook can serve as a tool in both the classroom and the writing lab.

The language of the exercises is usually moderately informal although references to appropriate usage are given when casual or overly formal forms are used. The vocabulary of the workbook's exercises is considerably simpler than that of the handbook's so that the students can clearly see the patterns which they are to uncover. However, since both workbook and handbook are designed for college-level composition classes, the students will encounter unabridged, realistic language.

Classroom or Lab Use

You are fortunate to be working with ESL students. You should think of these students as resources for insights into different ways of viewing and organizing the world. As you help ESL students enrich their abilities to communicate in English, remember that they are already members of complete cultures. Allow them to share their ideas and traditions with you and your English speaking students.

There are some basic guidelines to helping ESL students. First, recognize those grammatical errors which are peculiar to ESL students and are almost never made by native students. The most obvious are article usage and formation of verb forms. Since most ESL students will never completely master these areas, the sensible instructor will aim for reduction rather than elimination of these errors.

Second, make sure that ESL students have a conscious awareness of the patterns and principles of English grammar. This awareness is fostered by focused short repetitions of exercises emphasizing the regular forms rather than the exceptions. Unfortunately, most workbooks for native students emphasize the exceptions (for instance, *a bunch of roses is on the table*). This ESL workbook consists of very short exercises which concentrate on the regular patterns of English grammar.

Third, establish priorities and focus on one pattern error at a time. An ESL student has difficulty distinguishing between major errors which interfere with communication of ideas and minor errors which merely distract the reader. If you are unsure where to begin, you may wish to start with work on the count/mass distinction for nouns in Chapter 1. Then, you can continue on to Chapter 4 which introduces the regular patterns of the English verbal system. (From there, you may wish to consult the Contents for specific words or terms which trouble individual ESL students.)

Fourth, make ESL students revise. ESL students in particular learn English grammar at the revision stage of writing. The exercises in this workbook will make ESL students conscious of the patterns of English grammar, but only through revising sentences they have created will ESL students learn to incorporate these patterns effectively in their own compositions. Many ESL students are so concerned with grammatical errors that they forget that the purpose of writing is to communicate ideas. They must learn that the time to worry about grammatical correctness is once they have written a patch of English prose.

Teaching ESL students is not a matter of ignoring errors, but rather of teaching the ESL student to identify and correct those errors. ESL students, usually highly motivated, will repay the concerned teacher with solid work and with the traditional respect which most cultures afford the teaching profession.

I am grateful to the following colleagues for their helpful reviews of the manuscript: Robyn Browder, Tidewater Community College; Kathy Smith McCall, Gulf Coast Community College; Ziva Pilch, Pace University; Consuelo Stebbins, University Of Central Florida; Robert Viscount, Kingsborough Community College; Jean Zukowski-Faust, Northern Arizona University.

I am most indebted to the many students of English with whom I have worked who have allowed me to learn from them. I would like to thank my friends and colleagues in Memphis, Tennessee, and at Memphis State University for their support and advice: David Burton, Donald Carter, Marvin Ching, Teresa Dalle, Joseph Davis, Jeffrey Gross, Kevin Harper, Kathryn Helling, Jong Kim, William O'Donnell, Teresa Duma, and Magnolia Teh. In the preparation of the second edition Ron Metzler, Teresa Duma and Dawn Arrol were most helpful. A special note of thanks is due to Zeng Meili for her gracious comments and advice.

The staff at Holt, Rinehart and Winston deserve much thanks for their patient guidance and encouragement: Charlyce Jones Owen, Tod Gross, Lee Sutherlin, and Leslie Taggart.

Memphis, Tennessee
February 1988   C.H.

To the Student

You are reading this book for a purpose. You have something to say. The goal of all writing is communication, the communication of your ideas to someone else.

The goal of this workbook is to help you with matters of form, structure, and convention so that your reader or listener can concentrate on your ideas.

When you pick this book up, you might have a specific topic you have been assigned, or you might have been asking yourself questions about writing in English. It really doesn't matter which reason you have. You should still follow the same procedure.

First, use the table of contents to find the section of the book which seems to touch on your question. Sometimes your instructor will have already told you which sections you should review. Next, read through the explanations and the examples. Do the exercises in the workbook first. Then, try those in the handbook which relate to the same topic.

You will notice that the workbook contains exercises on topics which the handbook ignores. Those are areas which present challenges to English as a Second Language (ESL) students. You should concentrate on those areas.

The exercises are fairly short. It is important that you think each exercise through. Know why you are producing those forms or ideas. People are not parrots. We learn by thinking and analyzing. Isolated repetition and memorization will not help you improve your written or spoken English.

Finally, after you understand the concepts contained in a section, try to apply those concepts in your own compositions. Revision of your own compositions is the most important step in improving your English.

When a suggestion or correction is made in your composition, spend some time analyzing why you need to make a change. When you understand the *reason* for the change, make the revision. Keep your compositions in a folder if you are permitted to. When you work through a new section in the workbook or handbook, go back over a few of your old papers and revise a few sentences or paragraphs.

Communicating is hard work; communicating in a second language is even harder work. But it is also very rewarding when you finally know that someone else understands your ideas and thoughts.

Memphis, Tennessee   C.H.
July, 1989

Part I

□ Building Sentences: Words, Phrases, Clauses □

1

Nouns

1a. Proper and Common Nouns

Proper nouns are unique names and are always capitalized. They are *true* proper nouns if they are just sounds used as names. These words have no basic meaning.

George	Canada
Lee	Memphis

True proper nouns do not need *definite articles;* they are already definite.

Incorrect: *The* Canada is beautiful..

Other proper nouns are *derived* (formed) from common nouns and other words which already have general meanings.

General	Unique
states	the United States of America
ocean	the Indian Ocean
revenue	the Internal Revenue Service

Try Exercise 1-1 now.

Since these are unique, they are also *definite,* but we must show their definiteness with the *definite article.* (See THE ARTICLE SYSTEM, p. 169.)

Common nouns can be either *count* or *mass* nouns. Count nouns are nouns which can be counted; they have singular and plural forms.

Singular	Plural
one car	16 cars
a match	several matches

On the other hand, a mass noun **cannot** be counted; it has only a singular form although it can seem to refer to more than one object.

Mass
The agent had to talk to many people to get *new information.*
Everybody bought *some Basmati rice.*
Nobody likes to spend *much money* on food.

This distinction is very important in deciding which determiners, adjectives, and verb forms are used.

Try Exercise 1-2 now.

1b. Singular and Plural Nouns

Singular and plural nouns often interact differently with determiners, adjectives, and verbs. See those chapters for more information.

(1) Simple nouns

Most *count* nouns form their plurals by adding *-s*. However, several count nouns have the same form in both the singular and the plural.

<u>Singular</u>	<u>Plural</u>
a shrimp	six shrimp
one deer	many deer
that fish	those fish

Nonetheless, they are really plural. Remember that there are usually other clues (such as determiners or subject-verb agreement) in a sentence which allow you to decide if the noun is singular or plural.

Two very common nouns, *people* and *police,* are always plural even though they look like singular forms.

> The police *are* helpful.
> People *make* him happy.

Do Exercises 1-4 and 1-5.

(2) Count nouns

In English we **must** know if a count noun is singular or plural. If the count noun is plural, it does not need a *determiner,* a word which signals the presence of a noun (Section 6c).

> *Americans* can usually read and write.

However, we may use a *determiner* for other reasons.

> *Many* Americans can read and write a foreign language.

But if the count noun is singular, we **must** use a *determiner.*

> *An* American can usually read and write.

When we use a count noun in *questions* or *negatives* and we can't or don't need to specify an exact number, we normally use the plural form with the determiner *any* (see 6c).

> Does your family have any *pets?*
> I don't want any *rats* in my house.

Don't forget that *a* and *an* are really forms of *one*(1). When you use them, you have specified the number of the count noun.

> Do you want *a* dog? [Just *one* dog]
> She really doesn't need *an* injury in her career just now. [Just *one* injury]

Do Exercises 1-6 and 1-7 now.

1c. Possessive Nouns

It is very important to remember to add the *-s* ending on possessive nouns. Remember, the *owner* always is first.

Now do Exercises 1-8 and 1-9.

1d. Mass Nouns

Since mass nouns are very different from count nouns, you must be very careful that you learn just which nouns are mass nouns. Unfortunately, there is no formula; you must just learn them as you encounter them.

Although there is no formula to predict which nouns are mass nouns, there are tests to show if any specific noun is. If you see the noun modified by *much,* it is a mass noun.

> Bob spends too *much* money on clothes.

Try Exercises 1-3 and 1-10 now.

(1) Articles and mass nouns

Remember that the indefinite articles *a* and *an* are really forms of *one* (1). As a result, we cannot use mass nouns with these articles since we cannot count mass nouns.

Also, we do not use the definite article with mass nouns in English when we are speaking in general terms.

> *Correct:* Sugar is not always good for small children.
> *Incorrect:* *The* sugar is not always good for small children.

However, when we mean a specific example of a mass noun, we may use the definite article.

> *Correct:* *The* sugar I put into my coffee turned out to be salt.

Do Exercise 1-11.

(2) Determiners and mass nouns

Since mass nouns are always singular in form, we cannot use any of the determiners which count things.

> *Incorrect:* Both rice are ready. [*both* means *two*]

Try Exercise 1-12.

(3) Measure words for mass nouns

We can "count" nouns fairly easily.

> six geese   100 apples

But we must use special *measure words* when we are trying to "count" mass nouns.

> six *cartons* of milk   an *ear* of corn

Notice the pattern.

determiner	count noun	of	mass noun
an	*ear*		*corn*

This pattern allows us to "count" mass nouns. There are some very general measure words such as *bit* and *piece,* but often the measure words are very idiomatic and must be individually learned.

Now try Exercises 1-13 through 1-16.

(4) Subject-verb agreement and mass nouns

Since mass nouns are singular in form, they take singular verbs.

Current information *is* vital to our economy.

Even when they are modified by *percentages* or *fractions,* they are singular.

Eighty *percent* of the information *is* useful.
Fully *two-thirds* of the wheat *was* ruined by rats.

But if we use plural measure words, we must use a plural verb.

Six *cartons* of yogurt *were* broken in the kitchen.

Try Exercise 1-17 now.

(5) Using mass nouns as count nouns

Normally when we use a mass noun as a *count noun,* we mean it to be either *a kind of* or *a serving of* the mass noun.

These people brew a strange *tea*. [*tea* is normally mass]
These people brew a strange *kind of tea.*
Please bring me a *tea* from the machine.
Please bring me a *cup of tea* from the machine.

Try Exercise 1-18 now.

EXERCISE 1-1

NAME _____ **DATE**_____

Derive a proper noun from each noun with a general meaning.

Example: building   the Administration Building

1. house _____

2. canal _____

3. office _____

4. room _____

5. hotel _____

6. times (hint: newspaper) _____

7. street _____

8. college _____

9. states _____

10. university _____

Score _____

EXERCISE 1-2

NAME _____ DATE_____

Is each underlined noun a *proper, count,* or *mass* noun?

Example: The <u>man</u> likes to read <u>The New York Times</u> while drinking <u>coffee</u>.
<u>man</u> is a count noun
<u>The New York Times</u> (a newspaper) is a proper noun
<u>coffee</u> is a mass noun

1. Many <u>people</u> use <u>rice</u> to make <u>cabbage rolls</u>.

2. A <u>computer</u> can help your <u>staff</u> write better <u>newspapers</u>.

3. Here in <u>Tennessee</u>, <u>restaurants</u> serve <u>catfish</u> with <u>hush puppies</u>.

4. <u>Data</u> can be hard to interpret without the proper <u>statistics</u>.

5. If a <u>person</u> is smart enough, <u>information</u> can be had for the asking.

6. Ask the <u>waiter</u> to bring me a <u>glass</u> of <u>water</u>.

7. Those <u>kids</u> broke the <u>glass</u> in my <u>window</u>.

8. <u>Paper</u> is relatively cheap in <u>department stores</u>.

9. My <u>father</u> gives the <u>family</u> good <u>advice</u>.

10. The <u>saleswoman</u> told the <u>couple</u> that new <u>furniture</u> was expensive.

Score _____

EXERCISE 1-3

NAME _____DATE _____

Decide whether each underlined noun is a *singular, plural,* or *mass* noun. Remember, mass nouns are always "singular" in form.

Example: Sheep eat grass.
sheep—plural (note the plural verb form eat)
grass—mass

1. The men were amazed that they could catch so few fish with so much equipment.

    _____

2. In the kitchen, the class watched as milk was put into bottles._____

3. For the party, the servers put out big bowls of potato chips and popcorn.

    _____

4. Many fans circulated cool air and refreshing breezes through the enormous room.

    _____

5. The computer has made it easier for the police to gather information about people.

    _____

6. The kids were watching too much television._____

7. How often do most people need to get their hair cut? _____

8. The guest speakers were able to offer some really good advice. _____

9. The decorating firm tried to move the furniture again._____

10. Did the policeman bring the right equipment to do the job?_____

                                                              Score_____

EXERCISE 1-4

NAME _____ DATE_____

What is the plural form of each of these nouns?

Example: girl—girls

1. potato _____

2. house _____

3. mystery _____

4. wife _____

5. president _____

6. goose _____

7. judge _____

8. woman _____

9. lamp _____

10. bird _____

Score _____

EXERCISE 1-5

NAME _____DATE _____

What is the correct plural form of each of these compound nouns?

Example: mother-in-law   mothers-in-law

1. outlaw _____

2. bus station _____

3. newsman _____

4. cowboy _____

5. wheelchair _____

6. tablecloth _____

7. cab driver _____

8. television set _____

9. committee member _____

10. roller skate _____

Score _____

EXERCISE 1-6

NAME _____ DATE _____

Should there be a determiner in each blank?

Example: Does __(1)__ whale have __(2)__ scales?
1. Yes, a <u>whale</u> is singular.   2. No, <u>scales</u> are plural.

1. _____ newspapers were lying all over _____ floor.
       1.   2.

2. When _____ National Anthem is played, _____ people usually stand up.
            1.   2.

3. Have you ever heard _____ dog barking at _____ raccoons?
                          1.   2.

4. Ms. Atwood was selling _____ concert tickets at _____ cafe.
                            1.   2.

5. There really was _____ burglar hiding under _____ bed.
                       1.   2.

6. For _____ boys, _____fun was more important than _____ work.
         1.   2.   3.

7. Has _____ teacher shown you _____ texts you will be using?
         1.   2.

8. Why were there _____ potato chips all over _____ table?
                     1.   2.

9. Can _____ visiting writer also write _____ poetry?
         1.   2.

10. _____Visitors must sign in at _____ information desk.
        1.   2.

                                              Score _____

EXERCISE 1-7

NAME _____ DATE _____

Fill in the plural or singular form of the noun in parentheses. Why should that form be used?

Example: Maria doesn't want any (plant).
                  <u>plants</u> [unspecified number in negative]

1.   Maria doesn't want a single (plant).

2.   Do you have any (relative) in Cleveland?

3.   Why are they buying (banana)?

4.   I had never seen (race car) before.

5.   Where do they grow (mung bean) in Omaha?

6.   Have you ever seen an (elephant) before?

7.   Do you have any good (restaurant) in Albany?

8.   Don't buy (stock) right now.

9.   Since she started working hard, she hasn't had any (problem) with her homework.

10. The school rarely gives (scholarship) to rich people.

Score _____

EXERCISE 1-8

NAME _____ DATE _____

Make meaningful possessives from these words.

Example: the car/door
                  the car's door [the opposite <u>the door's car</u> is not very likely]

1. hands/Philip _____

2. the city/population _____

3. Andy/car _____

4. voice/James _____

5. the children/room _____

6. nest/the robins _____

7. the goat/horns _____

8. legs/a table _____

9. day/end _____

10. rice/protein content _____

Score _____

EXERCISE 1-9

NAME_____DATE_____

There are many missing possessive forms in these sentences. Rewrite these sentences with the correct form.

Example: my sister car
                    my *sister's* car

1. Do you know where my brother hat is?

2. I have never seen one of Neil Simon plays.

3. "A day pay for a day labor"

4. What is James last name?

5. Memphis population is almost 800,000.

6. She was taken to Doctors Hospital.

7. Where is the ladies room?

8. Where is the men room?

9. He had completely forgotten his mother-in-law birthday.

10. We really need to get the department chair permission to do that.

Score _____

EXERCISE 1-10

NAME _____DATE _____

Which of the following nouns are normally *mass* and which are *count*?

1. lotion _____

2. clothing _____

3. water _____

4. soda (pop)—soft drink _____

5. baking soda _____

6. information _____

7. marble (the stone) _____

8. news _____

9. furniture _____

10. rice _____

11. house _____

12. ink _____

13. luggage _____

14. equipment _____

15. marble (the toy) _____

16. bread _____

17. dinner roll _____

18. data [be careful] _____

Score _____

EXERCISE 1-11

NAME _____ **DATE** _____

If an indefinite article is needed, insert it; otherwise, put in an empty set (ø) to show that you know nothing *belongs* there.

1. When I drink _____ coffee, I like to put _____ milk and

   _____ sugar in it.

2. Then I also want _____ nice breakfast roll filled with _____

   honey and _____ butter.

3. Today, however, after I had finished _____ cup of coffee, there was

   _____ knock at _____ window.

4. I looked around to see which window it was. There in the window I could see

   _____ strange face looking at me.

5. I had fixed _____ bacon that morning and the sight of that face made me

   drop _____ strip of bacon on _____ clean clothing which I

   had just gotten out of the dryer.

6. I grabbed _____ piece of toast and threw it at the window.

7. I heard _____ loud laugh and the face was gone.

8. I have not had _____ moment's rest since then.

9. Whoever it was might return to give me _____ even bigger fright.

10. Since then, I have gathered _____ information on security systems.

                                                    Score _____

EXERCISE 1-12

Which of the following words and phrases count things and cannot be used with a mass noun? Provide a rough meaning of each.

Example: <u>a pair</u> can't because it means <u>two</u>

1. much

2. several

3. little

4. a little

5. many

6. every

7. all

8. each

9. a couple

10. a lot [only for extremely informal use]

11. few

12. a few

13. some

14. no

15. any

Score_____

EXERCISE 1-13

NAME_____ **DATE**_____

Fill in an appropriate measure word for each mass noun. There are often many correct answers.

Example: _____ of butter
                  <u>stick</u> of butter
                  <u>teaspoon</u> of butter

1. a _____ of bacon

2. two _____ of flour

3. a juicy _____ of gossip

4. a big _____ of beef

5. thirteen _____ of clothing

6. a good _____ of advice

7. several _____ of candy

8. a relevant _____ of information

9. many _____ of hair

10. six _____ of popcorn

Score _____

EXERCISE 1-14

NAME _____ DATE _____

Fill in an appropriate <u>mass noun</u> for each measure word.

Example: a pound of _____
a pound of <u>flour</u>

1. Open a jar of _____ for dinner.

2. She put six slices of fresh _____ on her sandwich.

3. Then the woman brought out an old bottle of homemade _____.

4. Can you cover a chair with a square yard of _____?

5. The merchants bought five metric tons of American _____ because of the

poor harvest in their country.

6. Several pieces of _____ fell from the window after the accident.

7. Give me a handful of _____ from your bowl!

8. Let me give you a good bit of _____ on how to succeed in this office.

9. If you hear a piece of _____ about things which don't concern you, forget

it immediately.

10. Since we don't have much money, we must buy one piece of _____ for

the living room at a time.

Score _____

EXERCISE 1-15

NAME _____ DATE _____

For many food items there are special measure words. We often use these special measure words even for some count nouns. Find out what the measure words for these nouns are.

Example: cabbage (real mass noun)
<u>a head</u> of cabbage (real measure word)
bananas (not a mass noun)
<u>a bunch</u> of bananas (not a real mass noun)

1. celery

2. lettuce

3. radishes

4. garlic

5. grapes

6. corn

7. bread

8. cauliflower

9. green onions

Score _____

EXERCISE 1-16

NAME _____**DATE** _____

There are some funny, old-fashioned measure words for *collectives* of animals.

> a *gaggle* of *geese*
> a *pride* of *lions*

Try to find a list of others in the library and write them here.

Score _____

EXERCISE 1-17

NAME _____ DATE _____

Would we use a plural or singular verb for each of these phrases?

Example: four slices of bacon   <u>plural</u>

1. one loaf of rye bread _____

2. two pounds of flour _____

3. a juicy bit of gossip _____

4. an enormous side of beef _____

5. thirteen tons of rice _____

6. a jar of mayonnaise _____

7. six slices of fresh tomato _____

8. an old bottle of homemade vinegar _____

9. several square yards of fabric _____

10. several pieces of onion _____

Score _____

EXERCISE 1-18

NAME _____ DATE _____

Rewrite the sentences so that the underlined nouns are used as mass nouns.

Example: The skinny man ate many <u>chocolates</u>.
            The skinny man ate many <u>pieces of chocolate</u>.

1. While I was in France, I had an interesting <u>wine</u>.

2. Along with the wine, I ate an interesting <u>bread</u>.

3. The bread seemed to be made of a <u>flour</u> I did not recognize.

4. The baker said it contained seven <u>grains</u>.

5. As I put three <u>sugars</u> in a <u>coffee</u> the baker gave me, I wondered if the bread would go with a <u>cheese</u> I had bought.

Score _____

2

Pronouns

Most pronouns are substitutes for nouns already mentioned in a conversation. The noun related to a pronoun is called the *antecedent*. The antecedent of any pronoun should always be clear to the reader or confusion can arise.

> My sisters went to stay with my cousins. But they hate them. (Is the antecedent for <u>they</u> *sisters* or *cousins?*)

In that example we cannot be sure just *who* hates *whom*. In Part II we will discuss ways to avoid these problems.

Do Exercise 2-1.

2a. Personal Pronouns

The personal pronoun system in English is much simpler than in many other languages. However, there are some problems which we will discuss in this section. The only formal difficulty is in the use of the few case forms which remain in Modern English (see Chapter 14).

(1) The "-self" personal pronouns

The *-self* pronouns are used when the subject of the sentence and an object refer to the same thing or group. This use is called the *reflexive*.

> *Jane* and *Alex* really know how to amuse *themselves*.
> *He* did it for *himself*.

In many parts of the United States, you will hear different reflexives.

> I'm going to buy *me* a new car.

That and other similar forms are not considered appropriate in writing or even in educated informal speech. Don't use them.

Many times reflexives are needed just to provide an object for a transitive verb (see Chapter 7). Some transitive verbs almost always occur in a reflexive situation.

> Bina was unable to *behave* herself.

At other times, the reflexive is used when the speaker doesn't really want or need to provide more specific information, but there must be an object for the transitive verb.

> We enjoyed *ourselves* at your party.

The speaker could also have said

> We enjoyed *the band* at your party.

There are two other major uses of the *-self* pronouns.

> *emphatic:* The duke *himself* will show us the castle. (Here emphasis is on the *duke.*)

> *adverbial:* No one helped her. It was difficult. But after years of backbreaking work, she can say she earned it *herself.* (This use excludes everyone else—similar to *by herself* or *alone.*

When used as an *emphatic,* the *-self* pronoun must follow the noun it emphasizes immediately. The *adverbial* use, however, must occur at the end of the clause which it "modifies."

Do Exercises 2-2 through 2-4.

(2) Gender of personal pronouns

Only in the third person singular (just *one* person or thing) for people and some animals do we need to refer to gender—the sex of the object or person.

> Sabina is a physicist, but *she* also drives race cars.
> Frank lives in Rome, but *he* is studying in Florence.
> The tree produced many apples, but we still cut *it* down.

Notice that in the last example the tree was clearly female, but in English we care only about the gender of people and some (usually domestic) animals. Everything else is *it,* although sometimes people still use *she* for ships, some countries, and cars that are special to their owners. However, you should always use *it* for these things.

Try Exercise 2-5.

(3) Possessive pronouns

The possessive pronouns (except *his*) have two forms to signal two different functions. First, possessive pronouns function as possessive *determiners* before a noun.

> *her* bike

When the possessive pronoun functions as a determiner, we still need the base noun.

> *Jamal's* composition   *his* composition

Do Exercise 2-6.

But a possessive pronoun can also substitute for the *possessed*.

> I haven't read *Jamal's composition* yet.   (I haven't read *his* yet.)

To show that we are using the possessive pronouns as pronouns, we must use a slightly different form. For the most part, this form is made by adding the possessive marker -s (without the apostrophe) to the determiner forms.

Determiner	Pronoun
your	yours
her	hers
our	ours
their	theirs

What happens when we try to add the -s to *his* and *its?*

his	his
its	its (This form is never used today.)

They, of course, stay the same since they already have an -s. Only one form is really different.

Determiner	Pronoun
my	mine

Although there is a historically valid reason why this form is used, just learn it as an exception.

Even though you will hear native speakers of American English use other forms such as *mines* and *hises,* don't use them.

Do Exercise 2-7 now.

(4) Dummy pronouns

English requires that every clause have a subject. Sometimes we must use *dummy pronouns,* pronouns that have no antecedents, to fulfill that need.

> *It* has been snowing for three days now.

Dummy pronouns are usually needed for expressions of distance, time, or weather. (See Chapter 8 for more information.)

Try Exercise 2-8.

2b. Demonstrative Pronouns

The demonstrative pronouns are really the determiners *this / these* and *that / those* (see Chapter 6, pp. 164-211) functioning as pronouns just as the possessive pronouns can.

> *Determiner:* Did you bring *that* snake in the house?
> *Pronoun:* I didn't do *that* (i.e., *bring the snake in the house*).

We can see in the last example that the antecedent for the demonstrative pronoun can often be a clause or phrase. Because of *that* (the fact that the antecedent can often be a clause or phrase), we must be careful that the antecedent of a demonstrative pronoun is quite clear.

Remember that you must make the pronoun agree with its antecedent in number (*singular* or *plural;* review Chapter 1 if you're not sure what *that* means).

You might be able to play many songs, but I don't think you will know *these* (antecedent is *songs*).

Do Exercises 2-9 and 2-10.

2c. Relative Pronouns

Relative pronouns allow two clauses to be joined.

> *Fritz* raises giant tomatoes.
> *Fritz* is my neighbor.
> Fritz, *who* is my neighbor, raises giant tomatoes.

In our example *Fritz* is the shared noun that allows us to combine these two clauses. If we put the second sentence into the first sentence, we have the following:

> Fritz [Fritz is my neighbor] raises giant tomatoes.

Notice we put the second sentence *immediately* after the first shared noun.

Try Exercise 2-11 at this point. Then, do Exercise 2-12.

Now we need to change the second noun into a pronoun. How do we change the second *Fritz* into a pronoun? When working with relative pronouns, we need to look for two dimensions: *case* and *humanness*. If you don't remember what case means, go to Chapter 14 before you try to do this exercise. At this point, let's just replace *Fritz* with the personal pronoun we would normally use:

> Fritz [*he* is my neighbor] raises giant tomatoes.

Do Exercise 12-13 now.

Finally we can substitute a *relative pronoun* for the personal one. But which one should we use?
First, we need to know if the pronoun refers to a person or a thing, since we can use different relative pronouns for each in writing. In informal speech, we can use *that* for everything. But in writing, for people we use the appropriate form of *who*. However, we cannot use those forms for things. For non-human nouns we use *which,* which we should not use for people. We see in our example that Fritz (*he*) is a human; therefore, we can use a form of *who*.

> Fritz [*who* is my neighbor] raises giant tomatoes.

Now we need to know what case it should be. We know that *he* is in the subjective form. This fact means that we can replace *he* with *who,* which is the subjective form of *who.* Fortunately, there are just a few relative pronoun forms.

Informal
that—for both people and things, both subjective and objective

Formal
who—only for people, only subjective
whom—only for people, only objective
which—only for things, both subjective and objective

Both informal and formal
whose—for both people and things, only possessive

Use this list to help you do Exercise 2-14 now. Then do 2-15 and 2-16.

If the relative pronoun is the object of a preposition and we are going to replace it with *whom* or *which*, we must move the preposition with it.

> *Base:* She photographs elephants. The people have respect for the elephants.
> *With pronoun:* The people have respect for *them*.
> *With relative pronoun:* The people have respect for *which*
> *Move the complete prepositional phrase to front of clause: for which* the people have respect.
> *Final form:* She photographs elephants for which the people have respect.

If we had decided to use the informal *that,* we must not move the preposition.

> *Base:* She photographs elephants. The people have respect for the elephants.
> *With pronoun:* The people have respect for *them*.
> *Replace with informal that:* The people have respect for *that*.
> *Move only that to front of clause: that* the people have respect *for*
> *Final form:* She photographs elephants that the people have respect for.

Since we must move prepositional phrases to the front of the clause if we use *which* or *whom,* we must be careful to distinguish between *prepositions* and *phrasal* <u>verbs</u> (see p.294 for more on phrasals). We do not move the particle of the phrasal even though it often looks like a preposition.

> *Preposition:* The store is noisy. We live *over* the store.
> *Relative clause:* The store *over which* we live is noisy.
> *Particle:* The article is boring. We must talk *over* the article. *talk over = discuss*
> *Relative clause:* The article *which* we must talk *over* is boring.

Remember to apply the following test to determine whether a word is a particle or preposition. If the verb would mean something else is we left off the preposition/particle, it is a particle. For example, *off* is a particle in the previous sentence. Why?

Of course, our first sentence would have been different if we had used *that.*

> *Preposition:* The store is noisy. We live *over* the store.
> *Relative clause:* The store *that* we live *over* is noisy.

Now try Exercise 2-17 and 2-18.

The relative pronouns which begin with *wh-* can combine with *-ever* when the speaker doesn't really have enough information to be more specific but knows that the general statement is correct.

> *Whoever* tried to sell you that didn't know what he was doing.

Here the speaker doesn't know the identity of *who,* but she does know that the person probably was inept.

We can substitute *the person who* for *whoever.*

> The person who tried to sell you that didn't know what he was doing.

Do Exercise 2-19.

2d. Interrogative Pronouns

The interrogative pronouns (and interrogative determiners) usually represent a request from the speaker for a missing piece of information.

Where are you going to spend this vacation?
In Alabama.

Their behavior is very similar to that of the relative pronouns; interrogative pronouns and determiners must be placed at the front of the question.

Do Exercise 2-10.

2e. Indefinite Pronouns

We will work only with the compound forms of indefinite pronouns in this section.

(1) Formation of indefinite pronouns

Compound forms are made up of a determiner (*some, any, every,* or *no*) plus an indefinite stem. The stem tells us to what the indefinite pronoun will refer.

> *Stems:*
> *-body*—an indefinite person [much the same as *-one,* but sounds less formal normally]
> *-one*—an indefinite person [often more formal than *-body*]
> *-thing*—an indefinite non-person

Do Exercise 2-21.

(2) Indefinite pronouns as subjects

When these indefinite forms are used as subjects, they are *always* singular. See 10e.

> *Correct:* Everybody *is* here on time.
> *Incorrect:* Everybody *are* here on time.

(3) Pronominal reference to indefinite pronouns

Many native speakers of English use a plural third person pronoun form when they need to refer to an indefinite pronoun.

> *Informal:* Does *everyone* have *their* book?
> *Formal:* Does *everyone* have *his* book?
> *Non-sexist:* Does *everyone* have *his* or *her* book? [wordy]

We should avoid the informal forms in writing, but in informal speech they are considered normal by many.

Now do Exercise 2-22.

EXERCISE 2-1

NAME _____ DATE _____

What is the antecedent for each underlined pronoun?

Example: Fritz was given a new car <u>which</u> <u>he</u> loves
which—a new car
he—Fritz

1. Rose and Marie were really sad when Alex told <u>them</u> that <u>he</u> had to leave the house
<u>which</u> <u>they</u> had rented to <u>him</u>.

    them _____

    he _____

    which _____

    they _____

    him _____

2. After <u>he</u> had given <u>them</u> his notice, Alex wanted to buy Rose and Marie a small present.
There was only one place to buy <u>it</u>.

    he _____

    them _____

    it _____

3. For years the women had wanted a sundial <u>which</u> <u>they</u> had seen in the hardware store

    next to their own store, but they had never wanted to spend the money on it.

    which _____

    they _____

    it _____

4. Since <u>they</u> would not buy <u>it</u> for <u>themselves</u>, Alex would.

   they _____

   it _____

   themselves _____

5. When Alex showed <u>them</u> where he had placed <u>it</u> as <u>he</u> was leaving, both women thanked <u>him</u> quietly, excused <u>themselves</u>, walked back to the door, and shut <u>it</u>.

   them _____

   it _____

   he _____

   him _____

   themselves _____

   it _____

Score _____

EXERCISE 2-2

NAME_____DATE_____

Fill in the correct reflexive pronoun. Use the underlined words as clues.

Example: Since no one else deserves it, <u>I</u> will give it to <u>myself</u>.

1. As she turned the corner, <u>she</u> saw _____ in the broken mirror.

2. The unexpected image of _____ frightened <u>her</u>.

3. <u>She</u> said only to _____, "Watch it! You really need to get hold of

    _____ ."

4. Slowly the <u>image in the mirror</u> began to change _____ into another face,

    one she did not recognize.

5. The unknown <u>man</u> in the mirror seemed quite pleased with _____ .

6. He whispered, "Perhaps <u>I</u> should introduce _____ ?"

7. <u>Ruth</u> was barely able to control _____ .

8. She bravely shouted, "Identify _____ ."

9. The <u>image</u> slowly gathered mist around _____ and disappeared.

10. For weeks, <u>Ruth</u> did not trust _____ to be alone in the upper hall.

Score _____

EXERCISE 2-3

NAME _____DATE _____

(a) Supply the correct reflexives. (b) Would these sentences be grammatical without the reflexive? (If you do not understand this question, see Chapter 4.)

Example: a.   Sarah prided <u>herself</u> on her ability to fix any jet engine made.
    b.   The reflexive is essential; the verb <u>pride</u> cannot occur without an object.

1. a. Laura and her parents had always enjoyed _____ so much in the

    evening.

    b.

2. a. As a result, Laura was unable to live by _____ .

    b.

3. a. Laura's brother Ian, an artist, could barely support _____ with his art.

    b.

4. a. Ian was so poor that he couldn't afford new razor blades to shave _____

    with.

    b.

5. a. Ian and Laura asked _____ if all this trauma was necessary.

    b.

6. a. But Ian thought, "I will really have to behave _____ if I return home."

    b.

7. a. Finally, they convinced _____ it was not and moved back to their

    parents' house.

    b.

8. a. Back in their parents' house, they did not have to do anything for

    _____.

    b.

9. a. The parents pushed _____ to be able to provide everything for the two.

    b.

10. a. Oddly enough, the two never thought of _____ as lazy even as long

    years passed by.

    b.

Score _____

EXERCISE 2-4

NAME _____ DATE _____

Insert the appropriate reflexive pronoun for the underlined noun or pronoun. Use the context of the sentence to determine whether the adverbial or emphatic form is appropriate.

Example: The <u>president</u> spoke to our graduating class.
                     The president <u>himself</u> spoke to our graduating class. [emphasis on the
                       <u>president</u>, not on his being alone]

1. Lost in the woods, <u>Cathy</u> had to start a fire.

2. Although <u>she</u> had never started a fire even with the help of her instructors, she wasn't too worried.

3. She assumed that the <u>matches</u> she had would start the fire.

4. In fact, <u>Fred</u> had told her not to worry if she got lost.

5. Although <u>Fred and his wife Debbie</u> owned the woods, many other hunters used it.

6. Because everybody else was gone, <u>Debbie</u> had to go look for Cathy when she noticed she had been gone too long.

7. Cathy thought, "If I am going to survive, <u>I</u> must do this."

8. Finally <u>Debbie</u> was able to find Cathy.

9. In this situation, what would <u>you</u> do?

10. Have <u>you</u> ever had to solve a difficult problem?

Score _____

EXERCISE 2-5

NAME _____ DATE _____

Would you use <u>it</u>, <u>she</u>, or <u>he</u> for the following?

Example: a floppy disk—it

1. book _____

2. your pet female bird _____

3. a car _____

4. a lizard in the zoo _____

5. Canada _____

6. The Queen Elizabeth II (a boat) _____

7. a waitress _____

8. a male flight attendant _____

9. a bull _____

10. a dog on the street _____

Score _____

EXERCISE 2-6

NAME _____DATE _____

This is a two-step exercise. First, in (a) fill in the full possessive noun for the underlined word or words.

Example: The desk belongs to <u>James</u>. As usual, there is nothing on _____ desk.
a. James's

Now use the information in (a) to put the correct pronomial form in the blank.

Example: The desk belongs to <u>James</u>. As usual, there is nothing on <u>his</u> desk.
a. James's

1. That car is <u>Bob and Jim's</u>. I would never ride in _____ car.

   a.

2. That decision came straight from <u>Jeanne</u>, the president. And you really should believe

   she knows _____ business.

   a.

3. My <u>sister</u> inherited the books from _____ grandmother.

   a.

4. <u>You</u> and <u>Karen</u> are so messy! How can <u>you</u> find _____ work in that wreck?

   a.

5. That <u>elephant</u> has lost _____ calf.

   a.

6. Many of the <u>people</u> were unable to find _____ cars.

   a.

7. Several car <u>thieves</u> had been practicing _____ skills in the parking lot.

   a.

8. The <u>children</u> really were enjoying _____ game.

   a.

9. Has <u>Kris</u> finished _____ new play?

   a.

10. Why did those <u>candidates</u> renounce _____ campaign promises?

    a.

Score _____

EXERCISE 2-7

NAME _____**DATE** _____

The underlined word or words will provide you with clues to provide the appropriate pronoun form to be put in the blank.

Example: Susan forgot to pick up <u>her dry cleaning</u>, but Joe remembered to get <u>his</u>.

Joe remembered to get _____
Joe remembered to get <u>his</u>.

1. I have finished <u>my engineering project</u>. Have you finished _____ ?

2. Why are you and Sam sharing <u>your book</u>? Did he leave _____ at home

   again?

3. Mr. and Mrs. Wyatt got <u>their letter</u> yesterday. We hope to get _____ today.

4. She is really slow in turning back <u>her papers</u>, but I have already given

   _____ back.

5. <u>Her plane</u> landed on time, but I am still waiting for _____ to arrive.

6. This evening both John and Jane spoke at the mass rally. The crowd really didn't like

   <u>his speech</u>, but everybody clearly enjoyed _____ .

7. The other lawyer wasn't able to justify <u>his claims</u>, but I had no problem in justifying

   _____ .

8. Few playwrights plan <u>their plays</u> as carefully as he does _____ .

9. I forgot to bring <u>my new racquet</u>. Did you happen to bring _____?

10. You seem to have all of <u>your papers</u> with you. But what has Polly done with

_____?

Score _____

EXERCISE 2-8

NAME _____ DATE _____

Construct a sentence with a dummy subject from the words in slashes.

Example: to the university/not far/is
It is not far to the university.

1. a quick drive/used to be/from the airport

2. seems/from here to New York/far

3. later and later/was getting

4. looks like/outside/a gloomy, dreadful day

5. summer/next month/will be

6. tomorrow/clearer/will be

7. was/very easy

8. dark/has been/for hours now

9. seems to be/clearing up/now

10. had rained/all week/during the tennis matches

Score _____

EXERCISE 2-9

NAME _____DATE _____

Write out the antecedent of the underlined demonstrative pronouns.

Example: They wanted to buy a condo in Florida, but I urged them not to do <u>that</u>.
buy a condo in Florida

1.   Why did you insist on bringing Fred home for dinner? You know I don't want you to do <u>that</u>.

2.   I have already filled out those forms. Now I must fill out <u>these</u>.

3.   Ernie says he has chicken pox and can't come to work. What am I going to do about <u>this</u>?

4.   Do you want to wear these gloves or <u>those</u>?

5.   <u>That</u> is an expensive car.

6.   My wife usually stops to pick up the kids. But she is sick today and I must do <u>that</u> too.

7.   Once again you have forgotten to turn in your homework. What is the meaning of <u>this</u>?

8.   Jane went sailing last week. I have always wanted to do <u>that</u>.

9.   I don't have time to fix dinner. Can you take care of <u>that</u> for me?

10.   Heather tricked me into helping her move. She's never going to do <u>that</u> to me again.

Score _____

EXERCISE 2-10

NAME_____DATE _____

What would be the correct form if the underlined nouns were antecedents? Explain your answers.

Example: cars (this/these)   *these*, since *cars* is a plural form

1. summer vacations (that/those) _____

2. people (this/these) _____

3. newspaper (that/those) _____

4. lovely, fresh strawberries (that/those) _____

5. a clear view of the mountains (this/these) _____

6. police (those/that) _____

7. hundreds of sheep (this/these)_____

8. the heart of the issue (this/these) _____

9. the major criteria (these/this) _____

10. important data (those/that)_____

Score _____

EXERCISE 2-11

NAME _____ DATE _____

Write out the shared noun that would allow each of these pairs of sentences to be combined into one.

Example: Marina lives in Malaga. Malaga is in Spain. <u>Malaga</u>

1. Fred hates to do the dishes before he goes to bed. Every morning Fred dirties every

   pan in the kitchen. _____

2. Marta used to live next door to Renee in France. Renee is the world's worst

   housekeeper. _____

3. Because the maid quit, the poor woman's party was a disaster. The maid moved to

   California. _____

4. Everybody in Memphis looks forward to barbecue season. Memphis is the barbecue

   center of the USA. _____

5. She saw the strange girl. Every day for years the girls on her street had spoken about

   the strange girl. _____

6. I watched a small bird. A small bird was sitting on my steps. _____

7. People talk about movie stars. Movie stars become involved in scandal.

    _____

8. Some scandals are fun. Some scandals are not serious. _____

9. Although I have lived in many cities, I really prefer to walk. Many cities have excellent

    public transportation. _____

10. Identify the relative pronouns. The following sentences have relative pronouns.

    _____

Score _____

EXERCISE 2-12

NAME _____DATE _____

Put the second sentence where it should be in the first sentence. Don't use any pronouns yet.

Example: Marina lives in Malaga. Malaga is in Spain.
Marina lives in Malaga [Malaga is in Spain].

1. Fred hates to do the dishes. Fred dirties every pan in the kitchen.

2. Marta lived next door to Renee in France. Renee is the world's worst housekeeper.

3. Because the maid quit, the poor woman's party was a disaster. The maid moved to California.

4. Everybody in Memphis looks forward to barbecue season. Memphis is the barbecue center of the USA.

5. She saw the girl. The girls on her street had spoken about the strange girl.

6. I watched a small bird. A small bird was sitting on my steps.

7. People talk about movie stars. Movie stars become involved in scandal.

8. Some scandals are fun. Some scandals are not serious.

9. Although I have lived in many cities, I really prefer to walk. Many cities have excellent public transportation.

10. Identify the relative pronouns. The following sentences have relative pronouns.

Score _____

EXERCISE 2-13

NAME _____DATE _____

Look at your answers from Exercise 12. Write out the bracketed clause. Now substitute the appropriate personal pronoun for the shared noun.

Example: [Malaga is in Spain.] (from Exercise 12)
[it is in Spain.]

1.

2.

3.

4.

5.

6.

7.

8.

9.

10.

Score _____

EXERCISE 2-14

NAME _____DATE _____

Finish this table, which shows the correspondences between the personal and relative pronouns. Determine which relative pronoun would substitute for each personal pronoun. The first line is done for you.

Person	Number	Case	=	Relative Pronoun
I	singular	subjective		who/what
my				
you	sing/plural	subjective		
you	sing/plural	objective		
your				
it				
its				
she				
her		objective		
her		possessive		
he				
him				
his				
we				
us				
our				
they				
them				
their				
they				

Score _____

EXERCISE 2-15

NAME _____DATE _____

Now take your answers from Exercise 13 and write out the appropriate formal relative pronoun for the personal one you had filled in.

Example: [it is in Spain] (from Exercise 13)
                 [which is in Spain]

1.

2.

3.

4.

5.

6.

7.

8.

9.

10.

Score _____

EXERCISE 2-16

NAME _____**DATE** _____

Rewrite these faulty sentences so that the relative pronoun is in the right position.

Example: Fritz [I know <u>whom</u>] lives in Washington.
Fritz, <u>whom</u> I know, lives in Washington.

1. The university [I attend <u>which</u>] is really large.

2. Most of the students [you see <u>that</u> pay their own way].

3. They must work jobs [they hate <u>that</u>].

4. But in the long run, they are glad because they are able to get a college education, [they couldn't afford <u>which</u> otherwise].

5. Unfortunately, in the meantime there are classes [the exhausted students sleep through <u>that</u>].

6. We hope that these students, [we work <u>whom</u> so hard now], will succeed and make it a little easier for the next generation.

7. However, most international students [the university admits <u>that</u>] are prohibited from working.

8. That means that the money [the international students bring <u>that</u>] must be spent carefully.

9. Those students need to plan a budget, [they must carefully follow <u>which</u>].

10. Otherwise, the funds [they bring <u>that</u>] may not be enough.

Score _____

EXERCISE 2-17

NAME _____DATE _____

Make correct relative clauses from these pairs of sentences. Remember what we must do with prepositional phrases if we use *which* or *whom*.

Example: The elephant was shot by the doctor. <u>It</u> was eating the sugar cane.
The elephant <u>which was eating the sugar cane</u> was shot by the doctor.

1. The elephant was shot by the doctors. <u>They</u> hated to kill any living thing.

2. The doctors shot the elephant in the sugar cane. The elephant seemed to pose a threat to <u>them</u>.

3. The young doctor shot two elephants. <u>They</u> were eating the old doctor's sugarcane.

4. The doctors lurked in the shadows. The whole event seemed a game to <u>them</u>.

5. The doctor shot the elephant. <u>Its</u> tusk had gouged large holes in the shed.

6. The doctor shot the elephants. <u>She</u> hated to kill any living thing.

7. The officer has gone already. There is a message for <u>him</u>.

8. The second officer is even more polite. The first officer was replaced by <u>him</u>.

9. The guns were by the door. He shoots small game with <u>them</u>.

10. The company has been very successful. I have worked for many years with <u>it</u>.

Score _____

EXERCISE 2-18

NAME _____DATE_____

Decide if the underlined word is a preposition or particle. Then make relative clauses from the two sentences. First, use <u>which</u>. Next, use <u>that</u>.

Example: The apartment is really expensive. She lives <u>in</u> the apartment.
a. preposition
b. The apartment <u>in which</u> she lives is really expensive.
c. The apartment <u>that</u> she lives <u>in</u> is really expensive.

1. The problem is not serious. We did look <u>into</u> the problem.
    a.

    b.

    c.

2. The cave was dark and dangerous. We looked <u>into</u> the cave.
    a.

    b.

    c.

3. The bats were not rabid. The scientists came <u>across</u> the bats.
    a.

    b.

    c.

4. The border is heavily guarded. The smugglers ran <u>across</u> the border.
    a.

    b.

    c.

5. The stairs were old and rickety. He crawled <u>up</u> the stairs.

    a.

    b.

    c.

6. All stories are fiction. An author makes <u>up</u> stories.

    a.

    b.

    c.

7. The idea seemed workable. They were kicking <u>around</u> an idea.

    a.

    b.

    c.

8. That is a dangerous corner. You live <u>at</u> a corner.

    a.

    b.

    c.

9. The obstacle was accidentally put in the road. The runners had to go <u>over</u> the obstacle.

    a.

    b.

    c.

10. The proposal was accepted. I was able to put <u>across</u> the proposal.

    a.

    b.

    c.

Score _____

EXERCISE 2-19

NAME _____DATE_____

Substitute an -ever word for the underlined constructions in these sentences.

Example: He said that which came to his mind.
                  He said whatever came to his mind.

1. The person who brings in the most pledges will win the grand prize.

2. Discuss first the question which seems easiest to you.

3. We should really give it to the person whom you see first.

4. Pick out the jacket which you like the best.

5. They were only able to take that which fit into the small suitcase.

6. He simply chooses to discuss that which comes to his mind.

7. The car which you take will be fine with me.

8. That ticket is for the person whom the agency sends.

9. Any one which you think is pretty can be re-designed for your needs.

10. We will never understand that which made him do that awful thing.

Score _____

EXERCISE 2-20

NAME _____ DATE _____

Which question word would you substitute for the underlined word or words?

Example: The men had to work <u>in the bakery</u>.
                    <u>where</u>

1. <u>The older woman</u> seems to have finished first.

2. Lane talked to <u>a rather nasty receptionist</u>.

3. The newspaper printed <u>Eliot's</u> letter.

4. Dian lived in <u>that</u> house.

5. I left <u>because I got a better offer in Hawaii</u>.

6. I got there <u>by car</u>.

7. We needed to talk with <u>him</u>.

8. They arrived in <u>the yellow</u> car.

9. <u>By begging the principal not to expel him</u>, Fritz managed to stay in school.

10. The boys left <u>the guests'</u> luggage at the station.

                                    Score _____

EXERCISE 2-21

NAME _____ DATE_____

Combine the stems and determiners to produce the compound forms. All of them (except <u>no one</u>) are written as <u>one</u> word. Two examples are done for you.

	<u>some</u>	<u>any</u>	<u>every</u>	<u>no</u>
-body				
-thing			everything	
-one	someone			

Score _____

EXERCISE 2-22

NAME _____ **DATE** _____

Change the informal forms to formal ones. Do both the traditional form and the non-sexist form.

Example: Everybody needs their own reason for living.
               a. Everybody needs <u>his</u> own reason for living.
               b. Everybody needs <u>his</u> or <u>her</u> reason for living.

1. No one has turned in their semester project yet.

   a.

   b.

2. Does everyone pride themself [avoid this form; it is too informal] on their work?

   a.

   b.

3. Everybody had a really good time, didn't they?

   a.

   b.

4. I hope nobody has forgotten to sign their forms.

   a.

   b.

5. Anybody who knows the answer should raise their hand.

   a.

6. Has anybody worked out their schedule for next semester?

   a.

   b.

7. No one should attempt to do the exercise themself [again, this form is too informal].

   a.

   b.

8. Somebody is coming to relieve me at noon, aren't they?

   a.

   b.

9. Everybody really gave their best, but we still lost.

   a.

   b.

10. Anyone who wants to go must bring their money tomorrow.

    a.

    b.

Score _____

3

Adjectives and Adverbs

3a. Adjectives

Adjectives are fairly straightforward. The main problems you will encounter will be ones of position and formation.

(1) Position of adjectives

Adjectives occur (called *attributive adjectives*) before nouns.

> The *yellow* lilies last the longest.

Adjectives (called *predicate adjectives*) can also occur after linking verbs.

> The lilies appear *yellow* in this light.

These terms are useful because there are some adjectives that can occur in only one position or the other. Some adjectives can occur only in the *predicate* position.

Now do Exercise 3-1.

Although we cannot use them in the normal position before the noun, we can use them after the noun in phrases.

> The dogs, *sound asleep,* did not hear the burglar.

Do Exercise 3-2 now.

Usually when an adjective is used before a noun, it represents a permanent or normal situation.

> The *lost* money was never recovered.

But the same adjective used after a noun usually indicates a temporary or unique situation.

> The money *lost* was found in the bus terminal.

Try Exercise 3-3 now.

In English, *complex adjective phrases* cannot occur before the noun they modify.

> *Correct: Responsible* kids are usually well-adjusted.
> *Correct:* Kids *responsible for their own actions* are usually well-adjusted.
> *Incorrect: Responsible for their own actions* kids are usually well-adjusted.

Now do Exercise 3-4.

(2) Order of adjectives

Sometimes more than one adjective is needed to describe a noun.

> It is rare to see such a *lovely, large, square, red, stone* schoolhouse in this area.

Not all adjectives are the same. There are different categories of adjectives. It is the categories that determine the order adjectives will follow.

Basically, the more *intrinsic* an adjective is, the closer it comes to the noun. Let's look back at our example *lovely, large, square, red, stone* to produce some appropriate categories.

> origin—*stone*
> color—*red*
> shape—*square*
> size—*large*
> evaluation—*lovely*

Do Exercises 3-5 through 3-8 to see how these categories interact.

(3) Formation of adjectives

Some adjectives are basic adjectives; they are not derived from other elements.

> yellow   old   nice

But the adjectives can be *formed* from many other types of words. Most commonly, adjectives are derived from nouns. There are several suffixes that can be added to the noun.

> child + -ish   child + -like   wind + -y   courage + ous

We can even use sometimes the *-ly* suffix, which we normally associate with adverbs (as in *normally*). Remember this use of *-ly* makes an adjective because it is added to a noun.

> man + -ly   mother + -ly   cost + -ly

This very old suffix is often used with very basic vocabulary words such as immediate family names. It is not often used with less common words.

Two important suffixes of this category are *-less* and *-ful*. They are used often, and usually both can be used for the same noun.

> thought + ful   thought + less

Try Exercise 3-9 now.

One suffix of this category can cause problems because it can be added to *verbs* to mean *able to be X-ed*.

think + able = able to be thought	drink + able = able to be drunk
The very idea is unthinkable.	His wines are barely drinkable.
The idea cannot be thought.	His wines can barely be drunk.

Do Exercise 3-10.

Some adjectives are formed by removing the nominal suffix (which makes a root a noun) and adding the correct adjectival suffix.

silen*ce*	silen*t*
intelligen*ce*	intelligen*t*
gener*osity*	gener*ous*
curi*osity*	curi*ous*

Now do Exercise 3-11.

(4) Participles used as adjectives

Both the present (the *-ing* form) and the past (the *-en* form) participles of many verbs can be used as adjectives.

> The *running* water cleaned the driveway of debris.
> *Stolen* cars are often used to commit crimes.

The present participle adjective modifies the noun that does the action of the *-ing* verb.

> The *running* water cleaned the driveway of debris.
> The water *that is running* cleaned the driveway of debris.

On the other hand, a past participle adjective describes the subject of a passive sentence; it modifies what was the object of the action.

> *Stolen* cars are often used to commit crimes.
> Cars *that are stolen* are often used to commit crimes.
> Someone *stole* cars.

Do Exercise 3-12 before you go on.

The past participles of most intransitive verbs are not normally used as adjectives, since there can be no passives of intransitive verbs.

> *Correct:* A man was *walking*.
> *Incorrect:* The *walked* man was tired.

But the same form *that* comes from a transitive use can be used as an adjective.

> Eve is going to *walk the dog*. A *walked* dog is a happy dog.

The past participle of some intransitive verbs may be used as an adjective to show the condition of the noun it modifies.

> The *drunk* sailor was lying on the floor. He is no longer drinking. He was drunk.

Compare these sentences.

> The lifeguard was able to save the *drowning* child.
> Did you know the *drowned* man?

In the first sentence, the child was not dead but was still in the process of drowning.

Try Example 3-13 now.

(5) Adjective participles of emotive verbs

One important group of participles used as adjectives causes problems because they seem to function backwards.

> Many people are *interested* in dogs.

From what we saw in section (4), we might expect that the *-ing* form should be used. We might think that *people* is the subject of an active sentence.

> *Incorrect:* Many people are *interesting* in dogs.

However, *people* is not the subject but rather the *object*.

> Dogs interest many *people*.

Note that *dogs* cause the interest. As a result, when we are describing the *dogs* we use the *-ing* form.

> The dogs are *interesting*.

There are several common verbs that have this "reverse" pattern in which the subject causes the object to *experience* some emotion.

> *Verb:* His snoring *irritates* me.
> *Adjective:* His snoring is *irritating*.
> *Adjective:* I am *irritated* by his snoring.

Now try Exercises 3-15 and 3-16.

3b. Adverbs

The classification *adverb* is very open. As a result, many different types of words are called adverbs. Most problems with adverbs come from *formation* or *placement*.

(1) Formation of adverbs

Most adjectives can be made into adverbs by adding the suffix *-ly*.

Try Exercise 3-16 now.

(2) Sentence-final positions of adverbs and adverbials

Although grammar books often suggest that there is an easy fixed order for adverbs that occur within a sentence, that is, unfortunately, not really true. Rather than fixed orders, there are general *tendencies*.

The general tendencies are based on the *function* of the adverb (or adverbials) in the sentence. Basically, adverbials answer five questions.

> where—direction *to the store*
> when—time *at midnight*
> why—reason *because he was ill*
> how often—frequency *every day*
> how—manner *in a hurry*

As you read and hear more English, you will gradually learn how to place adverbials.

Try Exercise 3-17. Next, try Exercise 3-18, which should be somewhat challenging.

(3) Meaning and position of preverbal adverbials of frequency

Many adverbials of frequency (how often) can and sometimes must occur before the main verb (*preverbal position*).

> *Preverbal:* Fred *sometimes* does his homework.
> *Less preferable:* Fred does his homework *sometimes*.
> *Preverbal:* Sandy *often* makes breakfast for his friends.
> *Less preferable:* Sandy makes breakfast for his friends *often*.

Basically, the preverbal is put before the main verb and after the auxiliary verbs.

> Fred <u>can</u> *sometimes* <u>do</u> his homework himself.
>   (aux)   (main)

> Fred *often* <u>wants</u> to leave school and work.
>   (main)

Since *be* is somewhat like an auxiliary verb, the preverbal follows it.

> Indeed, Fred <u>is</u> *often* brilliant.
>   (be)

However, if the auxiliary (or *be*) is stressed, the preverbal adverb *precedes* the auxiliary.

> I worked at the university for four years and I <u>*never did*</u> meet the president!

Before you go on, try Exercise 3-19.

Preverbals generally *come before* the auxiliary in reduced sentences (see pp. 217-218 for discussion of ellipses and reduced sentences), although some other orders are acceptable in very formal speech ("I did never").

> Fred: Is Nancy late?
> Nina: She *always* is! [She is always late.]
> *Not normally acceptable:* She is *always*!

> Nancy: Does Nina *generally* complain about me?
> Fred: Yes, she *generally* does.
> *Acceptable to some native speakers:* Yes, she does *generally*.

Of course, *not* and adverbs modified by *not* must still be put in the normal position after the auxiliary.

> Fred: Was Nancy late again?
> Nina: No, she was *not!* [She was *not* late again.]

> Fred: Is Nancy late again?
> Nina: Yes, but she *isn't always*. [She is *not always* late.]

Try Exercise 3-20.

Preverbal adverbials of frequency modify the entire sentence. Often adverbs of frequency modify just a specific part of the sentence.

> *Preverbal:* Jason *never* takes the trash out.
> *never* [Jason takes the trash out]

> *Normal:* Jason takes the trash out *once a week*.
> Jason takes the trash out [*once a week*]

The preverbal makes a statement about the entire sentence; it is usually essential to the meaning of the sentence. The sentence-final adverbial just refines the sentence.

The adverbs that have negative meanings often cause problems, since Standard English does not allow "double negatives."

> *Incorrect:* She *can't hardly* understand his French.
>   (neg) (neg)

> *Correct:* She can *hardly* understand his French.

The most common negative or negative-like preverbals are

> *never*   *seldom*   *rarely*   *hardly*   *scarcely*

Try Exercise 3-21. Remember to use "formal" English.

3c. Adjective and Adverb Forms

Even though we are calling this section *adjective and adverb forms,* it really covers almost every part of speech in English, since basically the rules for expressing degree are the same for all parts of speech.

> *Noun comparison:* Fritz has *more books* than Kathy.
> *Verb comparison:* Fritz *sleeps more* than Kathy.

(1) Regular adjective and adverb forms

Comparative Forms

Let's first look just at the comparative (comparing *only* two objects) forms first.

The basic word you use for positive comparatives is *more*. In some cases, you can add this word to the end of an adjective or adverb as the suffix *-er*.

> short + *-er* = shorter

There are a few rules that allow you to determine when we may add the suffix *-er* to a word.

If the adjective or adverb only has *one* syllable and is not made *(derived)* from some other part of speech, you can add *-er*.

> *One-syllable basic adjective:* tall
> *One-syllable derived adjective:* curved (*curved* is made from the verb *curve)*
> *Correct:* tall + er
> *Incorrect:* curved + er

Try Exercise 3-22 before you continue.

If the basic form (or *stem*) of an *adjective* has two syllables and ends in *-y, -ple, -el, -ow,* or *-ble* (this is not the same as *-able),* we can add *-er*.

> filthy + *-er* = filthier [remember spelling rules]
> unhappy [stem *happy* has two syllables] + *-er* = unhappier
> simple + *-er* = simpler [pronounced in two syllables]
> narrow + *-er* = narrower [pronounced in three syllables]

Make sure that you do not confuse *-y* with the very common *-ly* ending. You cannot use *-er* with *ly.*

> Evan worked even *more slowly* than Tina.

Some adjectives that fit this rule do not use *-er*. For example, we normally use *more* with *ready.*

> I could not be *more ready* for my close-up.

Now do Exercise 3-23.

For all other adverbs and adjectives you should use *more.* There are some other two-syllable adjectives that can use either *-er* or *more,* but it is just easier to always use *more.* In that way, you will always be correct.

Always remember, you can *never* use both the *-er* ending and *more* with the same word.

> *Incorrect:* Bette is *more* witt*er* than any other actress.

Although you will hear many Americans using both *more* and *-er* in conversation, do not follow their example.

> *Correct:* Bette is *wittier* than any other actress.

Superlative Forms

The *superlative* is used when we are comparing *three or more* items. Just as with the comparative, there is a basic form—*the most*—which can occur as *the -est* in some cases. The rules for adding *the -est* are just the same as for the comparative ending *-er*.

If the adjective has only *one* syllable and is not derived (made) from some other part of speech, usually use *the -est.*

> One-syllable *basic* adjective: tall
> One-syllable *derived* adjective: curved (*curved* is made from the verb *curve)*
> *Correct: the* tall + *-est*
> *Incorrect: the* curved + *-est*

Try Exercise 3-24.

If the stem of an *adjective* has two syllables with the suffix *-y, -ple, -el* (also written *-le), -ow,* or *-ble* (this is not the same as *-able),* we can add *the -est.*

> filthy + *the -est* = the filthiest [remember spelling rules]
> unhappy [stem *happy* has two syllables] + *the -est* = the unhappiest
> simple [two syllables] + *the -est* = the simplest [pronounced in two syllables]
> narrow + *the -est* = the narrowest [pronounced in three syllables]

However, some adjectives that fit this rule do not use *-er.* For example, *the most* is normally used with *ready.*

> As usual, Sean is *the most* ready.

Do Exercise 3-25 before you go on.

For all other adverbs and adjectives you should use *the most.* There are some other two-syllable adjectives that can use either *the -est* or *the most,* but it is just easier to always use *the most.* If you use *the most,* you will always be correct.

Some words have a built-in superlative meaning. They should not be used in comparisons.

> *Incorrect:* Their float was the *most unique* in the parade.
> *Correct:* Their float was *unique.*

Others already have superlative-like endings (*-st).* You cannot normally use the comparative or superlative forms with these words.

> *Aida* was the *first* opera the group performed.
> Then, *Tosca* was the *next.* [pronounced *nekst*]
> But *Madame Butterfly* has been their *foremost* production.

Test your knowledge with Exercise 3-26 now.

(2) Irregular forms

There are several very basic adjectives and adverbs that have *irregular* (in other words, *non-predictable)* forms; you must memorize and practice these until you are able to produce them easily. Although they are listed in the handbook, we will review them here also.

The irregular forms of *good* and *bad* are the same whether they are used as adjectives or adverbs.

Positive:	good/well	bad/badly
Comparative:	better	worse
Superlative:	the best	the worst

> Alan skis very *well,* but Sheila really does ski *better.*
> (adverb)

> Alan had a *bad* sprain, but Sheila's was *worse.*
> (adjective)

The count/non-count distinction between *many* and *much* disappears in the comparative and superlative.

Positive:	many	much
Comparative:	more	
Superlative:	the most	

Count: The ruling party doesn't have *many* allies, but it has *more* than any other party.
Non-count: The ruling party doesn't have *much* power, but it has *more* than any other party.

The same irregular forms are used for *a lot,* which occurs only in *very* formal spoken English (ESL speakers should avoid using it in writing).

Positive:	many/much/a lot
Comparative:	more
Superlative:	the most

The count/non-count distinction does not normally disappear for *little/few* although for some Americans it does in speech.

Positive:	few	little
Comparative:	fewer	less
Superlative:	the fewest	the least

However, if *little* is being used as the opposite of *big,* we must use the comparative forms of *small* in Standard English.

Positive:	little (few)	little (small)
Comparative:	less	smaller
Superlative:	the least	the smallest

Two other important words have irregular forms. *Far* is always irregular and has two possible forms (*farther* and *further*). But *old* is irregular only when we are talking about age relationships among brothers and sisters. Many Americans no longer use these forms for *old.*

Positive:	far	old
Comparative:	farther/further	elder
Superlative:	the farthest/the furthest	the eldest

Formal: Faranak is my *elder* sister.
Informal: Susy is our *oldest* sister.

For some Americans there is a difference between *further* and *farther.* We use *farther* for physical distances and *further* for mental comparisons.

How much *farther* is it to Tulsa? [physical]
Management and the union were unable to compromise any *further.* [mental or abstract]

Use Exercise 3-27 to show you understand both the regular and the irregular forms.

(3) Negative comparisons

Just as we can make positive comparisons about objects, we can make negative ones by using *less* and *the least.*

Halloran is *more important* to the company than Claude is.
But Halloran is *less important* than Roddy is.

Since we cannot fuse this form onto any words, it is easy to produce the correct forms. The only difficulties are with *many/much*.

> *less + many = fewer*
> Lauren has *many* books, but she has *fewer* than Anna.
> *less + much = less*
> Lauren has *much* free time, but she has *less* than Anna.

(4) Equative and comparative structures

Equative structures tell us that two (or more) objects are *equal*.

> Fred is *as* intelligent *as* Frieda.

Of course, we can make a negative from that last example. Negative equative structures often replace comparatives.

> Fred is intelligent. But Fred is *not as* intelligent *as* Frieda.

In this last example the topic of our discussion is *Fred,* not *Frieda*. If we had used the comparative, we would have needed to use a different order. That new order would have changed the flow of the conversation to *Frieda*.

> Fred is intelligent. But Frieda is *more intelligent.*

We would expect the next sentence to be about Frieda. Notice in the equatives, we *cannot* use the *more* or *-er* markers.

> Incorrect: Fred is not as *more* intelligent as Frieda.

Although many ESL speakers try to use *than* with the negative equatives, that is incorrect since they are just positive equatives with a negative marker added.

> *Base:* Fred is *as* intelligent *as* Frieda.
> *Negative of base:* Fred is not *as* intelligent as Frieda.
> *Incorrect:* Fred is not as intelligent *than* Frieda.

Of course, the meaning of a negative equative is much closer to a comparative than to a positive equative. Often the negative equative is less blunt than the comparative.

> *Gentle:* Fred is not as bright as Frieda.
> *Comparative:* Fred is less bright than Frieda.
> *Correct but blunt:* Fred is stupid.

In the last set of examples we also see another problem with the equatives. Just because Fred is not as bright as Frieda does not really mean he *must* be stupid.

Do Exercise 3-28.

EXERCISE 3-1

Each of the underlined adjectives can be used only in the *attributive* position. Find a synonym to fill in the *predicate* version. Use a dictionary or thesaurus if necessary.

Example: She is the <u>main</u> reason he is staying in Memphis.
Is that reason good enough to be <u>primary</u>?

1. Are you sure that is the <u>total</u> inventory?

   Yes, the inventory is _____.

2. His party was an <u>utter</u> disaster.

   That's right. I have never seen any mess so _____.

3. She accepts his teaching on <u>sheer</u> faith.

   It must be nice to have a faith so _____.

4. That big one over there is the <u>chief</u> gorilla.

   Which gorilla did you say is _____?

5. This prize was a <u>mere</u> trip to the company's headquarters.

   Don't complain. Any free trip is nice, no matter how _____.

Score _____

EXERCISE 3-2

NAME _____ DATE_____

In the following discourses, use the underlined phrase after the noun.

Example: The dogs were <u>sound asleep</u>.
The dogs, <u>sound asleep</u>, did not hear the burglar enter the house.

1. The man was <u>aghast with horror</u>.
   The man stared at the creature in the window.

2. All of the students were <u>overwhelmed by the test</u>.
   The students broke down one by one.

3. The cows were <u>content with their lots</u>.
   The cows gave gallons of milk daily.

4. Because the anchor was broken, the boat was <u>dangerously adrift</u>.
   The boat was close to going over the dam.

5. <u>Suddenly</u>, the manager was <u>wide awake</u>.
   The manager opened the door to find the cause of the loud noise.

                                                Score _____

EXERCISE 3-3

NAME _____DATE_____

Decide from the context if the adjective should be put before or after the noun. If both cases seem to be possible, what would each mean?

Example: (available) Many of the children will go hungry today because the _____ food _____ is not enough to go around.

Many of the children will go hungry today because the food <u>available</u> is not enough to go around. (temporary state)

1. (given) On Tuesday, the contestants were not yet able to solve the problem with the

    _____ clues _____. Perhaps when the new one is given

    today, they will be able to.

2. (necessary) Sheila could enter the vault because she knew the _____

    code _____.

3. (requisitioned) You always put _____ items _____ on the top

    shelf.

4. (elected) Unfortunately, the _____ woman _____ was the

    president of the company and could not accept the position.

5. (volunteered) The _____ information _____ was not sufficient

    to convict the accused today, but as more information comes in we hope to finish by

    tomorrow.

6. (requisitioned) Some _____ items _____ are not available

    right now.

7. (designated) The _____ person _____ for this job was unable

   to attend.

8. (chosen) Normally, the _____ site _____ is in a warmer part

   of the country.

9. (chosen) This year, however, the _____ site _____ is in

   Minneapolis.

10. (reviewed) In this week's article, the _____ restaurant _____

    is in Boston.

                                        Score _____

EXERCISE 3-4

NAME _____ DATE_____

Take the underlined adjective phrase from (a) and put it after the underlined noun in (b).

Example:
    a. Teenagers are <u>allowed to drive</u>.
    b. Do you think that <u>teenagers</u> are more responsible?
    c. Do you think that <u>teenagers allowed to drive</u> are more responsible?

1. a. The clues were <u>given by the radio station</u>.
   b. On Tuesday, the contestants were not yet able to solve the problem with the <u>clues</u>.
   c.

2. a. A secret code was <u>necessary to turn off the alarm</u>.
   b. Sheila could enter the vault because she knew the <u>code</u>.
   c.

3. a. Some items are <u>normally forbidden to the general public</u>.
   b. You always put <u>items</u> on the top shelf.
   c.

4. a. The woman was <u>elected by a large majority</u>.
   b. Unfortunately, the <u>woman</u> was the president of the company and could not accept the position.
   c.

5. a. Much of the information was <u>volunteered by children</u>.
   b. The <u>information</u> was sufficient to convict the accused.
   c.

6. a. Some of the press was <u>impressed by his credentials</u>.
   b. The <u>newsman</u> failed to ask significant questions.
   c.

7. a. Those funds are <u>essential to the maintenance of the program</u>.
   b. Congress failed to pass the bill that contained the <u>funds</u>.
   c.

8. a. Those courses are <u>equivalent to the ones required for graduation</u>.
    b. She failed to take <u>courses</u>.
    c.

9. a. The argument was <u>believable in its simplicity</u>.
    b. Her presentation included a brilliant <u>argument</u>.
    c.

10. a. The family was <u>wealthy beyond dreams</u>.
    b. It was hard to believe that such a miser could come from a well-known <u>family</u>.
    c.

Score _____

EXERCISE 3-5

NAME _____ DATE_____

Using the categories <u>evaluation</u> and <u>origin</u>, put the adjectives in the correct order.

Example: [charming] [Italian] girl
the charming Italian girl
EVALUATION   ORIGIN

1. [plastic] [poor] statue

2. [delightful] [Swiss] cheese

3. [thoughtful] [Vietnamese] monk

4. [wooden] [hideous] bowl

5. [marble] [nice] chess piece

6. [nice] [American] cheerleader

7. [interesting] [Southern] mansion

8. [bronze] [spectacular] horse

9. [Brazilian] [fantastic] novel

10. [glass] [repulsive] table

Score _____

EXERCISE 3-6

NAME _____ DATE_____

Now add the categories <u>size</u> or <u>age</u>.

Example: [charming] [Italian] [<u>little</u>] girl
the charming, <u>little</u> Italian girl
EVALUATION SIZE ORIGIN

[charming] [Italian] [<u>young</u>] girl
the charming, <u>young</u> Italian girl
EVALUATION AGE ORIGIN

1. [plastic] [enormous] [disgusting] statue

2. [old] [elegant] [Swiss] cheese

3. [tall] [nice] [Vietnamese] monk

4. [wooden] [hideous] [ancient] bowl

5. [plastic] [cheap] [big] chess piece

6. [young] [polite] [American] cheerleader

7. [interesting] [enormous] [Southern] mansion

8. [bronze] [spectacular] [huge] horse

9. [Brazilian] [fantastic] [new] novel

10. [glass] [repulsive] [antique] table

Score _____

EXERCISE 3-7

NAME _____ DATE_____

Next try the categories <u>color</u> or <u>condition</u>.

Example: [charming] [Italian] [<u>dark</u>] girl
the charming, <u>dark</u> Italian girl
EVALUATION COLOR ORIGIN

               [little] [Italian] [<u>well-dressed</u>] girl
the <u>well-dressed</u>, little Italian girl
CONDITION   SIZE ORIGIN

1. [plastic] [enormous] [pink] statue

2. [old] [Swiss] [white] cheese

3. [tall] [healthy] [nice] [Vietnamese] monk

4. [wooden] [hideous] [ruined] bowl

5. [plastic] [beige] [big] chess piece

6. [polite] [frumpy] [American] cheerleader

7. [interesting] [Southern] [run-down] mansion

8. [bronze] [spectacular] [well-preserved] horse

9. [Brazilian] [fantastic] [green] book

10. [glass] [repulsive] [clear] table

Score _____

EXERCISE 3-8

NAME_____DATE _____

Normally we should try to avoid having more than *three* adjectives, but sometimes it is necessary. Try all these categories together in the following exercise.

Example: [charming] [Italian] [dark] [round] [old] church
the charming, dark, old round Italian church
EVALUATION CONDITION AGE SHAPE ORIGIN

Also possible:
[charming] [Italian] [dark] [round] [old] church
the charming, old round, dark Italian church
EVALUATION AGE SHAPE COLOR ORIGIN

1. [plastic] [enormous] [pink] [decrepit] statue

2. [old] [Swiss] [white] [expensive] cheese

3. [tall] [healthy] [nice] [Vietnamese] [well-dressed] boy

4. [wooden] [hideous] [ruined] [square] table

5. [plastic] [beige] [big] [modern] chess piece

6. [nice] [frumpy] [young] [American] cheerleader

7. [interesting] [Southern] [enormous] [run-down] mansion

8. [bronze] [spectacular] [well-preserved] [huge] horse

9. [Brazilian] [fantastic] [green] [old-fashioned] book

10. [glass] [repulsive] [clear] [antique] table

Score _____

EXERCISE 3-9

NAME _____ DATE _____

Make an adjective from the underlined word or phrase.

Example: That man's face looks <u>like a boy's</u>.
That man's face looks <u>boyish</u>.

1. She treats her office staff <u>like a mother</u> would. She is _____.

2. Many of his characters are <u>like children</u>. They are very _____ in their

   innocence.

3. Even though he is the president of a large corporation, sometimes he is <u>like a naughty</u>

   <u>child</u>. He is so _____.

4. We should treat everyone <u>like a brother</u>. We could all use a little more

   _____ love.

5. The child acted <u>like a wild animal</u>. The _____ child ate the steak with her

   hands.

6. Because of the scandal, he was <u>filled with malice</u>. He is very _____.

7. The couple were very decided to remain <u>without children</u>. They enjoy being

   _____.

8. The valley where they lived was <u>filled with peace</u>. But it had not always been so

   _____.

9. They often say stupid things <u>without giving thought</u> to what they are saying. It's so sad

   that such basically nice people are so _____.

10. We <u>didn't have a single penny</u>. As usual, we were _____.

Score_____

EXERCISE 3-10

NAME_____ DATE _____

From the clues given, supply the correct 'able' adjective.

Example: She cannot <u>forgive</u> the thief. His crime was <u>unforgivable</u>.

1. Which canvas can you <u>use</u>? Is this one still _____?

2. I like being able to <u>remove</u> these windows. It's nice having _____

   windows.

3. I cannot <u>imagine</u> the cost. Three billion dollars is not even _____!

4. Was that new dress <u>washed</u>? I really hope it was _____.

5. I'm sorry we didn't <u>foresee</u> those problems. But then, some problems will always be

   un_____.

6. I <u>believed</u> him when he was really lying the whole time. But he really did sound

   _____.

7. That package is not big enough to be <u>noticed</u>. Some things just aren't

   _____.

8. Our national anthem is hard to <u>sing</u>. Indeed, some have said that it is really not

   _____ at all.

9. Henry meant to <u>return</u> the shirt. Now it's been so long that the shirt is no longer

   _____.

10. The crowd was not even able to <u>think</u> about the man's problems. His actions were

    un_____.

Score _____

EXERCISE 3-11

NAME _____ DATE _____

Change these nouns into adjectives. Try to group nouns in categories. Use your dictionary if you need to find which pattern fits.

Example: utility   utilit<u>arian</u>

1. authority _____

2. silence _____

3. anxiety _____

4. society _____

5. religion _____

6. apprehension _____

7. suspicion _____

8. perception _____

9. intuition _____

10. nausea _____

Score_____

EXERCISE 3-12

NAME _____ DATE _____

From the clues given, fill in the correct form of a participle used as an adjective.

Example: She had eaten only half the apple. The <u>half-eaten apple</u> still lay on the floor.

1. Our team was really <u>winning</u>. I was glad because the _____ team got to go

   to Florida.

2. Some people do not <u>earn</u> their doctorates. An _____ doctorate is not the

   same as an honorary one.

3. The ducks were <u>flying</u> high. High _____ ducks are hard to shoot.

4. His company <u>pays</u> him an enormous salary. He is awfully well- _____ for

   someone his age.

5. My neighbor is always <u>intruding</u> in my affairs. Yesterday, my _____

   neighbor told me to cut my grass.

6. The children were <u>watching</u> the teapot. But we all know that a _____ pot

   never boils.

7. Finally, the water was <u>boiling</u>. We poured the _____ water over the tea

   leaves.

8. Many people <u>boil</u> potatoes. I personally don't care for _____ potatoes.

9. Now when apples are <u>stewed</u>, I am really happy. _____ apples can be

eaten night and day.

10. The boys <u>used</u> all of the paper towels to clean up the mess they made.

_____ paper towels were lying all over the living room when I got home.

Score_____

EXERCISE 3-13

NAME _____ **DATE** _____

Use the past participle of the underlined verb as an adjective in each sentence.

Example: The cheese was <u>aging</u>. <u>Aged</u> cheese is more expensive.

1. Many of the peaches are <u>ripening</u>. Some _____ peaches are in the kitchen.

2. The eggs are already beginning to <u>hatch</u>. Some of the _____ chicks are

    hiding in the corner.

3. Savings bonds <u>mature</u> in 20 years. _____ bonds can then be cashed in.

4. Wheat will <u>sprout</u> if placed on a damp cloth. Then you can eat the _____

    wheat as a vegetable.

5. My checks are starting to <u>bounce</u>. One _____ check came back today.

6. Some of my plants are <u>dying</u>. I had to throw one _____ plant out today.

7. Fortunately, I have more plants <u>growing</u> out back. Some of the _____

    ones are beginning to bloom.

8. Several of my flowering trees are <u>budding</u> now. I have taken many _____

    branches inside.

9. Those trees are <u>branching</u> out nicely. Well- _____ trees are usually

    healthier.

10. He had really been <u>drinking</u> too much. The _____ man was arrested

because he was trying to drive.

Score_____

EXERCISE 3-14

NAME _____ **DATE** _____

Use the simple sentence as your model to make the adjectival participles. Add <u>very</u> to remind yourself that these forms are adjectives, not verbs.

Example: Verb: The films <u>amaze</u> the audience.
Causes emotion: The films are very <u>amazing</u>.
Experiences emotion: The audience is very <u>amazed</u>.

1. Verb: The president's speeches <u>amuse</u> the school.

    Causes emotion:

    Experiences emotion:

2. Verb: Her efforts really <u>please</u> the administration.

    Causes emotion:

    Experiences emotion:

3. Verb: Her articles <u>upset</u> the administration.

    Causes emotion:

    Experiences emotion:

4. Verb: The story <u>confuses</u> people who don't read carefully.

    Causes emotion:

    Experiences emotion:

5. Verb: Her lectures <u>bore</u> entire classes.

    Causes emotion:

    Experiences emotion:

6. Verb: She <u>interests</u> the older students.

    Causes emotion:

    Experiences emotion:

7. Verb: Did the film <u>trouble</u> your children?

    Causes emotion:

    Experiences emotion:

8. The results <u>embarrassed</u> the entire audience.

    Causes emotion:

    Experiences emotion:

9. My sudden victory <u>surprised</u> everyone.

    Causes emotion:

    Experiences emotion:

10. Does the noise from the airport <u>annoy</u> you?

    Causes emotion:

    Experiences emotion:

Score _____

EXERCISE 3-15

NAME _____ **DATE** _____

Here is a report of a TV program. Fill in any appropriate *emotive* adjective (one that causes emotions). Look back at your answers in 3-14 for some ideas. Remember the present participle form (*-ing*) causes the emotion and the past participle (*-en* or *ed*) experiences it.

Example: Last night we saw a very <u>exciting</u> program on TV.

1. The program discussed a(n) _____ problem found in American society.

2. Many older Americans are very _____ with their daily life because they

   have nothing _____ to do with their time.

3. The program dealt with _____ ways some older Americans have solved

   this _____ problem.

4. Some are buying _____ pets to share their time with. When people are

   _____ in something such as an animal they are _____ about

   life.

5. Others are taking part-time jobs in fast-food restaurants to be able to share their

   _____ lives with the _____ teenagers who normally work

   there.

6. But it is _____ that many do nothing but sit around being

   _____ at their friends and children.

7. It is _____ to think of ways to allow our older citizens to share their years

   of experience and talents with younger ones.

8. Do you have any _____ ideas on the subject?

                                                        Score_____

EXERCISE 3-16

NAME _____ DATE _____

Change the sentences so that the underlined word or phrase is used as an adverb in the new sentence. Remember that you must first build an adjective that can then be changed to an adverb.

Examples: a. The monks ate their meals <u>in silence</u>.
b. The monks ate their meals <u>silently</u>.

a. He laughed at her <u>filled with hate</u>.
b. He laughed at her <u>hatefully</u>.

1. Marie entered the room <u>with apprehension</u>.

2. The front door of the house appeared to have been ripped off its hinges <u>by force</u>.

3. The house appeared to have been torn apart as though someone had been looking for something <u>in a hurry</u>.

4. She looked around <u>filled with fear</u> as she heard a loud crash upstairs.

5. She began to climb the stairs <u>without breathing</u> outside the door.

6. As she reached the top, she stood <u>without breathing</u> outside the door.

7. Marie lunged <u>with great courage</u> into the room.

8. She gasped <u>in hysteria</u> as she saw the body of her roommate, Elie, lying on the floor.

9. Marie ran <u>without hesitating</u> to Elie.

10. At that moment, Elie rolled over <u>with great care</u> and said, "Great party, too bad you were gone."

Score _____

EXERCISE 3-17

NAME _____ **DATE** _____

Identify the role each of the underlined adverbials plays in the sentence.

Example: They run (1) <u>to their English classes</u> (2) <u>quickly</u> (3) <u>in order to learn more</u>.
1. where—direction
2. how—manner
3. why—reason

A.   The monks must eat (1) <u>every day</u> (2) <u>promptly</u> (3) <u>at noon</u> (4) <u>because the kitchen must then be used for the poor</u>.

1.

2.

3.

4.

B.   Many people went (5) <u>to the mall</u> (6) <u>suddenly</u> (7) <u>today</u> (8) <u>in order to take advantage of the great unannounced sale</u>.

5.

6.

7.

8.

C.   But I didn't go (9) <u>there</u> (10) <u>till after lunch</u>.

9.

10.

Score _____

EXERCISE 3-18

NAME _____ DATE _____

First, tell what role each adverbial is playing. Then, from the order you observed in Exercise 17, try to rearrange these incorrect sentences in the correct order.

Example: Incorrect: She visits her aunt (1) <u>because she is old</u> (2) <u>every day</u>.
(1) why (2) how often
Corrected: She visits her aunt every day because she is old.

A.   Incorrect: They talk (1) <u>every day</u> (2) <u>quietly</u> (3) <u>there</u>.

    1.

    2.

    3.

    Corrected:

B.   Incorrect: She walks (4) <u>at midnight</u> (5) <u>to the store</u> (6) <u>silently</u>.

    4.

    5.

    6.

    Corrected:

C.   Incorrect: We left (7) <u>because the music was too loud</u> (8) <u>quickly</u> (9) <u>in order to save our ears</u>.

    7.

    8.

    9.

    Corrected:

D.   Henry swims (10) <u>at sunup</u> (11) <u>to lose weight</u> (12) <u>in the pool</u> (13) <u>every other day</u>.

    10.

    11.

    12.

    13.

    Corrected:

E.   Jean had to take the car (14) <u>yesterday</u> (15) <u>for a tune-up</u> (16) <u>to the service station</u>.

    14.

    15.

    16.

    Corrected:

Score_____

EXERCISE 3-19

NAME _____ DATE _____

Put the bracketed adverbial in the preverbal position.

Example: [rarely] We are using this computer.
We are <u>rarely</u> using this computer.

1. [continually] The girls are complaining about the heat.

2. [frequently] Nina watches foreign movies to forget the heat.

3. [never] Lisa stops trying to make the fan go faster.

4. [scarcely ever] As a result, she leaves her room.

5. [occasionally] The heat will bother me.

6. [hardly ever] But I would complain about it.

7. [always] It seems to make it hotter when you talk about it.

8. [generally] I can accept things the way they are.

9. [not always] But I am content to do that.

10. [rarely] But I think it is worth the effort to complain.

Score_____

EXERCISE 3-20

NAME _____ **DATE** _____

Make a reduced sentence from the question asked and add the cued preverbal. You might need to review the process for making reduced sentences on pp.217-218 before you do this exercise.

Example: Do you eat in fancy restaurants? [rarely]
No, <u>I rarely do</u>.

1. Have you been to Paris? [never]

    No,

2. But you have visited Dakar, haven't you? [seldom]

    Yes, but

3. Do you know where you will go next? [occasionally]

    Well,

4. Do you enjoy that life style? [generally]

    Yes,

5. Will you want a settled home someday? [never]

    No,

6. Did the boys finish their work? [not often]

    No,

7. Do you ever rent videos? [frequently]

    Yes, we

8. Have you been taking your medicine? [generally]

   Well, I

9. Do the doctors or the nurses perform these tests? [normally]

   The nurses

10. Will the administrators be checking up on the program? [often]

    Yes, they

Score _____

EXERCISE 3-21

NAME _____ DATE _____

Has a "double negative" been used? If it has, rewrite the sentence. Remember that you don't need <u>do</u> if you don't use <u>not</u>.

Example: She doesn't seldom go. [notice <u>does</u>]
                 She seldom goes. [you don't need <u>does</u>]

1. We can't hardly afford his paintings.

2. Sadly, his paintings don't never sell.

3. People aren't hardly talking about his work anymore.

4. Even though there isn't never an art magazine without an article about him, he won't hardly be mentioned at important cocktail parties.

5. However, he hasn't seldom mentioned the problem.

6. I personally think he doesn't scarcely care.

7. Nor does his agent hardly accept responsibility.

8. Oh well, few painters seldom become rich.

9. Anyway, my opinion scarcely matters to no one.

10. But I really hope that he never doesn't stop painting.

Score_____

EXERCISE 3-22

NAME _____ **DATE** _____

Add the -er suffix to the one-syllable basic adjectives or adverbs. If the word is derived, put an X next to that word and give the base form.

Example: short*er* [basic]
                  lost <u>X</u> [derived from <u>lose</u>]

1. loud _____

2. curved _____

3. fast _____

4. burnt _____

5. big _____

6. hard _____

7. near _____

8. fused _____

9. red _____

10. bent _____

Score _____

EXERCISE 3-23

NAME _____ DATE _____

If an adjective has a two-syllable stem that ends in -y, -ple, -el (also written -le), -ow, or -ble, add -er. Otherwise, put an X next to the word.

Example: sadly X [the ending is -ly]
              crazy *crazier* [don't forget spelling rules]

1. easy _____

2. ready _____

3. nimble _____

4. dizzy _____

5. cruel _____

6. gentle _____

7. thoughtful _____

8. shallow _____

9. lousy _____

10. feeble _____

Score_____

EXERCISE 3-24

NAME _____   **DATE** _____

Add the *-est* pattern to the one-syllable basic adjectives. If the word is derived, put an X next to that word.

Example: the short<u>est</u> basic]
lost <u>X</u> [derived from <u>lose</u>]

1. loud _____

2. curved _____

3. small _____

4. burnt _____

5. weak _____

6. sick _____

7. slow _____

8. fused _____

9. red _____

10. bent _____

Score _____

EXERCISE 3-25

NAME _____ DATE _____

If an adjective has a two-syllable stem with the suffixes *-y, -ple, -el* (also written *-le*), *-ow,* or *-ble,* add *the -est*. Otherwise, put an X next to the word.

Example: sadly X [not an adjective]
crazy the craziest [don't forget spelling rules]

1. easy _____

2. ready _____

3. nimble _____

4. dizzy _____

5. simple _____

6. loony _____

7. thoughtful _____

8. messy _____

9. shallow _____

10. pretty _____

Score_____

EXERCISE 3-26

NAME _____ **DATE** _____

Use the rules we have discussed to provide the correct form of the comparative (c) or superlative (s).

Example: (c) fat: Craig used to be _____.
Craig used to be <u>fatter</u>.

1. (s) pretty: Debbie is the _____ model we have ever had.

2. (c) petty: I did not think you could find a _____ issue to bother

me with, but I was wrong.

3. (c) near: They were very glad to move _____ to the university.

4. (s) important: The current chair thinks that her opinion is the

_____.

5. (s) blunt: All of the remarks were straight-forward, but his were the

_____; they were almost cruel.

6. (s) strange: Someone once said that April was the _____ month.

But in Memphis it is August.

7. (s) sad: *Sophie's Choice* was the _____ novel Ellie had ever read.

8. (c) fast: If the women wish to win, they must run _____ than last

week.

9. (c) dramatically: Only Sarah herself could have done it _____.

10. (s) gentle: In spite of his size, he was the _____ human ever.

Score _____

EXERCISE 3-27

NAME _____ DATE _____

Fill in the appropriate comparative or superlative form from the cued word.

Example: (short) That is _____ bank robber I have ever seen.
That is <u>the shortest</u> bank robber I have ever seen.

1. (bad) There had been _____ days, (good) but then there had also been

   _____ ones.

2. (boring) Working in the bank had been even _____ than the ice cream

   factory.

3. (easy) Jan thought, "There must be _____ ways to pay for college."

4. (near) Jan watched as a little old man came _____ to her window, (few)

   which had _____ people in line.

5. (long) Suddenly she remembered today was _____ day of the month.

   Social Security checks came out, and the day never seemed to end.

6. (old) Normally, Jan enjoyed waiting on _____ people (much)

   _____ than on young business types.

7. (important) But there was nothing _____ to senior citizens than their

   checks. As a result, everything went (slowly) _____ today.

8. (more) The old man finally got to her window and asked, "What's _____

   money you have ever had?"

9. (little) Jan thought and said, "I have never had _____ than today."

10. (far) But before she could get any _____ in her story, the old man pulled

    out a gun.

11. (deep) "Give me all your money!" he said in _____ voice Jan had ever

    heard.

12. (old) As she thought how her _____ sister would tease her at dinner, she

    began to stuff the money in the man's paper bag. (afraid) She had never been

    _____ .

13. (little) Just then _____ old lady Jan had ever seen walked over and took

    the gun from the man.

14. She said, "Don't mind him, honey. (good) He used to be _____ bank

    robber in Chicago. (short) Now he's just _____ ."

15. (exciting) Maybe working in the bank was _____ than the ice cream

    factory.

Score _____

EXERCISE 3-28

NAME _____ **DATE** _____

Form equatives from the formulas given.

Example: Fred/Frieda/be bright
                 Fred is as bright as Frieda.

1. my house/your house/not be nice

2. The girls/the boys/eat much

3. *Giant/West Side Story/* not be interesting

4. Bonnie/Cary/read many books

5. This clock/that clock/not run well

6. Dan/Dawn/not be funny

7. Frank/Gloria/not be tall

8. Walking/eating/be important

9. Jack/William/act dumb

10. Swimming/watching movies/not good for you

Score _____

4

Verbs and Verb Phrases

The English verb system presents many challenges to the ESL learner. But you can learn to avoid many predictable errors if you understand the principles behind the verb system.

4a. Basic Forms

Each English verb phrase must contain a basic form. You must learn to recognize, produce, and *predict* the required basic form. Let's look at each of the basic forms and see how they interrelate. We are trying to find *patterns* that make learning easier.

Regular Verbs

Most English verbs are called *regular*, which means they follow the most common verbal pattern. Their forms are easy to predict.

base:	walk
-s form:	walks
past:	walked
past participle:	walked
present participle:	walking

Irregular Verbs

Most of the verbs we call irregular (see "Irregular Verbs" in the handbook's "Glossary of Grammatical and Rhetorical Terms") are not really *irregular*. Rather, they follow uncommon verbal patterns (for example, *sing, sang, sung,* and *ring, rang, rung*) in which the *vowels* change to form the basic forms. In this chapter, we will call verbs that follow these vowel patterns *strong* verbs. Although their forms are predictable, there are not many examples of each pattern. However, you should always practice two or more of these verbs together to remind yourself that there is a pattern to be found.

There are, however, verbs that are really *irregular*; their forms are not predictable (for example, *go, went, gone*). The most irregular verb is also the most common: *be*. The forms of these verbs must be memorized and practiced until you can produce them naturally.

Do Exercise 4-1.

Base (Infinitive)

The English base (or infinitive) form doesn't need a suffix to show that is the infinitive form. Only one verb, *be*, has an irregular base form.

Past

Because of its formation, this form is also called the *-ed* form: *drag* plus *-ed* equals *dragged*. Don't let the name "past" confuse you; this form is also used in constructions that have nothing to do with past time.

> *Past time:* I *travelled* to Chicago *last week*.
> *Future time:* If I *travelled* to Chicago *tomorrow*, could I catch a flight to Singapore on Thursday.

Do Exercise 4-2.

The strong verbs have a different pattern in forming their past forms. There is an *internal* change in the vowel and no *-ed* suffix is added.

Strong Base	Strong Past
write	wrote

Finally, there is a very small group that do both. They add *-ed* (which sometimes shows up as *-t*) and change an internal vowel. Some people call these verbs *mixed*, since they use both processes.

| leave | left |
| sell | sold |

Past and Present Participles

Each verb has two participles: the past and the present. These are very awkward names; these forms are used in contexts that have nothing to do with the past or the present.

Another name for the past participle is the *-en* form to distinguish it from the *-ed* or past form. This *-en* name comes from the suffix that many strong verbs use for their past participles.

Strong Base	Past	Past Participle
write	wrote	written
eat	ate	eaten

Regular verbs form their past participles by adding the *-ed* suffix. In isolation, there is no difference between the past form and the past participle for regular verbs.

Regular Base	Past	Past Participle
laugh	laughed	laughed

The *present participle* is made for all verbs by adding *-ing* to the base. Remember spelling rules.

Base	Present Participle
be	being
try	trying
get	getting

4b. Auxiliaries and Verb Phrases

Most often, we do not use simple verb forms. Verbs are normally combined with *auxiliaries*.

In a verb phrase the last verb is always the main or lexical verb; it is the verb with the real content. All others are auxiliaries. However, there can be several auxiliaries in a verb phrase. But only the first auxiliary can be a *tensed* form. All other auxiliaries must be *non-tensed* forms.

(1) *Be* auxiliary

Be can be followed only by the *-ing* (present participle) or *-en* (past participle) form. Any other verb form is incorrect. A form of *be* and the present participle form the *progressive*.

> He *was eating* lunch at the time.

Be and the past participle form the *passive*.

> The cat *was given* to the children on Sunday.

We will discuss the uses of these forms later. Now just be sure that you understand that no other forms are possible.

Do Exercise 4-3.

(2) *Have* auxiliary

Have can be followed only by the *past participle*. This combination is called the *perfect*.

> *Present perfect:* I have forgotten the keys again. (Notice that *have* is in the *present* tense.)
> *Past perfect:* She had already given me the book. (Notice that *had* is in the *past* tense.)

Try Exercise 4-4.

(3) Modal auxiliaries

The modals are unique. They only have one form, which is always *tensed*. As a result, the modals cannot be used in any of the structures that use non-tensed forms such as participles of infinitives. Notice also that the modals must be followed by the *base* (infinitive form).

> *Incorrect:* (perfect) I have *could* go.
> *Incorrect:* (progressive) She is *must* leaving.
> *Incorrect:* (infinitive) She hopes *to can* leave.

Now do Exercise 4-5.

Since the modals have only a tensed form, they must always be the first verb in a verb phrase. If you want to use the modals in those forms that need non-tensed forms, you must use *periphrastic* modals. (*Periphrastic* means using more words to do the same thing fewer words could.) These periphrastic modals are actually *phrases* that have just about the same meaning as the modals.

> *Modals, always tensed:* can
> *Periphrastic modal, all forms possible:* be able to

I *can* go today, but I don't think that I will *be able to go* tomorrow.

Now do Exercise 4-5.

(4) *Do* auxiliary

We call the auxiliary *do* the periphrastic auxiliary.

> *Without do:* I tell you, Cybill knows my name!
> *With periphrastic do:* I tell you, Cybill *does* know my name!

One of the unpredictable functions of *do* is the emphatic form, which we saw in the last example. You should try not to use those forms too much. Did you notice that the *base* form must follow *do?*

Even though the emphatic use must be determined from context, there are many uses of the *do* auxiliary that are *predictable and required*.

Do Exercise 4-7 before you go on.

Question Formation

Questions need a special form to let the reader know that they are special. Other related languages just *invert* subject and verb to show that special quality. English allowed this inversion for a long time. If you read earlier works in English (such as anything by Shakespeare), you will encounter this form.

> *Normal:* She walks to the store.
> *Inverted for question:* Walks she to the store?

But this inversion is no longer acceptable in Modern English because we require the *main* verb to follow the subject. Still we needed some way to signal the question. Now we use the auxiliary *do* to allow us to do both: change word order and keep the subject before the main verb.

Auxiliary	Subject	Verb
Does	Don	study every night?

Now try Exercise 4-8.

Remember, only the first verb in a verb phrase can be tensed; the others must be non-tensed: a base or a participle. When we add *do* to the verb phrase, we must take the tense from the main verb and transfer it to *do*. If we put the tense on *do*, then the first verb is tensed. That means the verb that follows *do* must be the base form.

> *Normal:* She walked to the beach. (past tense)
> *With do:* She *did* walk to the beach. (*did* is the past of *do*)

Do Exercise 4-9 before you go on.

If there is another auxiliary or *be* is the main verb, we don't need to add *do*. In fact, it is incorrect in English to mix *do* with the other auxiliaries or the main verb *be*.

> *Incorrect:* Do you be on time for once?
> *Correct: Are* you on time for once?

Negatives

We need to use *do* with negatives to make sure we negate the correct part of a sentence. We normally need to place the negative right after the first verb in the verb phrase so that it is firmly inside the verb phrase.

> *Incorrect:* Eve *not* (has gone) apple picking.
> *Correct:* Eve (has *not* gone) apple picking.

However, if we do not have any auxiliaries, the *not* would be outside the verb phrase.

> *Incorrect:* Eve (went) *not* apple picking.

To prevent that, we must use *do*.

> *Correct:* Eve (*did* not *go*) apple picking.

With *be* we do not want the *not* inside the verb phrase because we are usually negating the rest of the predicate, not the verb.

> *Correct:* Eve *was* (not the first American astronaut).

Now do Exercise 4-10.

Inversions

There are a few really strong *negative* words that require a special inversion of the first verb and the subject. If there are auxiliaries or *be* is the main verb, everything is fine.

> *Inverted: Rarely have* I eaten so much!
> *Inverted: Never is* he to be let back in this house!

If there are no auxiliaries, however, we must use *do;* otherwise, we would put the main verb in front of the subject.

> *Regular word order:* Jason grasps the main idea *only rarely.*
> *Inverted for emphasis: Only rarely does* Jason grasp the main idea.

4c. Tense

Tense is really a statement about the relationships among related events. Time and tense are not necessarily the same.

> *Present tense but past, present and future time:* He goes to camp
>   every summer.

Since the handbook contains a complete chart of the verb tenses, we won't include one here. Now try Exercise 4-12.

4d. Progressive Forms

Whether to use a progressive form (made with some form of *be* and the *-ing* participle) or a simple form is often a problem. If we compare the basic functions of these forms, we can avoid some of the more obvious errors.

Present Progressive and Present

The progressive has three major uses. First, use the progressive when you are interested *in the process of* doing something.

> *Are* you *talking* on the other line at this very moment?

In this example, we want to know if the person is in the *process* of making a single conversation. We don't care how many conversations that person has had or not had.

When the progressive is combined with certain adverbials, this construction indicates *future time* of a single event.

> *Tomorrow* Fritz *is taking* me to lunch.

If *tomorrow* were not in that sentence, it would mean now or, at best, in the *very* near future.

> A: Fritz *is taking* me to lunch.
> B: Oh, today?
> A: Well, no, but someday.
> B: Don't hold your breath.

Finally, when combined with other verbs such as *go, begin, become,* or *start,* the progressive stresses the *beginning* of a *single* event.

> She is *going* back to school. (She is *not* in school now.)
> My hay fever *is beginning* to bother me. (It just barely has *started* to bother me.)

Simple Present and Present Progressive

The simple present forms are often used for events that generally occur more than once or for *eternal* truth.

> Fritz *takes* me to lunch *every* Friday.
> The world *is* round.

On the other hand, the present progressive usually refers to just one occurrence of an event or to an ongoing event.

> Fritz *is taking* me to lunch *this* Friday.
> The world *is recovering* nicely from a recession.

Since the progressive describes a state of an event, you do not need to use the progressive with verbs that already describe states. Instead, just use the present with these *verbs of state.*

Fred *seems* very bored in his new job. (no end, no beginning)
Do you *think* so? (we are in the process of thinking)

With certain adverbials, even the present can be used to describe the future time.

The final exam *is tomorrow.*

When we use the present tense for future time, the event seems unavoidable; on the other hand, the progressive seems less certain. In certain parts of the country one hears *to be fixing to* as a future form. Although you should understand it, you should avoid using it.

Nonstandard: We *'re fixing to* leave for the movies.
Standard: We're ready to leave for the movies.

Simple Past and Past Progressive

The differences between the simple past and the past progressive are not as great as for the present forms. Basically, the progressive stresses the process of doing something (the event may never have been finished) while the *past* (and *past perfect*) tells of an event *completed* in the past.

We *were talking* when the ceiling *fell* in. (past progressive; past)
The boy *was throwing* stones when we *asked* him the question. (past
    progressive; past)
The farmers *had* already *left* when we *arrived.* (past perfect; past)

Progressive, Perfect, and Past

The perfect forms signal indefinite lengths of time that might have a definite beginning but have no specific ending.

The girls have visited France. (no beginning, no specific ending)
They have worked here since 1979. (specific beginning, no specific ending)

The past tense is for events that are over.

The girls visited France. (but they are in Florida now)
They worked here. (but now they work somewhere else)

The past can be used with prepositions that have an "end." But they cannot be used with prepositions that have an indefinite length of time (e.g., no specific end).

Correct: We worked *until* 7:30. (exact end)
Incorrect: We worked *since* 7:30. (no end)

The present perfect or past perfect progressive stresses a process that began in the past and is (was) still valid at the time of the event.

We *have been going* to the river for years now. (still going on even though it began in the past)

The present doesn't tell us when something began. In fact, it cannot be used with prepositions that "start" events.

Correct: We live in Memphis. (who knows how long we have been here)
Incorrect: We live in Memphis since 1978. (a beginning of an event: our living in Memphis)

Although the present progressive doesn't tell us when something began, it stresses the *now,* which might be subject to change.

> We *are living* in Memphis right now. (but I might be transferred again)

The present progressive can't be used with prepositions that "start" events either.

> *Incorrect:* We *are living* in Memphis since January.

Do Exercises 4-14 and 4-15.

4e. Voice

When we have a transitive verb, we can usually make a passive of an active sentence.

> *Active:* Someone *checks* the figures.
> *Passive:* The figures *were checked.*

The passive allows you to put an object in the subject position. Sometimes you can try to use the passive to get away with things.

> A: Did you check those *figures?*
> B: The figures *were checked.* (no agent)
> A: No, I asked if *you* checked those figures.
> B: No, I didn't.

Many American writers and educators dislike the passive. However, if you are in the sciences, you will need to learn when the use of the passive is appropriate. Ask your instructors about their attitudes toward the passive.

Formation

It is not difficult to make the passive in isolation; the difficult part is using it correctly. Let's do the easy part.

> *Base:* The nasty children broke the beautiful vase.
> (subject) (verb) (object)

> *Substitute form of be for main verb: were* since *broke* is simple past plural:
> (the nasty children) *were* (the beautiful vase) *(broke)*

> *Change main verb to past participle: broke* becomes *broken*

> *Insert participle after form of be:* (the nasty children) *(were broken)* (the beautiful vase)

> *Reverse positions of subject and object; add* by: (the beautiful vase) (were broken) (by the nasty children)

> *Make* be *agree with new subject (old object):* The beautiful vase *was* broken by the nasty children.

> *It is very important to check (new) subject-verb agreement.*

Now do Exercise 4-16.

If we wanted to hide the fact that it was *the nasty children* who broke *the vase,* we could just delete the *by* phrase.

> The beautiful vase was broken.

We can make any sentence type passive, although imperatives rarely sound natural.

> *Not very natural: Be regarded* as a leader of your community! Sign up for our leadership classes!

In English you can make *indirect* objects passive with ease. This operation is not possible in all languages.

> The committee awarded *the poet* the prize.
> The poet *was awarded* the prize by the committee.

However, you cannot make passive certain locatives, as other languages can.

> *Base:* Someone washes clothes *here.*
> *Incorrect: Here* is clothes washed. (*here* cannot be the subject)

Get *and* Be *Passives*

In colloquial English, we often use *get* as the passive marker rather than *be.* We seldom use the agent with the get passive.

> Fred *got* arrested for driving without a license.
> Fred *was* arrested for driving without a license.

Do not use these forms in writing. In speech, there is a difference in emphasis; the get passives focus on the process while the be passives focus on the state. As a result, the get passives are often more emotionally charged than the be passives.

There is one important difference. *Get* is *not* an auxiliary, so you must use the auxiliary *do* if it is needed.

> Jan *was* arrested last night.
> Jan *got* arrested last night.
>
> Where *was* he arrested?
> Where *did* he get arrested?

Do Exercise 4-17 now.

4f. Mood

Modern English is losing many of the special verb forms that signal different moods. However, in writing we must observe the formal forms.

(I) Indicative mood

This is the normal mood of most sentences in conversation. This is the form we have been discussing in this chapter so far.

(2) Imperative mood

The *imperative* is another name for command forms used when someone tells *you* to do something. Command forms are simple in English. To form the imperative, just delete the *you* and make sure the verb is in the base form (a problem only with *be*).

Try Exercise 4-18.

The negative is formed by adding *don't/do not* in front of the imperative. Notice that in this case we allow *be* to be combined with *do*; in all other structures that is incorrect.

> *Don't* be late!
> Don't leave home without it!
>
> *Incorrect:* You *don't be* a famous movie star, do you?
> *Correct:* You aren't a famous movie star, are you?

Now do Exercise 4-19.

Many times in English we use forms that sound like questions but are really imperatives. Some people call these forms *whimperatives*.

> *Whimperative:* Would you shut the door?
> *Imperative:* Shut the door!

Do Exercise 4-20.

(3) Subjunctive mood

For the most part, the subjunctive is disappearing in Modern English. However, one construction that uses the subjunctive is actually growing.

Mandative Subjunctive

The *mandative subjunctive* is the formal name for the subjunctive that must be used in *American* English after certain *that* clauses of *demands*. Many Americans still do not use this form, but it is imperative that it *be* used.

To form the mandative subjunctive, just use the base (infinitive). This form will look odd for the third person singular and for all forms with *be* and negatives. Many native speakers will not use modals (remember they have no base form) in this construction.

> It was essential that he *not be* elected president.
> We are requiring that each student *bring* a new book.
>
> *Incorrect:* We require that each student *will* bring a new book.
> *Correct:* We require that each student bring a new book.

Notice that this form doesn't change even when the main clause is in the past or any other form; the mandative subjunctive is always the same.

> We *insist* that he *be* well-groomed.
> We *insisted* that he *be* well-groomed.

Since this form is growing in use, you may encounter some confusion from native speakers about whether a specific verb or adjective requires this form or not.

Now try Exercise 4-21

EXERCISE 4-1

NAME _____**DATE** _____

Look at the IRREGULAR VERBS list in the glossary of the handbook. Find *five* pairs of verbs whose *vowels* "rhyme." In other words, find verbs that have the same pattern.

Example: ride   rode   ridden
         write   wrote   written

1.

2.

3.

4.

5.

Score _____

EXERCISE 4-2

NAME _____ **DATE** _____

Provide the past form (*-ed* form) for each of these regular verbs. Remember spelling rules.

Example: wish   wished

1. work _____

2. interact _____

3. try _____

4. exercise _____

5. remember _____

6. apply _____

7. generate _____

8. account _____

9. cover _____

10. lag _____

11. stay [careful] _____

12. mix [careful: *x* equals *ks*] _____

Score _____

EXERCISE 4-3

NAME _____ DATE _____

Supply the correct form for the form requested.

Example: (passive) She has been *asks* to leave.
                 She has been *asked* to leave.

1. (progressive) Why have you been *gotten* to work late?

2. (progressive) We are *became* tired of your tardiness.

3. (passive) If you don't improve, you will be *firing*.

4. (progressive) The situation hasn't been *improves* much this week.

5. (passive) Now you have been *warn*.

6. (progressive) Last week I was *drove* from Santa Fe to Dallas.

7. (passive) Part of the road had been *washing* out by a sudden storm.

8. (passive) Some animals were *kills* by the water.

9. (progressive) Some of the animals were still *run* around looking for shelter.

10. (passive) Fortunately, not too much had been *destroy* by the storm.

Score _____

EXERCISE 4-4

NAME _____ DATE _____

Make sure that a past participle (*-en* form) follows any form of *have*.

Example: a. She has *being* fired.
                b. She has *been* fired.

1. a. Have you *enjoying* the evening?

    b.

2. a. The girls will have *leave* by now.

    b.

3. a. He has *breaked* his arm.

    b.

4. a. I have *being* forgotten by the computer again.

    b.

5. a. Earlier, we had *went* to the zoo.

    b.

6. a. The judge has *give* her a light sentence.

    b.

7. a. Computers have *changing* our world.

    b.

8. a. Research has *be* made easier.

    b.

9. a. Some people have *cut* their fingers on the sharp edges of the desk.

    b.

10. a. Jane had *betted* on the favorite.

    b.

Score_____

EXERCISE 4-5

NAME _____ DATE _____

Supply the correct form of the verb that follows the modal auxiliary.

Example: a. She must <u>went</u> to the store.
                 b. She must <u>go</u> to the store.

1. a. Sadly, she should <u>cooks</u> dinner for the family.

    b.

2. a. We're afraid it will <u>being</u> a disaster.

    b.

3. a. She is a great mathematician, but she cannot <u>was</u> trusted with even the simplest dishes.

    b.

4. a. Yes, I think tonight would <u>was</u> a good night to eat out.

    b.

5. a. He should <u>avoids</u> the traffic in the morning.

    b.

6. a. Where would you <u>liking</u> to dine? Franco's?

    b.

7. a. My friend will <u>left</u> on Friday.

    b.

8. a. Will you <u>insisting</u> on his resignation?

    b.

9. a. When should we <u>hoped</u> to see you again?

   b.

10. a. What should the class <u>being</u> doing now?

    b.

Score _____

EXERCISE 4-6

NAME _____ DATE _____

Using the correct form of the periphrastic modal in brackets, replace the modal that has been used incorrectly.

Example: [be able to] I hope to <u>can</u> study medicine.
I hope to <u>be able to</u> study medicine.

1. [have to] To study medicine, I will <u>must</u> work hard.

2. [be permitted to] You haven't <u>may</u> declare your major, have you?

3. [be able to] After you take your exams, you might <u>can</u> declare that you are a pre-med.

4. [need to] Because of your grades, you won't <u>should</u> worry.

5. [be required to] Others might <u>must</u> take remedial courses, but you won't.

6. [be able to] Will you <u>can</u> watch my cat while I am gone?

7. [need to] Have you <u>should</u> visit the office again?

8. [be permitted to] <u>May</u> he go on the class trip?

9. [have to] They were <u>must</u> replace the water every day.

10. [be required to] They hope not to <u>must</u> buy a new license for their boat this year.

Score _____

EXERCISE 4-7

NAME _____ DATE _____

Supply the correct form of the verb that follows <u>do</u>.

Example: a. Did you ever <u>visited</u> that city?
                b. Did you ever <u>visit</u> that city?

1. a. Carmen didn't <u>had</u> the chance to visit the capitol.

    b.

2. a. She says she still does <u>wanting</u> to see it.

    b.

3. a. Lee doesn't <u>believes</u> her.

    b.

4. a. Nor did he <u>understood</u> that new interest of hers in architecture.

    b.

5. a. Why doesn't he <u>accepts</u> her statements at face value?

    b.

6. a. Rarely does a case of abuse of power <u>comes</u> to the court.

    b.

7. a. She didn't <u>had</u> the right key with her.

    b.

8. a. Only in Florida does one <u>needs</u> sunglasses at Christmas!

    b.

9. a. His actions did <u>tended</u> to make us think he was guilty.

    b.

10. a. Why does the nastiest customer always <u>complains</u> the most?

    b.

Score _____

EXERCISE 4-8

NAME _____ DATE _____

Change these sentences to questions.

Example: She did buy the new car yesterday.
                 Did she buy the new car yesterday?

1. They did visit their grandmother in Florida.

2. The clock did stop running last night.

3. The girls did miss their plane because of it.

4. Both girls did enjoy the visit.

5. The grandmother did have a nice time, too.

6. Your sister does live in Southport.

7. She did bring the right key today.

8. The thieves did steal everything.

9. His associate did win the prize.

10 Belinda did know the answer to the question.

Score_____

EXERCISE 4-9

NAME _____ DATE _____

(a) Label the tense in the first sentence. (b) Take the tense from the main verb; transfer it to the correct form of <u>do</u>. (c) Make a question of the sentence. You might need to review the section on tense (4c) before you try this exercise.

Example: a. Ron gives out the checks. <u>present</u>
b. Ron <u>does</u> <u>give</u> out the checks.
c. Does Ron give out the checks?

1. a. India produces most of the world's rosewater. _____

    b.

    c.

2. a. You completed the form yesterday. _____

    b.

    c.

3. a. Mr. Ginnis lost his form again. _____

    b.

    c.

4. a. The government lent you the money. _____

    b.

    c.

5. a. A teacher needs to learn to think on his feet. _____

    b.

    c.

6. a. The computer changed the way we work. _____

   b.

   c.

7. a. They wrote the book on a word processor. _____

   b.

   c.

8. a. Sheila took her vacation in May. _____

   b.

   c.

9. a. Today we need to cut the hedge. _____

   b.

   c.

10. a. You want to go with us. _____

    b.

    c.

Score _____

EXERCISE 4-10

NAME _____   DATE _____

Correct the following so that the <u>not</u> is right after the first auxiliary. If there are no auxiliaries, provide the correct form of <u>do</u>.

Example: We have gone not shopping in years.
                    We have <u>not</u> gone shopping in years.

                    We left not the keys in the restaurant.
                    We <u>did</u> not <u>leave</u> the keys in the restaurant.

1. The boss wrote <u>not</u> the letter for Willy.

2. Vera would have <u>not</u> gone if we had been nicer.

3. Could you pick <u>not</u> me up at six? [Careful—where's the first verb?]

4. The Keltics were <u>not</u> the first inhabitants of England.

5. Taylor will have been forgotten <u>not</u> by then.

6. She takes <u>not</u> vitamins.

7. Give <u>not</u> him the cookies!

8. Why have you asked <u>not</u> to go with us?

9. Did you leave <u>not</u> the dog some water?

10. You will be visiting <u>not</u> this summer, will you?

Score _____

EXERCISE 4-11

NAME _____ **DATE** _____

Move each underlined strongly negative phrase to the front of the sentence. Then, invert the subject and first auxiliary. If there is no auxiliary, you need to add <u>do</u>.

Example: Bennie <u>rarely</u> tries to help around the house.
<u>Rarely</u> does Bennie try to help around the house.

1. Yvonne is <u>seldom</u> seen anymore.

2. Carl has <u>only recently</u> recovered from the shock.

3. The team <u>hardly ever</u> wins anymore.

4. The prince can <u>never</u> leave the castle again!

5. We went to the beach <u>only occasionally</u>.

Score _____

EXERCISE 4-12

NAME_____ DATE _____

Using the charts on tenses in the handbook, label the tense of each sentence. Then, label the time.

Example: Andrew <u>now</u> marches in the college band.
                    Tense is present, time is present.

1. In 1876, there was a horrible yellow fever epidemic.

   Tense: Time:

2. We have lived in Memphis for six years now.

   Tense: Time:

3. First, we ate dinner with my friends.

   Tense: Time:

4. The races start tomorrow.

   Tense: Time:

5. Yesterday, she performed at the Student Union.

   Tense: Time:

6. The boys have already gone home.

   Tense: Time:

7. She had performed at the Union before.

   Tense: Time:

8. In 1990, she will have lived here exactly 30 years.

   Tense: Time:

9. The earth turns very quickly.

   Tense: _____   Time: _____

10. The warriors had already seen the enemy camp.

    Tense: _____   Time: _____

Score _____

EXERCISE 4-13

NAME _____ DATE_____

Decide whether the present or the progressive tense should be used. Justify your answers.

Example: [live] Where _____ you _____ these days?
[live] Where <u>are</u> you <u>living</u> these days?
in the process of one [very slow] event

1. [study] I _____ right now. Leave me alone.

2. [study] Fred and I _____ together every night.

3. [have] We think Fred _____ a physics exam tomorrow.

4. [like] [want] Because he _____ physics, he _____ to do well

    on the exam.

5. [make] In fact, he normally _____ fairly good grades in school all the time.

6. [remind] [burn] But then, Fred always _____ me that he

    _____ the midnight oil.

7. [fail] However, this semester Fred _____ some subjects.

8. [wonder] [have] His mother _____ if he _____ the motivation

    to succeed this year.

9. [view] His parents _____ success as a moral question.

10. [be] [improve] But Fred and I _____ sure that he _____

    because of our extra study sessions.

Score _____

EXERCISE 4-14

NAME _____ DATE _____

Decide whether the past, past perfect, or past progressive tense is most appropriate. Justify your answers.

Example: [think] [know] The judge _____ he _____ the inmate well.
[think] [know] The judge <u>thought</u> he <u>knew</u> the inmate well. [verbs of state]

1. [watch] [leave] Yesterday was an exciting day for my neighbor's family. While the girls

    _____ television, their father _____ to go to the video store.

2. [hope] [be] He _____ that the video store _____ not busy on

    Sunday evenings.

3. [want] [get] [have] He just _____ to pick up an educational video for his

    family, who _____ bored with the tapes they _____ .

4. [have] [try] Indeed, they _____ problems right then with their eldest

    daughter, who _____ to convince her father to buy her a car.

5. [ring] [fade] [shout] Suddenly, shots _____ rang out and

    _____ away quickly. For a long time, someone _____ .

6. [be able to] [have] Finally, the father _____ to get off the ground, where

    he _____ fallen during the shooting spree.

7. [seem] [be] Although no one _____ to be hurt, everyone

    _____ visibly shaken.

8. [return] [tell] [hear] [be] After he _____ home and

   _____ his story to his family, they _____ on the television

   that a disgruntled former employee _____ questioned at that very

   moment.

9. [be] [be] [laugh] [think] Just then, a film of the scene _____ shown and

   there the father _____ right on TV. Everyone _____ but they

   all _____ how tragic it could have been. [Careful in the last sentence; there

   is a trick.]

10. [go] Finally, they all _____ to bed early.

Score _____

EXERCISE 4-15

NAME _____ DATE _____

Supply the appropriate form. Justify your answer.

Example: [visit] She _____ her friends every year until last.
[visit] She <u>visited</u> her friends every year until last. [repeated action in the past]

1. [check] [miss] An auditor _____ the figures last month. Still millions of

   dollars _____ .

2. [raid] [gather] [ring] All at once, the police _____ our offices. The whole

   time the police _____ evidence, the phones _____ madly.

3. [calm] [march] [start] Just as most of the secretaries _____ down, my uncle

   _____ in and _____ yelling.

4. [rant] [be] [plan] He _____ that his rights _____ violated and he

   _____ to sue everybody.

5. [be able to] [want] [tell] Finally, when the police _____ explain what they

   _____ there, he _____ them the money was safe under his

   mattress at home.

6. [not go] [seem] He _____ to leave all that money in a bank; they

   _____ to be unsafe.

7. [live] [visit] When the family _____ in Washington, they _____

   the National Gallery every Sunday.

8. [live] [have] In 1985, after Maureen _____ here for five years, she

_____ to move.

9. [work] [force] Although she _____ on a degree at <u>that</u> time, the move

_____ her to drop out of college.

10. [stay] [grow] Every summer when my brother and I _____ with our

grandparents, we _____ tomatoes, cucumbers, and radishes.

Score _____

EXERCISE 4-16

NAME _____ DATE _____

Make these sentences passive if they are active and active if they are passive. You may need to supply a new subject. Double-check [new] subject-verb agreement.

Example: She was asked to be on the program.
                    <u>Someone</u> asked her to be on the program.

1. The boys were telling stories about ghosts and ghouls.

2. My friend bought that big, old house on the corner.

3. No ghosts or ghouls were found in there.

4. Why were you given this office by the dean?

5. When was the dean last seen?

6. Do many people enjoy your music?

7. Where are your compositions sold?

8. Can the recordings be found in the library?

9. Are you really being awarded the Curtis Prize by the committee?

10. Have the folks over there ever fed their dog?

Score _____

EXERCISE 4-17

Change the *be* passives to *get* passives and the *get* passives to *be* passives.

Example: She was fired yesterday.
                She <u>got</u> fired yesterday.

1. I am getting hurt every time I do this.

2. Many people were employed by the new plant.

3. The scholars have finally gotten published.

4. Many people were killed in the accident.

5. Some of the audience were confused by the trick.

Score _____

EXERCISE 4-18

NAME _____ DATE_____

Change the sentences to the imperative.

Example: You are on time.
                 Be on time!

1. You write this letter, Dawn.

2. You finish that liver first.

3. Don, you buy me a camera while in New York.

4. You try to talk with them more.

5. You are able to change a tire.

6. Kevin, you study those last three chapters.

7. You enjoy your trip to Spain.

8. You name her after me, David.

9. Guy, you grow tomatoes in this bed.

10. You wash the car on Saturday.

Score _____

EXERCISE 4-19

NAME _____   **DATE**_____

Change each sentence to a *negative* imperative.

Example: You are late.
                  Don't be late.

1. You write her an excuse for that day.

2. You finish the last piece of cake, Dawn.

3. You buy me any clothes in New York.

4. You try to be nice to them, Jeffrey.

5. You are ready to leave.

6. You forget those last three chapters.

7. You enjoy your trip to Spain too much.

8. You name her after me.

9. You grow tomatoes in this bed.

10. You wash the car on Saturday.

Score _____

EXERCISE 4-20

NAME _____ **DATE** _____

Change these sentences to questions that are used as commands.

Example: You are on time.
                  Would you be on time?

1. You write her an excuse for that day, Alice.

2. You finish the last piece of cake.

3. You buy me some clothes in New York.

4. You even try to be nice to them anymore.

5. You are ready to leave on time, Teresa.

6. You study those last three chapters.

7. You watch your step.

8. You name her after me.

9. You grow tomatoes in this bed.

10. You wash the car on Saturday.

Score _____

EXERCISE 4-21

NAME _____ **DATE** _____

Change the sentence in brackets to the mandative subjunctive form.

Example: It is essential that [the students will study]
                   It is essential that the students study.

1. It is imperative that [the city pays the bills]

2. It is extremely important that [we don't meet again]

3. The government insisted that [we should apply for an extension]

4. I recommend that [he isn't allowed to drive]

5. The hijacker demanded that [the airplane flies to New Orleans]

6. The king requires that [the prince marries someone rich]

7. Would you suggest that [he is not given any more antibiotics]

8. Have you ever tried insisting that [all employees wear uniforms]

9. They had been demanding for years that [the land is given back to them]

10. I recommend that [another candidate is not chosen]

Score _____

5

Verbals and Verbal Phrases

A verbal functions in a sentence as something other than a verb.

> <u>Winning</u> is not everything.

Here winning is the subject.

Now do Exercise 5-1.

5a. Infinitives and Infinitive Phrases

Infinitives and infinitive phrases are compact forms. You can use them to reduce the amount of material in conversation. For example, the following pairs mean about the same thing.

> Samsi was very anxious. He wanted to leave.
> Samsi was very anxious *to leave*.
>
> The boys were so tired that they could not sleep.
> The boys were too tired *to sleep*.
> [Notice that *so* changed to *too*.]

Do Exercise 5-2. Then do Exercise 5-3.

5b. Participles and Participial Phrases

You may wish to review 3a (4) for work on participles used as adjectives.

5c. Gerunds and Gerund Phrases

Gerunds (*-ing* forms) used as nouns have all the properties of a regular noun.

> The *ticking* of the clock helps me sleep.

A gerund phrase should also be treated as though it were one "long" noun. You can pretend that gerund phrases come from *that* clauses or *the fact that* clauses.

> Ed regrets *that he must go to school in summer.*
> Ed regrets *having to go to school in summer.*
> Ed was upset by *the fact that he moved in the school year.*
> Ed was upset by *moving in the school year.*

One aspect of gerund phrases causes both native speakers and ESL learners problems. In standard English, the subject of the gerund phrase becomes a *possessive.*

> [That *Ed* goes to school in summer] pleases me.
> *Standard:* *Ed's* going to school in summer pleases me.

> [That *he* goes to school in summer] pleases me.
> *Standard: His* going to school in summer pleases me.

Do Exercise 5-4. Then do Exercises 5-5 and 5-6.

Gerund, Infinitive, or that *clause?*

The most difficult aspect of the verbals is deciding which one to use. On occasion, it does not matter; however, most of the time we must be very careful or our sentences will be ungrammatical. Even worse, they may be grammatical but misleading. For example, let's suppose you want to tell someone that you followed their advice and *took* vitamins for two weeks. If you use the wrong form, you will be saying that you *never* took any vitamins but you thought about it.

> I tried *to take* vitamins for two weeks. [You didn't take any vitamins.]

The only correct form in this case would be the gerund form.

> I tried *taking* vitamins for two weeks.

Let's try to establish when we should use each form.

Phrasal Verbs and Prepositions

If the verbal follows a preposition or the particle of a phrasal verb, you *must* use the gerund form.

> *Preposition:* The leaders argued *about* his going for hours.
> *Phrasal:* The group never *got over* not being invited back.

Infinitives and Gerunds

In many cases, the infinitive is used after verbs that express unfulfilled events. These are events that did not happen or have not yet happened.

Lane wants *to meet* that nice girl. But he hasn't yet.
Last week, I was hoping *for Lennie to hear* that new record. But he didn't have the time to visit me.

On the other hand, gerunds are used with verbs that deal with *fulfilled* events. These events are taking place or already have taken place.

The spy admits *stealing* the documents. He has stolen documents before.
The spy denied *stealing* the documents. He says (but we don't believe him) that he *didn't* steal the documents.

Some verbs allow both the infinitive and the gerund. See if you can determine when to use which from just these two examples.

Remember *to feed the dog* before you leave for school later today.
Do you remember *feeding the dog* yesterday? Well, you gave him my special, expensive ground steak.

Did you guess that we use the infinitive for events that are yet to take place or were unfulfilled?

The school tried *to give* each student a book. But there weren't enough books. [unfulfilled]

On the other hand, we use the gerund for events that were fulfilled.

The school tried *giving* each student a book. Each student *did* get a book. But the students kept losing the books. [fulfilled]

This distinction explains the difference between *like* and *would like*.

Raccoons *like digging* around in garbage cans. In fact, they turn mine over every night. [fulfilled]
The dancers *would like to see* the Bolshoi, but they haven't had the chance. [unfulfilled]

Do Exercise 5-7 now.

A similar distinction is made for events that are felt to be *concrete/near* or *abstract/far*. However, this distinction is so subtle that most native speakers are not consciously aware of it.
Notice both these sentences with *like*. From the last example we would expect *gerunds*.

The kids really *like visiting* you *here,* Fred. [concrete/near]
I don't know, Fred. The kids *like to visit* you normally, but they really want to go to the beach this weekend. [abstract/far]

Although only a few verbs allow this distinction, they are very common, important verbs such as *hate* and *love*.

Now review everything in Exercise 5-8.

5d. Absolute Phrases

Absolute phrases are *sentential adverbials* [*sentential* means *entire sentence*]. The absolute phrases are very similar in function to *sentential adverbs,* adverbs that tell us how to interpret an *entire sentence.*

Sentential adverb: Fortunately, we found the keys.
Absolute phrase: The game already won, we just enjoyed ourselves.

The absolute phrase sets the stage for understanding the entire sentence. We can often substitute a dependent clause (such as *since we had already won the game*) for an absolute phrase that begins a sentence.

Unless your instructor asks you to, you should probably avoid using these forms. It would be better for you to practice clause forms.

EXERCISE 5-1

NAME _____ DATE _____

How does the underlined verbal or verbal phrase function in each sentence?

Example: Sheila went to the kitchen <u>to throw away trash</u>.
<u>adverb</u> [<u>why</u> she went to the kitchen]

1. After years of saving, their family was really glad <u>to be in Memphis</u>.

2. They had never expected Memphis <u>to be so green</u>.

3. They enjoyed <u>visiting Mud Island, a museum</u>.

4. The family had come <u>to see Graceland, the home of Elvis Presley</u>.

5. Those people have a tendency <u>to ignore the many other fine attractions of Memphis</u>.

6. <u>To understand the motivation behind this fascination with Elvis</u> requires hours of explanation and sociological analysis.

7. It surprises many people for <u>Elvis still to be so popular</u>.

8. Now there are thousands of young Europeans <u>fascinated with Elvis and his life</u>.

9. <u>Visiting the important sites of their hero's life</u> is the major concern of these fans.

10. Many Memphians never understand the fan's <u>wanting to be able to touch objects that he once touched</u>.

Score _____

EXERCISE 5-2

NAME _____ DATE _____

Who (or what) is the "subject" of each of these underlined infinitive phrases?

Example: a. We decided <u>to go</u>.
                 b. We

1. The committee hoped <u>to elect a new president</u>.

    _____

2. The committee planned <u>for Jane to be there</u>.

    _____

3. It was strange <u>for Carl not to visit his sister</u>.

    _____

4. It seems odd <u>for her to be able to afford that new car</u>.

    _____

5. Lane hopes <u>to be married by next year</u>.

    _____

6. All of us hope <u>for her to be married by next year</u>.

    _____

7. Parents should expect their children <u>to be well-mannered</u>.

    _____

8. <u>For Lonnie not to call us</u> is very disturbing.

   _____

9. Have you applied <u>to go to graduate school</u>?

   _____

10. It was interesting <u>to visit the White House</u>.

    _____

Score _____

EXERCISE 5-3

NAME _____ DATE_____

Make the underlined infinitive or infinitive phrase negative.

Example: She plans <u>to go to the beach</u> while at the conference.
She plans <u>not to go to the beach</u> while at the conference.

1. The party hoped <u>to need a new president</u>.

2. The committee planned <u>for Jane to accept the offer</u>.

3. It was appropriate <u>for Candy to visit his sister</u>.

4. It seems odd <u>for her to be able to afford a new car</u>.

5. Lane hopes <u>to be working there next year</u>.

6. They have a tendency <u>to use the correct form in their writings</u>.

7. Parents should expect their children <u>to be vulgar</u>.

8. <u>For Lonnie and his wife to call us</u> is very normal.

9. Have you decided <u>to go to graduate school</u>?

10. <u>To visit the White House</u> while you're in Washington would be a shame.

Score _____

EXERCISE 5-4

NAME DATE

Supply the correct *possessive* form for the cued word.

Example: [Ellen] I don't mind _____ lecturing me.
                 [Ellen] I don't mind <u>Ellen's</u> lecturing me.

   [they] Peter detests _____ eating pizza for breakfast.
   [they] Peter detests <u>their</u> eating pizza for breakfast.

1. [he] The girls adored _____ singing of that song.

2. [the boys] _____ arriving ahead of schedule created problems for us.

3. [I] _____ screaming bothers the upstairs neighbor.

4. [the men] The waitress complained about _____ not tipping at least fifteen

   percent.

5. [we] By _____ buying your grandmother's house is our friendship at

   stake?

6. [she] _____ singing is very beautiful.

7. [you] The class really enjoyed _____ bringing in that raccoon to show us.

8. [the data] I can't understand _____ being so easy to gather.

9. [the horses] _____ playing and running amused the small girl.

10. [James] I wasn't shocked by _____ giving his money to that charity.

Score_____

EXERCISE 5-5

NAME_____ DATE_____

Change the underlined *that* clauses to gerund phrases. If the subjects of the gerund phrase and the main clause are identical, you can leave out the gerund's subject.

Example: We were saddened by <u>the fact that Sheila would go</u>. [Subjects are not identical]
We were saddened by <u>Sheila's going</u>.

We were saddened by <u>the fact that we would go</u>. [Subjects are identical]
We were saddened by <u>going</u>.

1.   The audience was amazed by <u>the fact that the elephant disappeared into thin air</u>.

2.   <u>That someone tries to save money</u> is difficult. [You can delete the subject of the gerund when it is <u>someone</u>.]

3.   Imagine <u>that you are able to meet anyone in the world</u>.

4.   <u>The fact that who is receiving the prize</u> is thrilling for the entire community. [careful]

5.   The professor mentioned <u>that he would not be there tomorrow</u>.

6.   <u>The fact that the women have been invited to speak in Oslo</u> was front-page news today.

7.   Do the police really deny <u>that Gary was involved in that strange incident</u>?

8. The case depends on <u>the fact that Gary must be able to establish an alibi</u>.

9. <u>That Olive will buy that book for the library</u> is encouraging, isn't it?

10. <u>That someone gives up free time to help people learn to read</u> is a sign of dedication and hope.

Score_____

EXERCISE 5-6

NAME _____ DATE _____

Change the first sentence into a gerund phrase in the second sentence.

Example: a. He can judge people's character.
b. His job depended on _____
c. His job depended on <u>his being able to judge people's character</u>.

1. a. David goes to Detroit for his company.

    b. The case was similar to _____.

    c.

2. a. He brought in several new clients.

    b. Every day he reminds me of _____ while I lost some.

    c.

3. a. People long for absolute truth.

    b. Next semester this course will take up _____.

    c.

4. a. The criminal steals money.

    b. The criminal finally gave up _____. [Since the subjects

    are identical, you can delete the subject of the gerund.]

    c.

5. a. The choir will visit Vienna.

   b. The choir plans on _____. [Since the subjects are

      identical, you can delete the subject of the gerund.]

   c.

6. a. Karen stood him up.

   b. You need to help him forget about _____.

   c.

7. a. You would study chemistry.

   b. Your father and I would like to talk over _____.

   c.

8. a. He wants to be a lawyer.

   b. That unresolved issue hangs over _____.

   c.

9. a. The corporation will pay for dinner.

   b. I insist on _____.

   c.

10. a. Do you want to go or not?

    b. Have you decided on _____.

    c.

Score _____

EXERCISE 5-7

NAME _____ DATE _____

(a) Which of these underlined words deal with *unfulfilled events* and which with *fulfilled* ones? Should a gerund or infinitive follow it? (b) Change the clause in brackets to the appropriate verbal form. Don't forget to add *for* if it is necessary.

Example: I <u>hope</u> [she does well]
a. unfulfilled, infinitive
b. I hope <u>for</u> her to do well.

1. The administration <u>expects</u> [it has a balanced budget].

    a.

    b.

2. Most children <u>enjoy</u> [they swim in a pool].

    a.

    b.

3. Have they <u>decided</u> [they will go to Dallas next week]?

    a.

    b.

4. His mother <u>defended</u> [he acted strange in the past].

    a.

    b.

5. Have you <u>finished</u> [you clean out the refrigerator]?

    a.

    b.

6. The woman was <u>determined</u> [we would learn French].

   a.

   b.

7. The insurance salesperson <u>failed</u> [he shows up].

   a.

   b.

8. Most teachers really don't <u>mind</u> [students ask questions].

   a.

   b.

9. It is <u>advisable</u> [someone shouldn't leave money in a hotel room].

   a.

   b.

10. The kid <u>enjoy</u> [the kids takes hikes in the summer].

    a.

    b.

Score _____

EXERCISE 5-8

NAME _____ DATE _____

Answer the question about the first sentence. Then, using your answer, decide if you need a gerund or infinitive phrase. Provide the correct form.

Example: a. When Fred walked in, he saw Alice, whom he hadn't seen in years. So he
                        stopped [he talks to her].

                  b. Was Fred talking to Alice as he walked in? No action unfulfilled means
                        infinitive.

                  c. So he stopped to talk to her.

1.   a. After all these years of having lunch, Frances was finally mad enough at Robert to
        stop [she talks to him] forever.

     b. Has Frances talked to Robert already?

     c.

2.   a. Every day Diana goes to aerobics. She is trying [she becomes an instructor].

     b. Is Diana an aerobics instructor yet?

     c.

3.   a. Tim cannot open his apartment door. He forgot [he takes his keys].

     b. Does Tim have his keys with him now?

     c.

4.   a. Tim cannot open his apartment door because he does not have his keys; however,
        that is strange because he remembers [he took his keys when he left this morning].

     b. Does Tim think he should have his keys with him?

     c.

5. a. Normally, most people hate [they get wet], but since they are playing water polo right now, they don't mind [they get wet].

    b. The people get wet. Are they upset now?

    c.

6. a. Thanks for bringing me here. I really <u>love</u> [I watch movies on the big screen].

    b. Are they watching a movie on a big screen?

    c.

7. a. Thanks anyway. Normally, I like [I hike in the mountains], but I have no time this weekend.

    b. Will the speaker go to the mountains this weekend?

    c.

8. a. Thanks, I'd love to go! I really like [I hike in the mountains]. When do we leave?

    b. Have they left yet?

    c.

9. a. Well, Henry thinks he would like [Henry visits France this summer]. It would be his first trip to Europe.

    b. Has Henry visited France yet?

    c.

10. a. This is the last exercise. These students hate [these students have no more exercises to do].

    b. Are these students concrete or are they unknown, abstract students?

    c.

Score _____

6

Function
Words

6a. Prepositions and Prepositional Phrases

Basically there are three types of problems with prepositions in English.

1. The wrong preposition will be used.

   Incorrect: The women stayed at Memphis. [should be in]

2. A preposition that is not needed in English will be used.

   Incorrect: Then we salute *to* the older generation. [*to* is not needed]

3. A preposition that is needed in English won't be used.

   Incorrect: Next they will go _____ Nashville [should use *to* here]

If you record your own problems with prepositions in your English notebook, you can work specifically on them.

(1) The wrong preposition

There are two main causes for using the wrong prepositions: *required co-occurrence* and *semantic use.* Many verbs and adjectives in English must be used with only one specific preposition; that is *required co-occurrence.* For example, *mad* as in *angry* must be used with *at;* any other preposition would be incorrect. That means you must learn the required preposition as though it were a part of the noun or verb.

There are three important pairs of prepositions that co-occur. Learn these pairs as units:

> *from/to* (distance, time): They drove *from* Chicago *to* Tulsa *from* 6 A.M. *to* noon.
> *from/till* or *from/until* (only time): Sheila has to work *from* 6 A.M. *till* noon.
> *out of /into* (change): *Out of* the frying pan *into* the fire.

It's actually easy to use the co-occurrence prepositions, since they can be memorized.

Do Exercise 6-1 and 6-2 before you go on.

164

It is a little harder to understand the *semantic* uses of prepositions. Let's start with the easiest and yet the most often misused, *spatial*. Spatial just means space.

In English, there are three dimensions of space. Each dimension has its own preposition for movement *toward, away,* and for a *stable* position in that dimension. Thus, each dimension could use three different prepositions.

The first dimension is the *point* when we first intersect with something. The line drawing will help you understand.

Frank is driving *to* Little Rock.

It's not nice to be expelled *from* school.

There are traffic lights *at* corners where streets intersect.

The second dimension is a *line*.

Frank is putting the can *on* the table.

Excuse me, you are standing *on* my foot.

Thank you for getting *off* my foot.

The third is a *plane* or *cube*.

Sean is moving into a new apartment.

But there are already six guys *in* the apartment.

I think a few had better move *out of* the apartment first.

Now try Exercise 6-3.

Another relatively straightforward area is the use of *temporal* prepositions. Temporal refers to time. If we use the three dimensions we just established for spatial relations, the temporal relations are easier to understand.

If something happens at a specific point, we use *at*.

> You must be there *at* 8:45. [exact point]
> We eat lunch *at* noon. [noon is 12:00, so it is an exact point]
> The ship sails *at* dawn. [when the sun rises, an exact point]

In English we think of *days* as *lines,* so we use *on* for days of the week and dates.

> *On* Tuesday, the power will be out for two hours.
> I was born *on* January 24.
> That family always mows their lawn *on* Sundays.

For longer periods of time (centuries, years, seasons, months), we think of them as *areas,* since we are surrounded by them. As a result, we use *in* or *during*.

> *In* summer the living is easy.
> *During* summer we must mow the grass often.
> I was born *in* 1965.

Additionally, we think of parts of the days as small *areas*.

> In the morning, bring me your workbook.

Do Exercise 6-4 now.

In addition to signalling temporal and spatial relations, prepositions signal relations among people and/ or things. We call these *case* relations. Several of the most common prepositions carry most of the burden. We will explore some of the common relations in the next exercise.

Do Exercise 6-5 at this point.

(2) Unnecessary prepositions

When you are told that you put a preposition where none is needed, you usually need to look at the verb of the sentence. There are many verbs that can appear to need prepositions sometimes and sometimes not to need them.

> The salesman was traveling *to* New York on business.
> The film crew traveled _____ the country.
>   (no preposition needed)

Actually, the use or non-use of the preposition changes the meaning of the verb slightly. In the first example *traveling* could be replaced with *going*. However, in the second *visited* would be more appropriate.

Now do Exercise 6-6.

(3) Forgotten prepositions

Often English requires prepositions where other languages do not; these are called *forgotten prepositions.*

Incorrect: The class is going Washington.
Correct: The class is going *to* Washington.

6b. Conjunctions

Conjunctions are like road signs that guide us through our texts. Some make us go on small detours; others change the direction of our text radically. If you learn the basic message of each of the major conjunctions, you will both understand the internal structure of other people's writing and be able to improve your own skills.

When we use conjunctions, we impose order on our texts. Sometimes we want to be very specific and other times intentionally vague. But it is you, the writer, who can decide which is appropriate. When writing for an American audience, however, it is best to try to be as precise as possible with conjunctions.

(1) Coordinating conjunctions

Let's first examine the basic *direction* in which each of the coordinating conjunctions guides the text.

and: continue on, everything is fine [A and B]
I went to the store *and* to the cleaners.

but: major change of direction as we come to the element introduced by *but* [A changes to B]
I went to the store, *but* I could not go to the cleaners.

or: a choice must be made [either A or B]
I can go to the store *or* the cleaners.

yet: a small change of direction is occurring [A changes mildly to B]
Ian went to the store, *yet* he wanted to go to the cleaners.

nor: continue on in the *negative* [not A and not B]
Ian could *not* go to the store, *nor* could he go to the cleaners. [could *not* go to the cleaners]

for: *only* for independent clauses; the first clause is caused by the *next* clause [A is caused by B]
Ian went to the cleaners, *for* his clothes were dirty. [A is caused by B]

so: *only* for independent clauses; the first clause causes the *next* clause [A causes B]
Ian's clothes were dirty, *so* he went to the cleaners. [A causes B]

Now try Exercise 6-8.

2) Correlative conjunctions

These pairs of words or phrases *frame* elements so that our attention is clearly turned to them. They emphasize elements.

Both . . . and: notice these elements and continue on
Both Janet *and* Fred were going to Paris.

not . . . but: notice these elements and change direction to the second element
You're wrong. It was *not* Janet *but* Fred

either . . . or: notice these elements and make a choice
Either Janet *or* Fred will go.

not only . . . but also: there's more than you thought; notice these elements and
    continue; very emphatic; can cause inversion
Regular: We will take *not only* Janet *but also* Fred.
Inverted: *Not only* will we take Janet *but also* Fred.

neither . . . nor: notice these elements and continue in the negative; *nor* can cause
    inversion.
Regular: *Neither* Janet *nor* Fred could go.
Inverted: *Nor* could she stay.

(3) Subordinating conjunctions

Subordinating conjunctions are essential to clear writing. For work on subordinating conjunctions, see Chapter 7.

(4) Comparative conjunctions

These pairs of words or phrases serve to frame or emphasize specific elements of degrees or qualities.

as . . . as: stresses similarly
Ron is *as* old as Bill. They are the *same* age.

When *as . . . as* is used for a negative sentence, it presupposes that the similarity had been assumed or suggested.

Ron is *not* as old as Bill, although most people assume they are twins.

Try Exercise 6-10.

so . . . that: indicates that a degree of something has been reached that allows or causes a
    second event.
The policeman was *so* angry *that* he arrested the driver. [*so* X *that* Y happens]

Notice that *so* modifies verbs, adjectives, or adverbs; it acts as an adverb. If we want to modify a noun (usually already modified and *always indefinite*) we must use *such . . . that,* which allows *such* to act as a determiner.

Randall is *such* a good student *that* he didn't need to take his finals.

Now do Exercise 6-11.

6c.   Determiners

Without a doubt, determiners pose the greatest structural challenge for the ESL learner. They are especially a problem because most determiners can also function as pronouns. As a result, there are many chances for confusion. However, there are some important concepts that can help you avoid many predictable errors in your compositions.

(1) The article system

Before we discuss how we use the article system in English, let's quickly review the forms we need to know.

Forms

Remember, we have *indefinite* and *definite* articles in English. In English, nouns *must* be preceded by some form of an article (even if it is "nothing") or other determiner.

The *indefinite* articles are *a, an,* and nothing. We use *a* for *singular* count nouns, *an* for singular count nouns that begin with a vowel sound, and nothing for *singular* non-count nouns and *plural* count nouns. If you remember that *a* and *an* are really unstressed forms of *one* (the number "1"), the distribution of these three forms makes more sense.

> *Singular count nouns:*
> There is *one pigeon* on the table.
> There is *a pigeon* on the table.

> *Singular count nouns with vowel sound:*
> Is there *one opening* in the roof?
> Is there *an opening* in the roof?

> *Singular non-count nouns:*
> *Incorrect:* There is *one jam* on the floor!
> *Correct:* There is _____ jam on the floor!

> *Plural count nouns:*
> *Incorrect:* There are *one ants* all over the food [there is no plural of *one* (1) in
>   English.]
> *Correct:* There are _____ *ants* all over the food.

Now try Exercise 6-13.

The definite article is much easier. There is only one form: *the.* Remember, you cannot do anything to this form. Please do not try to add an s or to change this form in any way.

In using *the,* it helps to remember that *the* is (semantically) related to *this, that, these,* and *those,* which also begin with *th.* Those are the forms. But why do we need them in English?

Article Usage: Specificity

The article system reflects many concepts, but the most important is *specificity. Specificity* simply means we think we know *which* particular object or objects we are talking about. The indefinite article [*a, an*] means that the speaker thinks either the speaker or hearer doesn't yet know which particular object they're talking about.

> *Speaker knows, hearer doesn't:* I have a friend.
> *Speaker doesn't know, hearer doesn't:* Look! There's a plane landing in our driveway.
> *Speaker doesn't know, hearer does:* Why did you tell a lie?

The definite article is used only when the *speaker* thinks both the speaker and hearer know definitely which object they're talking about.

> *Speaker and hearer both know:*
> A: Where are *the* keys?
> B: In the kitchen.
> *Speaker thinks both know:*
> A: Where is *the* book?
> B: Which book are you talking about?

Now carefully do Exercise 6-14.

Article Usage: Abstract Nouns

Unlike many languages, English does not require the use of articles with abstract nouns. When we use *the* or *a/an* with an abstract noun, it means a specific case of the abstraction.

> *Abstract: Pride* goes before the fall.
> *Specific case:* He was *the* pride of the Midwest.
> *Specific case:* His eyes showed *a* special pride.

We also do not use articles for *abstract states,* which often use the preposition *in* (such as *in love, in crime, in trouble,* or *in need*).

> *Abstract state:* The actress is *in film*. But she will also do TV work.
> *Specific case:* The actress is in *a* film that has yet to be released.

Article Usage: Proper Nouns

Normally, true proper nouns do not take any articles, because they are already *definite*. But derived proper nouns (called *unique common nouns*) usually need a definite article to remind the hearer that a *definite,* specific object is under discussion.

> *Common and indefinite:* Is there *a university* in Florida?
> *Derived and definite:* Where is *the University of Florida?* [*the* specific X of Y]

This form [*the* specific X of Y] allows us to make many titles and names.

> *the* President of the United States
> *the* Duke of Windsor
> *the* League of Nations
> *the* Book of Ruth

There have been many presidents of the United States, so the specific "X" of the formula could change.

However, if we use a title as an appositive, we do not need *the,* since the specificity has already been established by the proper name.

> Fritz, King of Fools, laughs with ease.
> The King of Fools, Fritz, laughs with ease.

We could also allow X to stay the same and change its description. We can do this with adjectives.

> the Y/X
> *the* adjective *noun*
> the United *States*
> the German Democratic *Republic*

There is another pattern that does not allow the X of the formula to change.
Y/X

> noun/noun
> Memphis State University
> Florida State University
> New York City

In this pattern, there can be no other example of X. As a result, we do not need *the* to establish specificity.

Try Exercise 6-15.

Article Usage: Religious Texts

The names of many religious texts have become true proper nouns, but they still use *the* as though they were unique common nouns.

> *the* Torah [there is only one]
> *the* Koran [there is only one]
> *the* Bible [there is only one]
> *the* Upanishads [there is only one]
> *the* Sunna [there is only one]
> *the* Mishna [there is only one]

Notice that they are also not underlined, as the titles of books should be. However, the names of the individual parts of these books do not use *the:*
> Esther
> Genesis

Of course, if we use any pattern such as *the book of* or *the second verse of,* we must use *the.*

Article Usage: Geographical Names

We have already discussed the formation and usage of most political designations for areas. Unfortunately, geographic designations (such as *lake, desert,* or *valley*) are fairly complex in Modern English.

Some of the patterns are standard; just use the rules we have established for all proper nouns.

the noun of noun	*the* adjective [understood, but deleted noun]
the Gulf of Mexico	*the* Northeast [region]
the Straits of Florida	*the* Midwest [region]

Some appear to be standard, but there really is another reason why we must use *the* for the nounsthat fit this pattern.

the adjective noun
the Persian Gulf
the Indian Ocean

We will return to these examples in a moment to see the real reason for the use of *the*.
If the proper name follows the geographic designation, we normally do not use *the*.

Geographic	*Proper*
Lake	Michigan
Mount	Everest
Cape	Kennedy

The primary deciding factor in determining whether one should use *the* or not is *size*. We do not use *the* with relatively small **geographical** names. (of course, there is some problem in defining exactly what *small* is.)

Small	*Large*
Golden Pond	the Andaman Sea
Hidden Lake	the Atlantic Ocean
Nonconnah Creek	the Nmai River
Tampa Bay	the Gulf of Mexico
Sandy Beach	the Ivory Coast
Dry Gulch	the Grand Canyon
Blue Bayou	the Erie Canal
Larchmont Street	the Florida Turnpike

Related to size is *quantity*.

One	*Several*
Sardis Lake	the Great Lakes
Pike's Peak	the Himalayas
Stone Mountain	the Grand Tetons

Unfortunately, this system does not work perfectly. For example, we must say *the Great Salt Lake,* but then that does sound as though we were trying to distinguish it from some other *Salt Lake.* Use this information to do Exercise 6-16 now.

Article Usage: Locative Nouns

We normally don't use any article with locative [place] nouns that aren't specified. This use helps distinguish general locatives from non-locative uses of the same nouns.

Locative: She is at *work*.
Non-locative: She is doing *the work* now.
Locative: She is at *home*.
Non-locative: We need to find *a* new *home* for our cat.

Notice in the locative uses, we don't really need to know where her *home* or *work* is. They aren't really specific. They are used adverbially. There is one American idiomatic use of *the home* that you should know.

We visited my grandmother at *the home*.
[*the home* = nursing facility for elderly people]

On the other hand, in American English we always say *the hospital* even if we do not specify which hospital it was.

American: I visited my friend in *the hospital*.
British: I visited my friend in *hospital*.

This last use of *the* in American English extends to public places that might be unique [only *one*] in a small American city or area such as *train station, airport, harbor* or even *the store* even though we now normally have more than one in a city.

Can you take me to the airport?
Do you need to go to the store?
But: I'm going over to school. [normally more than one]

Article Usage: Temporal Phrases

We do not normally use *the* with general phrases of time when we use *at, until,* or *till;* however, we do use *the* with *in* or *into*.

Non-specific
Until: We will need to wait *until evening*.
Till: Indeed, we will need to work *till morning*.

In: We will need to work *in the evening*.
Into: Indeed, we will need to work *into the night*.

Specific: Did you enjoy *the evening?*
        Have you ever seen *a more beautiful dawn?*

We use *the last* with these temporal words (such as *day, night* or *year)* for any specific date: *last* by itself must be the one just before this one.

The last year I was in Stockholm was 1974.
Last year, I was in Stockholm. [this year minus one]
The last night in Venice was beautiful. Of course, it was in 1932 when the world was young.
Last night was wonderful. I hope to see you again soon, perhaps tonight? [Notice *tonight* has
    even become one word.]

Now review these uses of articles with Exercise 6-17.

Article Usage: Diseases

Unfortunately, you must memorize whether a specific disease uses *the (the flu)*, *a (a cold)* or is a mass noun which uses neither *(aphasia)*. You should practice these forms as units.

> My sister has *a cold*.
> Fortunately, she does not have *the flu*.
> But she does have *a horrible headache* and *a fever*.
> NOTE: She has *a temperature*. [meaning a higher than normal temperature]

Article Usage: Generic Ideas

Count nouns have three different levels of usage with generic ideas—ideas that do not apply to a specific case.

> *Colloquial:* A crocodile is a dangerous animal.
> *Informal:* Crocodiles are dangerous animals.
> *Formal: The* crocodile is a dangerous animal.

Of course, mass nouns can have only one form for generic usage.

> *All levels:* Rice is a staple for many cultures.
> *Incorrect: The* rice is a staple.
> *Incorrect:* A rice is a staple.

Practice this usage in Exercise 6-18.

(2) Possessive pronouns and possessives

Possessive pronouns and other possessives function as determiners; they signal that a noun follows.
There are no variations in form for the possessive determiners. You must remember not to use the *pronominal forms* as determiners, however.

Determiner form	*Pronominal Form*
my	mine
our	ours
your	yours
her	hers
his	his
its	(not used in English)
their	theirs

The possessive determiners *cannot* occur with the articles.

> *Incorrect:* his *the* car
> *Correct:* your every glance

The only real difficulty with these possessive determiners is determining when they should be used instead of the definite article. In English, we use possessive determiners where many other languages would use a [pronoun + *the* noun] sequence.

Incorrect: I broke me *the* arm.
Correct, but awkward: I broke *the* arm.
Correct: I broke *my* arm.

Any possessive fulfills the requirement that a noun be preceded by some determiner. Possessives cannot occur with the possessive determiners or articles.

Incorrect: Ellen's *the* arm was broken in the crash.
Incorrect: The Ellen's arm was broken in the crash.
Correct: Ellen's arm was broken in the crash.

However, you must be careful because an article might be part of the possessive.

Possessive: the lady's
Therefore, correct: the lady's hat

The possessed noun (*hat*) takes on the definiteness of the possessive noun. That means in the last example the entire noun phrase (*the lady's hat*) is *definite.*

Now do Exercise 6-19.

(3) Demonstrative pronouns

We often use the demonstrative pronouns (*this, that, these,* and *those*) in their determiner function.

Determiner: Did you see *that* flash of light?
Pronoun: No, I don't believe *that.*

They cannot co-occur with articles of possessives. But remember, they might be part of the possessor noun phrases.

Correct: That man's house

This and *that* are singular while *these* and *those* are plural. Additionally, *this* or *these* is used for near [both physically and mentally] objects while *that* and *those* are used for things farther away. We signal our closeness to an object by our choice.

Mentally distant: I don't like *that* idea. It won't work.
Mentally close: We appreciate *this* offer. It is very nice.

DoExercise 6-20.

(4) Indefinite pronouns

The indefinite pronouns are not a unified group. They can even look, at first glance, as though they were definite.

Indefinite determiner: Some Memphians flew on the Concorde. But I don't know which ones.
Indefinite pronoun of a definite group: Some of *the* Memphians flew on the Concorde. But part of the group took the QEII home.

These forms cannot occur with articles. But some can be used with possessives if they are numerical (in other words, *absolute*) in meaning. If they comment on *group relationships* (in other words, *relative*) they can't.

>*Absolutes*
>his *any* and *every* wish [*any* one of his wishes]
>his *many* friends [his *16* friends]
>his *few* friends [his *2* or *3* friends
>his *other* friends [not this group]
>
>*Relationships within a group*
>*Incorrect:* his *all* friends [*all* of his friends]
>*Incorrect:* his *less* money [*less* of his money]
>*Incorrect:* his *either* parent [*either* of his parents]
>*Incorrect:* his *some* friends [*some* of his friends]

Indefinite Usage: A few, A little

We also need to include *a few* (for count nouns) and *a little* (for mass nouns) in this group. They are less *negative* in attitude than *few* and *little*.

>*Positive:* Well, we still have *a little* money left.
>*Negative:* Horrors, we have *little* money left. What will we do?
>*Positive:* Thank goodness, we still have *a few* friends left.
>*Negative:* Since we lost our fortune, we have such *few* friends left.

Since they mean about the same thing and differ only in outlook, you must be careful to use the correct one or you will confuse your listener.

>A looks in his wallet, sees $2000 and *smiles* at B, who also sees the money.
>*Correct:*
>A: I have *a little* money left. Do you want to go to the movies?
>B: [smiles] Good, let's go.
>
>A looks in his wallet, sees $2000 and *smiles* at B, who cannot see the money.
>*Incorrect:*
>A: I have *little* money left. Do you want to go to the movies?
>B: [looks puzzled] Shouldn't you save it for an emergency?

Now do Exercise 6-21.

Indefinite Usage: Any *and* Some

We normally use *any* for negatives and questions, while *some* is used for everything else. Don't forget that the negative can be fairly subtle.

>*Negative:* She *hardly* has *any* time for me.
>*Positive:* But she does have *some,* doesn't she?
>
>*Question:* Does Mr. Hardy have *any* time for me?
>*Positive answer:* Of course, Mr. Hardy has *some* time for you.
>*Indirect question:* We *asked* if she had *any* time for us.
>*Negative answer:* But she answered that she *rarely* had *any* time even for herself.

However, if we are almost sure that we will get a positive answer to out question, we can use *some* to show that expectation.

> *Positive answer expected:* A husband asks his wife the day *after* payday: Do you have *some* money for me?
>
> *Not sure:* A husband asks his wife the day *before* payday: Do you have *any* money for me?

Indefinite Usage: Another, Other / Others, the Other / the Others

These forms can be confusing; however, it you notice that *another* is really *an other,* much of the confusion will disappear.

If you already have *one* of something, you can have *another.* In other words, *another* means *a second.* It is, of course, *indefinite* because of the built-in *an,* the indefinite article.

> *Pronoun:* Finish that piece of cake before you take another!
> *Determiner:* There's another car coming up to the house.

Since *another* has a built-in *an,* it cannot be used with *plurals* or *mass nouns.* We must use just plain *other* for those cases.

> *Plural count noun:* I don't like these. Do you have any *other styles?*
> *Mass noun:* This has caffeine. Do you have any *other coffee?*

To use *the other,* we must have a definite noun in mind.

> *Singular:* I put two pieces of cake on the table. One is still here. Where is *the other piece?* [specific *piece*]
> *Plural:* Six are already at the table. But where are *the other guests?* [specific *guests*]
> *Mass noun [acceptable]:* I bought two kinds of bread. One was very tasty, but *the other bread* was stale.
> *Mass noun [preferred]:* I bought two kinds of bread. One *kind* was very tasty, but *the other kind of bread* was stale.

If we use *the other* as a pronoun, we must be careful because we must add an -*s* if the noun is plural. Notice that *other* is the only determiner that requires this marking.

> *Singular:* Here is one answer. Where is *another?*
> *Mass noun:* This water is not safe to drink. Where is the *other?* [sounds formal]
> *Plural:* Here are some of the guests. Where are *the others?*

Do Exercise 6-22.
Review the determiners with Exercise 6-23.

(5) Interrogative pronouns

Even the interrogatives can function as determiners.

> *Determiners:* She is not sure *how many* people will be there.
> They could not remember *what* color the walls had been.
> *Pronouns: Which* of the scholars would care to comment?

(6) Cardinal numbers

The numbers *one, two,* and so on can serve as determiners. They may also function as pronouns. Most importantly, they can mix with all of the other determiners except, for logical reasons, those that refer to relative quantity.

> She drank *all* six cans?
> Have you seen *the* five new neighbors?
> Where did he put *his* four books?
> *Incorrect:* Where did he put *many* four books? [many refers to quantity]
> *Incorrect:* Now he has only eight *few* books.

Of course, you can use numbers with the determiners that signal *changes* in quantity.

> Now we have only six *more* books to put away.
> After we leave, he will have five *fewer guests.*

Number Usage: Specific and General

There are some differences in British and American usage of numbers, but let's ignore those and discuss just American usage.

Whenever a numerical unit is used to give a *general estimate* of a number, we add *-s* and *of,* if it is being used as a "determiner."

> There were *hundreds* of sea gulls at the beach today.
> He made *millions* in stocks.
> I order the pens by *tens.*
> You need to buy *thousands* of shares.

However, when you use a *specific* number with these same units, you may *not* add an *-s* in American English. Additionally, you cannot use the *of* construction.

> There were *six* hundred sea gulls at the beach today.
> *Incorrect:* There were six hundreds of sea gulls at the beach today.

> He made *thirteen million* in stocks.
> *Incorrect:* He made thirteen millions in stocks.

> I order the pens *sixty* at a time. [*-ty* means ten]
> *Incorrect:* I order the pens by *six tens.* [ten must be combined with the specific number: *sixty*]

> You need to buy *thousands* of shares.
> *Incorrect:* You need to buy *forty* thousands *of* shares.

Number Usage: Measurements

We make a distinction when using measurements between the *predicate* use and the *prenomial* use.

> *Predicate use:* The car really does weigh 2400 *pounds.*
> *Prenomial:* A 2400-*pound* car is not that heavy.

Notice that the -*s* must be dropped. Really it is the *plural* form that is dropped, as we note in the following example.

> *Predicate use*: Roses are rarely over six *feet* tall.
> *Prenomial*: A six-*foot* rose is rare.

The irregular plural *feet* returned to the singular form *foot*. You should also note that measurements are not determiners; they are modifiers. That means that you must have a real determiner before the determiner requirement is satisfied.

> *Incorrect*: Have you seen twenty-foot snake? [missing determiner]
> *Correct*: Have you seen *a* twenty-foot snake?

Number Usage: Plural Nouns

In many languages and some dialects of English when we use a specific number with a noun, we do not need the plural marker anymore, since the specific number is obviously plural. In Standard English, however, the plural marker must be present.

> *Nonstandard*: Give me six *cent*.
> *Standard*: Give me six cents.

6d. Expletives

Normally, the subject of a sentence is reserved for *old information*, information we already know, while the predicate of a sentence is for new information.

> *Old*   *New*
> She is going to Tahiti.

We must already know who *she* is for this sentence to make sense. However, there are times when even the subject is new because we are introducing or changing the subject.

> *New*
> A new store   is
> That she is here is probable.

When this is the case, we use *expletives*, filler words, to act as *dummy subjects* so that the new subject can appear to be part of the predicate, where we expect most new information.

> *Dummy*   *New Information [real subject]*
> There is   a new store.
> It is   probable that she is here.

Remember that every English clause must have a (recoverable) subject. However, sometimes it is not clear what the subject would be. This is the case for most weather occurrences and environmental descriptions. In these cases, we add *it* as the dummy subject.

No real subject
_____rains.
_____is really messy in here.
_____is windy.

With dummy [expletive] subject

It rains.
It is really messy in here.
It is windy.

Now do Exercise 6-24.

EXERCISE 6-1

NAME_____   **DATE**_____

We don't even need a context to know which preposition follows these words. Fill in the right preposition for each noun or adjective. If you aren't sure, a good dictionary will list them.

hostile _____

consist _____

triumph _____

exclude _____

interested _____

restrain _____

afraid _____

include _____

rely _____

digress _____

allergic _____

detract _____

There are many others; be sure to keep a list of the ones pointed out to you in your papers.

Score _____

EXERCISE 6-2

NAME _____ DATE _____

Fill in the right preposition. You may need to look some words up in the dictionary.

Finally, it was Friday and we were going to drive _____ [1] town _____ [2]

the mountains. I wasn't really interested _____ [3] mountains, but my friend, Sheila,

has loved them _____ [4] the time she was just a child _____ [5] now. As a

matter _____ [6] fact, she dabbles_____ [7] mountain climbing.

_____ [8] the other hand, I am actually afraid _____ [9] heights. Although

my friend sympathized _____ [10] me, she still insisted _____ [11] going.

She thought that I would lose my fear _____ [12] mountains quickly after we had

gone _____ [13] the urban traumas _____ [14] the natural beauty. She was

mistaken _____ [15] her judgment. _____ [16] the moment we left Memphis

_____ [17] the moment we returned _____ [18] the flat, safe Mississippi

Delta, our trip consisted _____ [19] frightening moments when I had to rely

_____ [20] her to guide me because I am so susceptible _____ [21] vertigo.

Next year, we are going _____ [22] the Netherlands, which is composed almost

entirely _____ [23] nice, flat areas.

Score _____

EXERCISE 6-3

NAME _____   DATE _____

For each sentence, fill in the correct preposition and draw a line drawing that shows what is happening. Remember *point, line,* and *area.*

Example: Fred enjoys sitting _____ the step and talking.

_____x_____

Fred enjoys sitting *on* the step and talking.

1. Ali is standing on _____ the sidewalk.

2. Eve just walked _____ the house into the garden.

3. Ike just put the cat _____ the floor.

4. There are large holes _____ the floor. [the holes go *through* the floor]

5. Some kids run away _____ home. [here it is only important where *home* ends and the "world" begins]

6. Hang the picture _____ the wall.

7. There was a rather serious accident _____ the corner. [where two streets intersect]

8. Rima is really glad her house is not _____ the corner. [the *area* between two streets that cross]

9. Cats hate to walk _____ wet, tall grass.

10. Sometimes if there is an icy crust, you can actually walk _____ the snow.

Score_____

EXERCISE 6-4

NAME_____   DATE_____

In addition to filling in the correct preposition, draw the symbol that represents the dimension used.

Example: _____ 6:04   at 6:04 •

1. _____ the 20th century

2. _____ June 24

3. _____ June

4. _____ full moon

5. _____ 15 April 1975

6. _____ 1987

7. _____ the morning _____ 5:36 _____ August 12

   _____ the year 1654

8. _____ November 27, 1986

9. _____ 11:30 a.m.

10. _____ Tuesday

Score _____

EXERCISE 6-5

NAME _____ DATE _____

For each case, provide an additional sentence that illustrates the relation expressed.

Example: agent—by The painting was done by Paul.
Everyone was upset by Paul.

1. accompany—*with* He went to the concert with her.

2. benefit —*for* The dancer performed for the audience.

3. dative—*to* Joyce presented the trophy to the winner.

4. goal—*to* Joyce brought the trophy to the dining room.

5. instrument—*with* I opened the window with a knife.

6. join—*with* The floor was covered with garbage.

7. means—*by* You went by bus?

8. separate—*of* They cleared the city of crime.

9. source—*from* Those toys came from our factory in Albany.

10. substitute for—*for* Since Bea can't go, Lee will go for her.

Score_____

EXERCISE 6-6

NAME _____ DATE _____

Find a substitute or paraphrase for each of the underlined verbs.

Example: a. With preposition: She <u>walked</u> to the dog.
           b. Without preposition: She <u>walked</u> the dog.
           a. went up to the dog
           b. took the dog for a walk

1. a. With preposition: Valerie screamed at Fred to stop.
    b. Without preposition: Valerie screamed.

    a.

    b.

2. a. With preposition: I have never heard of that record before.
    b. Without preposition: I have never heard that record before.

    a.

    b.

3. a. With preposition: The waitress served on the committee.
    b. Without preposition: The waitress served the committee.

    a.

    b.

4. a. With preposition: They studied in Germany.
    b. Without preposition: They studied Germany.

    a.

    b.

5. a. With preposition: Dennis ran to the store.
    b. Without preposition: Dennis ran the store.

    a.

    b.

6. a. With preposition: Pat and Chris parked in the car. [slang, not for formal use]
    b. Without preposition: Pat and Chris parked the car.

    a.

    b.

7. a. With preposition: I traveled to the western United States.
    b. Without preposition: I traveled the western United States.

    a.

    b.

8. a. With preposition: They delayed three days on the trip.
    b. Without preposition: They delayed the trip three days.

    a.

    b.

9. a. With preposition: The bankers could not approve of the check but had to cash it.
    b. Without preposition: The bankers could not approve the check and could not cash it.

    a.

    b.

10. a. With preposition: The children turned around the corner.
    b. Without preposition: The children turned the knob.

    a.

    b.

                                        Score _____

EXERCISE 6-7

NAME _____ **DATE** _____

Fill in the appropriate preposition if needed.

When we go shopping _____ [1] antiques in Atlanta, we need to know

exactly what we are looking _____ [2]. Otherwise, we could spend days

wishing _____ [3] objects we have no use _____ [4].

Even after we have found _____ [5] the perfect something, we must wrestle

_____ [6] our budget before we can spend any money _____ [7]

the treasure we have just uncovered. Even then, we must compare it _____ [8]

every other similar object we have looked _____ [9]. Finally, when we have

agreed _____ [10] a price that seems fair _____ [11] all of us, we

write a check _____ [12] the amount and walk _____ [13] the door,

dreaming _____ [14] our next visit _____ [15] the antique rooms.

Score _____

EXERCISE 6-8

NAME _____   **DATE**_____

Which coordinating conjunction can fit in the blanks? Some might allow two or more. Describe what each would mean.

Example: She works days _____ wants to work nights.
<u>but</u> change of direction

1. Lee wanted to stop to eat, _____ they had not eaten that day.

2. He punched me in the nose, _____ I punched him back.

3. At the restaurant I saw Jim _____ Bob. I don't know which.

4. Eddie seems happy. _____ I wonder if he really is.

5. Mark doesn't want to work, _____ does he want to study.

6. Normally we are open till five, _____ tonight we are closing at four.

7. The boy _____ the dog seemed to be hungry.

8. You must do your homework _____ you won't be allowed to watch TV

    tonight.

9. I enjoy flying, _____ I joined the Air Force.

10. We needed to stop, _____ we were having too much fun.

Score _____

EXERCISE 6-9

NAME _____ DATE _____

Replace the normal coordinating conjunctions with the corresponding correlative ones. Sometimes more than one answer is possible.

Example: Our hotel is clean <u>and</u> modern.
Our hotel is <u>both</u> clean <u>and</u> modern.
Our hotel is <u>not only</u> clean <u>but</u> modern.

1. When Pam <u>or</u> Jeanne can be found, I will leave.

2. Jan <u>and</u> Fritz can go to Paris.

3. It was <u>not</u> Jan <u>and not</u> Fritz.

4. Do you want eggs <u>or</u> rolls for breakfast?

5. We did <u>not</u> walk <u>and</u> we did <u>not</u> ride. [Watch word order!]

6. The new convertible is fast <u>and</u> safe.

7. She is going to work in Florida <u>or</u> Georgia.

8. Biology <u>or</u> botany will fulfill that requirement.

9. Barry enjoys skiing <u>and</u> ice skating.

10. Ellen lives in this building <u>or</u> did live here.

Score _____

EXERCISE 6-10

NAME _____ DATE _____

Combine these sentences with <u>as . . . as</u> and delete what you can.

Example: Roy can sing very well. Ellie sings as well.
                 Ellie can sing as well as Roy.

1. The Canadians are very friendly. The Mexicans are just as friendly.

2. Your car is old. But my car is not.

3. There are many snakes in Texas. There are many snakes in Arizona. [Delete as little as you can.]

4. There are many snakes in Texas. There are many snakes in Arizona. [Delete as much as you can.]

5. Kathy is not rich. I thought she was rich.

6. The fajitas at Molly's are good. The fajitas at Mi Casa are also good.

7. Gertrude sings well. Does Bob sing well, too?

8. I have enjoyed visiting Japan. I also enjoyed visiting Singapore.

9. Philip dances well. Randy dances well.

10. Did Sam do well at graduation? Fred did well at graduation last year.

Score _____

EXERCISE 6-11

NAME _____ **DATE** _____

Combine these sentences these <u>so . . . that.</u>

Example: The policeman was very angry. He arrested the driver. [normally, he wouldn't]
The policeman was <u>so</u> angry <u>that</u> he arrested the driver.

1. I am very busy. I need help.

2. The new car was extremely expensive. I couldn't afford it.

3. There were many people at the concert. The band could not be heard.

4. Eve has many cats. The neighbors called the authorities.

5. Their trip was exciting. They will do it again.

6. They were so excited. They danced around the room.

7. Jeffrey arrived early. I was not ready.

8. The cakes are delicious. I will eat another.

9. His efforts were beneficial. He was given an award.

10. Her story was very moving. I wept.

Score _____

EXERCISE 6-12

NAME _____ DATE _____

Should we use <u>so . . . that</u>, <u>such . . . that</u>, or <u>as . . . as</u>? Choose and then combine.

1. We were tired. We went straight to bed.

2. She is a rich woman. She doesn't need any more money.

3. Fritz is happy. He is buying me lunch.

4. Fritz is successful. Now his wife is successful.

5. Harold and Gary are bitter enemies. They will not say hello to each other.

6. The class was a success. It will be offered again next semester.

7. We were happy in Washington. We were also happy in Seattle.

8. Her range was dynamic. She was given a recording contract.

9. Manny is a great cellist. He was a soloist at sixteen.

10. They were very surprised. They let out a little scream.

Be sure to review *comparatives* and *superlatives* (pp.64-68) if you need any more work on these topics.

Score _____

EXERCISE 6-13

NAME _____ DATE _____

Fill in the correct form of the indefinite article. If "nothing" [no determiner is needed] is the correct form, use an empty set to show that you have thought about it. Then classify each noun. You might need to review the difference between count and non-count nouns in Chapter 1, pp. 1-5 first.

Example: _____ clock
                      a clock—singular count noun
                      _____ clocks
                      ø clocks—plural count noun

1. _____ pocket

2. _____ rituals

3. _____ apple

4. _____ data [be careful with this form]

5. _____ lettuce

6. _____ information

7. _____ criteria [be careful with this form]

8. _____ unicorn

9. _____ roses

10. _____ bosses

Score _____

EXERCISE 6-14

NAME _____ **DATE** _____

For each of these mini-dialogues determine if the definite [specific] or indefinite [non-specific] article is appropriate.

Example: In the grocery
A: Do you sell _____ keys?
A: Do you sell ø̲ keys?

1. At home

   A: I parked on the street.

   B: Are you sure _____ car is safe there?

2. At school

   A: Have you read _____ chapter?

   B: I haven't even bought _____ book yet!

   A: Then you haven't even read _____ single word.

3. At the cafeteria

   A: Where is _____ cashier?

   B: He is by _____ left front door.

4. At the cafeteria

   A: Where is _____ cashier? I'm in a hurry.

   B: I'm sorry, but they all seem to be in _____ kitchen.

5. In the park

 A: Do you hear _____ music or am I losing my mind?

 B: You're OK. _____ music is coming from _____ concert

 shell.

6. In the concert shell

 A: Do you hear _____ music? I can't.

 B: No, there seems to be _____ problem with _____ sound

 system.

7. In Kuala Lumpur, Malaysia

 A: When are you going to _____ United States?

 B: I need to take _____ business trip home first.

 A: Oh, I didn't know.

8. Still in Kuala Lumpur, the next day

 A: When are you going to _____ United States?

 B: Have you forgotten _____ business trip we talked about yesterday?

 A: Oh, yeah.

9. One policeman approaches two policemen who are looking at something that is

 covered up with a blanket.

 A: What seems to be _____ problem? What's under _____

 blanket?

 B: _____ body.

10. A detective approaches two policeman who are looking at something that is covered

    up with a blanket.

    A: OK, thanks for the call. Where's _____ body? Who is it?

    B: You're in luck. It's _____ man you were asking us about.

    A: We've changed procedures, so you'll need to fill out _____ new form

      when you get back to _____station. Wait for me there.

                                                    Score _____

EXERCISE 6-15

NAME _____ DATE _____

Label the pattern. Determine if we need *the* based on that pattern. If *the* is needed, fill it in; otherwise, put an empty set in the blank

Example: _____ America
                      ø America [true proper noun]
                      _____ United Nations
                      the United Nations [derived adjective/noun]

1. _____ California

2. _____ City of London

3. _____ Rhodes College

4. _____ United Arab Emirates

5. _____ Congress of the United States

6. _____ Library of Congress

7. _____ Supreme Court

8. _____ Memphis

9. _____ Tammy, _____ Queen of Country

10. _____ Secretary of State

Score _____

EXERCISE 6-16

NAME _____ **DATE** _____

From the size (or quantity) decide if we need to use *the*.

Example: _____ Sargasso Sea
          <u>the</u> Sargasso Sea [large]

1. _____ Amazon River

2. _____ Finger Lakes

3. _____ Indian Ocean

4. _____ Panama Canal

5. _____ Bayou Teche

6. _____ San Diego Freeway

7. _____ Belvedere Boulevard [not very big]

8. _____ Sahara Desert [large and growing]

9. _____ Staten Island

10. _____ Bahamas [several islands]

11. _____ Upper Peninsula [of Michigan, fairly large]

12. _____ Lighthouse Point [smaller than a peninsula]

13. _____ Everglades

14. _____ Hudson Bay

15. _____ Okefenokee Swamp [large]

Whenever you find a new geographical designation, try to fit it into this system. If it won't fit, memorize it as an exception.

Score _____

EXERCISE 6-17

NAME _____ **DATE** _____

Decide if the definite article, indefinite article, or nothing is needed. Use the empty set if nothing is needed.

Example: Have you gone to _____ bank yet?
Have you gone to <u>the</u> bank yet?

At _____ [1] school, we needed to be in _____ [2] bed by

midnight. However, at _____ [3] university we didn't need to be in

_____ [4] dorm till _____ [5] 2 AM. Sometimes when we had gone

to _____ [6] movies, we didn't get _____ [7] home till very late in

_____ [8] night.

We would sneak over _____ [9] wall that surrounded _____

[10] campus and run madly towards _____ [11] bushes under our windows.

When we reached _____ [12] windows, we would throw _____

[13] stones at them till _____ [14] people upstairs would sneak down to

_____ [15] door and let us in. Occasionally one of _____ [16]

assistants would catch us and we would be cleaning in _____ [17] showers

during _____ [18] break _____ [19] next day. But

_____ [20] showers were never really that dirty since there were always

_____ [21] students on _____ [22] report. _____ [23]

last year I was at _____ [24] university, I began to study till _____

[25] morning.

Even _____ [26] today I sleep in _____ [27] whenever I am at

_____ [28] home. Then about _____ [29] noon, I struggle out of

_____ [30] bed and head to _____ [31] airport to catch

_____ [32] flight to _____ [33] day's first destination.

_____ [34] today my life is really different from _____ [35] life of

_____ [36] student.

Score _____

EXERCISE 6-18

NAME _____ DATE _____

Provide the correct form for the given level.

Example: Americans are industrious.
Formal:

Formal: Americans are industrious.

1. Water is necessary for life.
Colloquial:

2. The panda is a cute animal.
Informal:

3. Rabbits are very good to eat.
Colloquial:

4. Reindeer live in many countries.
Formal:

5. Tea is the national drink of many countries.
Colloquial:

Score _____

EXERCISE 6-19

NAME _____ DATE _____

Determine if the phrases are correct. If they are not, correct them.

Example: a. the Kathy's car
            Kathy's car
            b. the United States' GNP
            correct

1. a nice boy's problem

2. the Holland's famous cheeses

3. child's the temperature

4. tiger's den

5. a prince of Lombardy's a palace

6. many girls' dreams

7. many girl's dreams

8. sister her breakfast

9. the George's broken foot

10. the lucky man's million dollars

Score _____

EXERCISE 6-20

NAME _____ DATE _____

Provide a correct demonstrative determiner and state whether the noun is singular or plural.

Example: [far] _____ gentlemen
                 [far] <u>those</u> gentlemen [plural]

1. [near] _____ table

2. [near] _____ tables

3. [far] _____ data [be careful with this form]

4. [far] _____ water

5. [near] _____ man's children

6. [near] _____ man's child

7. [far] _____ silly swans

8. [near] _____ people's obnoxious laughter

9. [far] _____ scary film of theirs

10. [near] _____ people

Score _____

EXERCISE 6-21

NAME _____ **DATE** _____

From the clues, fill in the correct phrases in these mini-dialogues.

Example: Woman looking at the strawberries at a good market asks politely
A: Do you have _____ fresher strawberries?
A: Do you have <u>some</u> fresher strawberries?

A. Man upset at restaurant that has run out of everything

  A: Well, do you have _____ [1] food left?

B. Smiling international student talking to several Americans [little/a little]

  A: Of course, I needed _____ [2] luck to be able to study here. At first, I

  had _____ [3] hope that I would be selected from so many. But then after

  _____ [4] hard work and _____ [5] help from my parents, I

  was selected _____ [6] bit after everybody else.

C. At a party [many/many of]

  A: Goodness, there are _____ [7] people here, but I don't seem to know

  _____ [8] the people here.

  B: You're right. _____ [9] times when I've been here there were

  thousands having a good time.

  A: There seem to be _____ [10] internationals here. But there don't seem

  to be _____ [11] the internationals from our school.

D. Choosing between two colleges [either/either of] [neither/neither of]

A: _____ [12] college is <u>anywhere</u> exciting. But that means that

_____ [13] the two will have any parking problems.

B: _____ [14] one would be interesting. Does _____ [15] have

a swim team for you?

E. At an election [a few/few] [many/many of]

A: It has been disturbingly empty here today at the polls. Why do you think so

_____ [16] voters have stayed at home?

B: I think _____ [17] people bothered to vote. They didn't think

_____ [18] the issues were important. Furthermore,

_____ [19] people were out of town for _____ [20] days

because of the holidays.

Score _____

EXERCISE 6-22

NAME _____ **DATE** _____

Fill in the correct form of *other*.

Example: Where are the _____ guests?
Where are the <u>other</u> guests?

A. Do you know where there might be _____ [l] restaurant? This one is closed,

and we're from out of town.

B. Do you want to see the new film by Kubrick. Have you seen his many

_____ [2]? No, I'll see it _____ [3] day.

C. The Curtis twins are so different. One is nice and pleasant, but _____ [4] is a

terror.

D. Oh, I don't know. Perhaps _____ [5] are disturbed by his actions, but in

_____ [6] environment he might do just fine.

E. Well, just _____ [7] day he and that _____ [8] rascal, Peter,

broke _____ [9] of my windows. And he still hasn't paid for

_____[10], all six of them!

Score _____

EXERCISE 6-23

NAME _____ DATE _____

In each of these sentences, there is some problem with one or more of the determiners.
Find the errors, correct them and explain why the original was incorrect.

Example: a. She swatted the several flies.
           b. She swatted <u>several of</u> the flies.
           c. indefinite part <u>of</u> a definite group

1. a. Why did you buy this books?

    b.

    c.

2. a. She could not decide the which scholarship to accept.

    b.

    c.

3. a. He is ignoring his much responsibilities.

    b.

    c.

4. a. I hope I have few more friends at school this year.

    b.

    c.

5. a. Tom sold six millions dollars worth of real estate.

    b.

    c.

6. a. Give an example of every.

    b.

    c.

7. a. Did you ride train to Little Rock?

    b.

    c.

8. a. The sunflower grew 16-foot tall.

    b.

    c.

9. a. The last dance was fun. Let's dance other.

    b.

    c.

10. a. They have served billion and billion worldwide.

    b.

    c.

11. a. That was really yours problem.

    b.

    c.

12. a. Then they found an eight-inches worm in the fruit.

    b.

    c.

13. a. The statisticians could not interpret thises data.

  b.

  c.

14. a. Some soldiers were allowed to go home for the holidays.

  b.

  c.

15. a. Don't worry about the burned rice. I have another.

  b.

  c.

Score _____

EXERCISE 6-24

NAME _____ DATE _____

Add expletives to these phrases, clauses and sentences. Assume that they are all introducing new information into the conversation.

Example: That the government will collapse <u>is</u> clear to me.
It is clear to me that the government will collapse.

1. To dare to go where no one has ever gone before <u>is</u> her goal.

2. A new store <u>is</u> in the mall.

3. Six new houses <u>are</u> being built on my street.

4. That the forces of justice will succeed <u>seems</u> clear to everyone but the criminals.

5. That neither plan will work <u>appears</u> to be most unlikely.

6. <u>Rains</u> in the mountains every day.

7. In the classroom <u>is</u> noisy.

8. People <u>are</u> waiting in the hall.

9. To achieve excellence <u>is</u> often difficult.

10. <u>Was</u> brewing up a real storm outside.

Score _____

7

Clauses and Sentences

If you learn to manipulate the basic patterns of clauses and sentences, you will avoid many of the most common writing problems.

7a. Clause Patterns

Most of the variety in clause patterns comes from the structure of the predicate. Remember that the predicate consists of the auxiliaries, the main verb, and all the verbal modifiers.

Intransitive verbs cannot take objects. However, intransitive verbs may be modified. Indeed, some intransitive verbs *must* have some adverbial modification to be correct.

> *Incorrect*: Each day I would just *lie*.
> *Correct*: Each day I would just lie *by the pool*.

Some verbs can be either transitive or intransitive.

> *Transitive*: The police *broke down* the door.
> *Intransitive*: Finally, the spy *broke down* and told all.

Usually, transitive verbs must have a direct object. Additionally, they may have an *indirect object*. Most transitive verbs *must* have a direct object before they can have an indirect object.

> *One object, must be direct*: The artist made *the statue*.
> *Two objects*: The artist made the statue *a new base*.

Notice when both objects are nouns, the indirect object comes before the direct object.

Now do Exercise 7-1.

There is another position for the indirect object: in a prepositional phrase after the *direct* object.

>The artist made a beautiful statue *for me*.

But which preposition should you use? Most of the time if a verb has a sense of direction or motion, you should use *to* as the preposition.

>[direction/motion] She sent *me* the nicest gift.
>She sent the nicest gift *to* me.

Otherwise, you should use *for*.

>[no direction/motion] My father would make *me* hot chocolate.
>My father would make hot chocolate *for* me.

We can even use both prepositions for one verb depending on its use.

>[direction/motion] Bring *me* your new brochure when you come to visit.
>Bring your new brochure *to* me.
>[no direction] While you're at it, bring *Cathy* one.
>While you're at it, bring one *for* Cathy. [implied *to me*]

The use of *of* is very unusual and should be learned as an exception.

>Let me ask *you* a favor.
>Let me ask a favor *of* you.

Do Exercise 7-2 now.

This process of using prepositional phrases [called *dative movement*] becomes more complex if we use pronouns. Let's look at this process a little bit at a time.

>*Two nouns, no pronouns*: Mimosa baked Stan cookies.
>*Optional*: Mimosa baked cookies for Stan.
>*Indirect object pronoun*: Mimosa baked him cookies.
>*Optional*: Mimosa baked cookies for him.
>*Direct object pronoun*: Mimosa baked them for Stan.
>*Incorrect*: Mimosa baked Stan them.

Do Exercise 7-3 before you go on.

We must put the indirect object in a prepositional phrase if the direct object is a pronoun.
Both pronouns: Mimosa baked them for him.
Incorrect: Mimosa baked him them.

In other words, when the direct object is a pronoun, we must use the prepositional form. Practice these forms in Exercises 7-4 and 7-5.
Some verbs allow *object complements,* which either modify the direct object or rename the direct object.
Modifying the direct object: The chemicals made *the air unsafe*. [The air is unsafe.]
Renaming the direct object: The lawyer called *the defendant a crook*. [The defendant is a crook.]

Now do Exercise 7-6.

Some verbs change their meanings when they are used in these object complement structures.

> The president *called* Fred, his best friend, on the telephone and said, "Hi Fred!"
> called = spoke to

> The president *called* Fred his best friend on the telephone while he was talking to the
First Lady.
> called = named

Do Exercise 7-7 now.

Related to object complements are the linking verbs [e.g., *seem* or *feel*]. The most important problem associated with linking verbs is remembering to put them in. Remember that every English clause *must* have a tensed element. This is especially true with *be* and both adjective and noun subject complements.

> *Adjective subject complement*: Their house *was* hot. [noun is adjective]
> *Noun subject complement*: Those clowns *are* doctors. [noun is noun]

Do Exercise 7-8.

Since an adjective subject complement describes the subject, a noun, you must use the adjective forms. If you used an adverb form, you would be modifying the verb. Since many of the linking verbs can be used as intransitives also, you can sometimes have a few problems.

> *Adjective*: The rose smells *good*. It has a sweet smell.
> *Adverb*: The rose cannot smell *well*; it has no nose.

There is only one irregularity of importance in this pattern. If someone is asking about your health, you must use *well* in the answer.

> How are you doing?
> I am *well*, thank you.
> means: I am in good health.

In this one case, *well* is an adjective of good health because using *good* would be a judgment of your *moral* quality.

> I am good.
> means: I do not do evil things.

Now do Exercise 7-9.

One of the standard ways to express possession in English is with *be* and a *possessive subject complement*.

> The key was *Henry's*.

Try Exercise 7-10 now.

Remember that every clause must have a tensed verb. In many languages, no linking verb is needed for an adverb subject complement, but it is most definitely in English; otherwise, we produce a fragment.

Sentence: The class is at noon.
Fragment: The class at noon.

For the adverb subject complement, the linking verb *be* is really just there as the required tensed element. It really doesn't do much else.

Now do Exercise 7-11.

7b. Independent Clauses

Independent clauses stand by themselves. If we forget part of an independent clause (for example, the subject or the tensed verb), we have a fragment. See pp. 251-257 for work on making fragments complete independent clauses.

7c. Dependent Clauses

Dependent clauses act as modifiers or nouns. As a result, dependent clauses cannot occur alone. We have many words and phrases that tell us that a dependent clause is following. You will need to learn to recognize and produce them.

(1) Adverb clause

We normally use subordinating conjunctions [*subordinate* is the same as *dependent*] to tell us how to interpret the dependent clause that follows.

Do Exercise 7-12 to explore the different types of relationships adverb clauses can express. Then do Exercises 7-13 and 7-14 to practice them.

(2) Adjective clauses

Adjective clauses are often called relative clauses. The formation of relative clauses is explained in Chapter 2.

(3) Noun clauses

These are clauses that are used where a noun could be used. In other words, a noun clause can function as a subject, object, or complement.

Syntactic Types of Noun Clauses

There are two types of noun clauses. The easier is simply a complete clause with *that* used to signal subordination. If there is no chance for ambiguity, *that* may be deleted.

Independent clause: The aerobics class won't be cancelled.
That subordinator: *that* the aerobics class won't be cancelled.
Used as noun clause: I hope *that the aerobics class won't be cancelled.*
That deleted: I hope *the aerobics class won't be cancelled.*

The other type of noun clause looks more like a blend of a relative clause and an indirect question.

> *Noun clause: Whatever he wants* is fine with me.
> *Relative clause:* That is the gift *that he wants.*
> *Indirect question:* Ask him *what he wants.*

As in a question, the *wh-* word indicates a missing piece of information. In our last example we do not *know* or even *care* what it is that he wants. This construction allows us to make statements about information we don't have yet.

In this construction, you must choose between the fairly specific *wh-* question words (such as *what, when*) and the very vague *-ever* forms (such as *whenever, whatever*). Normally, we use the *-ever* forms when there is no specific reference and the normal *wh-* forms when there is.

> Professor, where shall I begin playing?
> *Specific reference:* [Where we left off last time] is fine.
> *No specific reference:* [*Wherever* you want] is fine. It all sounds bad.

Do not move prepositions to the front of the noun clause.

> You are pointing *at something.* It is moving closer.
> [*Whatever* you are pointing *at*] is moving closer.

Noun Clauses as Subjects

If a *that* noun clause is used at the beginning of a sentence, we cannot delete the *that* since we need *that* to let the reader know that what follows is not the main sentence.

> *Correct:* That he is not very bright is common knowledge.
> *Incorrect:* He is not very bright is common knowledge.

We normally replace a *that* noun clause used as a subject with *it*, an expletive, and move the clause to the end of the sentence. If you need work on the expletives, see Chapter 6.

> With expletive: It is common knowledge that he is not very bright.

We do not use the *wh-* noun clause as a subject very often in writing, but it is used frequently in informal speech.

> *Explicit: What you are trying to do with that class* is impossible.
> *Vague:* That's impossible.

Now do Exercise 7-15.

Noun Clauses as Objects of Prepositions

Noun clauses can be used as objects of prepositions. In this case, the only problem is to remember that the wh- word is part of the noun clause and not the object of the preposition. If you forget that fact, you may be tempted to use *whom* when we need to use *who.*

> *Correct:* They just stood around and talked about [*whoever* walked through the door].
> *Incorrect:* They just stood around and talked about [*whom*ever walked through the door].

7d. Elliptical Clauses

Many constructions in English allow us to omit parts that are recoverable.

> *Comparatives*: She is taller than he *is tall*.
> She is taller than he.
> *Subordination*: She is sure *that* he is taller.
> She is sure he is taller.
> *Restrictive relatives*: The girl *whom* you know is here.
> The girl you know is here.

We discussed the deletion of *that* earlier in this chapter. Let's turn to the other two constructions.

There are certain rules that govern what may be deleted. The first is that a tensed verb cannot occur without a subject. That means that if you are going to delete the subject of a construction, you must delete the tensed verb (or change it to a non-tensed form). Look at the next example. It shows what happens if you try to delete a relative marker that is also the *subject* of a relative clause.

> *Base*: The woman [*who* is running for mayor] is talented.
> *Delete relative marker*: The woman [*is* running for mayor] is talented.
> *Tensed verb must be deleted since it has no subject*: The woman [running for mayor] is talented.

If you didn't delete the tensed verb, then the reader would try to make a subject of the noun that came just before the tensed verb.

> *Incorrect*: [The woman is running for mayor] is talented.

Try Exercise 7-16 now.

Adverb Clause Deletion

Deletion of adverb clauses follows the same rule as relative clause deletion except that there must be a form of *be* to delete or we can't delete anything.

Form of be *in Clause*

> *Deletion possible: While he was living in America*, he wrote several of his best books.
> *After deletion: While living in America*, he wrote several of his best books.

> *No Form of* be *in clause*
> *No deletion possible*: While the critics praised him, he starved.
> *Incorrect*: While the critics praised, he starved.

However, you can change the sentence to a passive form, which contains a form of *be*.

> *Passive: While he was being praised by the critics*, he was starving.
> *Deletion possible: While being praised by the critics*, he was starving.

In order to avoid repetitiveness, you can often alter sentences to be able to delete elements.

Predicate Deletions

When you ask a question or compare two things, you will want to delete the repetitive parts so that you can focus on the pertinent part.

> *Deleted, focused:* Fritz is crazier than *Fred.*
> *Repetitive, not focused:* Fritz is crazier than Fred is crazy.
> *Deleted, focused:* Who is at the door? Fred.
> *Repetitive, not focused:* Who is at the door? Fred is at the door.

As you can see in those examples, subjects can stand without their predicates. However, there is a tendency in Modern English not to allow pronouns to stand without some tensed verb. Usually you need to retain one of the auxiliaries.

> Who *will* bring me proof of his capture?
> *Grammatical but stilted:* I!
> *Grammatical:* I *will!*
> *Grammatical:* Fred!

If there is no auxiliary, you need to use the correct form of the *periphrastic do.*

> Who *wants* to visit the castle?
> *Grammatical but stilted:* I!
> *Grammatical:* I do!
> *Grammatical but stilted:* Fred talks more than *he.*
> *Grammatical, normal:* Fred talks more than he *does.*

You can also delete predicates if they are recoverable.

> *Base:* Be on time if you can *be on time.*
> *Deleted:* Be on time if you can.

Of course, to delete a predicate, you must still leave a subject and a tensed element. If there is no auxiliary verb, you must supply the correct form of the periphrastic *do.*

> *Base:* Bring a friend; however, if you *bring a friend,* please bring some more chips.
> *Deleted predicate with added* do: Bring a friend; however, if you *do,* please bring some more chips.

You can delete only units. For example, you could not delete the object of a transitive verb and leave just the verb since a transitive verb must normally have an overt object.

> *Base:* Bring a friend; however, if you *bring a friend,* please bring some more chips.
> *Incorrect deletion:* Bring a friend; however, if you *bring,* please bring some more chips.

If you used an intransitive verb, you could delete the modifying elements since they are not essential.

> *Base:* Do you really want to go to that awful school in the city? Well, if you decide to *go to that awful school in the city,* I will come visit you.
> *Correct deletion:* Do you really want to go to that awful school in the city? Well, if you decide to go, I will come visit you.

Now do Exercises 7-17 and 7-18.

7e. Kinds of Sentences

A composition with only one kind of sentence is usually boring and uninteresting. Let's quickly look at the four basic kinds of sentences that allow us to vary the length and complexity of our sentences.

(1) Simple sentences

The simple sentence has one and only one subject-predicate sentence. Although it is basic, you must avoid just using one type. Make sure that every simple sentence has a tensed element.

> He works in the city. He likes the city.

Now do Exercise 7-19.

(2) Compound sentences

When we combine two or more independent clauses, we have a compound sentence. We can use a semicolon (see Chapter 22) to join two independent clauses together.

> He works in the city. He is an engineer for Ford.
> He works in the city; he is an engineer for Ford.

Try Exercise 7-20 now.

(3) Complex sentences

In compositions, you use many complex sentences to show explicit relationships with subordinating devices. For example, both this sentence and the one you just read are complex sentences.

(4) Compound-complex sentences

If we join a compound and a complex or two complex sentences together, we have a compound-complex sentence.

> The nation hoped they could avoid the issue, and although they filled, the issue was resolved without bloodshed.

Now you should do Exercise 7-21 to help you understand how English texts use the different kinds of sentences.

EXERCISE 7-1

NAME _____   **DATE** _____

Put the cued word in the appropriate place in the sentence to make an indirect object.

Example: [Tim] The artist made a beautiful statue.
             The artist made Tim a beautiful statue.

1. [the girls] Mother knitted new gloves.

2. [the class] My friend baked cookies.

3. [a sick friend] Americans send flowers.

4. [the students] The teacher read the correct answer.

5. [David] She bought a new car.

6. [the horse] I gave sugar.

7. [Nancy's cousin] The board awarded five thousand dollars.

8. [the university] The scholar offered his books.

9. [your neighbor] Have you made your special cranberry bread yet?

10. [Tom's brother] Why was the university sending a notice?

Score _____

EXERCISE 7-2

NAME _____   **DATE** _____

Using the word in brackets, make a prepositional phrase with an indirect object.

Example: [Tim] The artist made a beautiful statue.
The artist made a beautiful statue <u>for Tim</u>.

1. [the girls] Mother bought new gloves.

2. [the class] My friend sent cookies.

3. [a sick friend] Americans wire ["send"] flowers.

4. [the students] The teacher gave the correct answer.

5. [David] She sold a new car.

6. [the horse] I offered sugar.

7. [Nancy's cousin] The board lent five thousand dollars.

8. [the university] The scholar sold his books.

9. [your neighbor] Have you given your special cranberry bread yet?

10. [Tom's brother] Why was the university mailing a notice?

Score_____

EXERCISE 7-3

NAME _____ DATE _____

Change the word in brackets to a pronoun. Now, using that pronoun, build an indirect object. If two forms are possible, give both.

Example: [the boy] The artist made a beautiful statue.
The artist made <u>him</u> a beautiful statue.
The artist made a beautiful statue <u>for him</u>.

1. [the girls] Mother bought new gloves.

2. [the class] My friend sent cookies.

3. [a sick friend] Americans wire ["send"] flowers.

4. [the students] The teacher gave the correct answer.

5. [David] She sold a new car.

6. [the horse] I offered sugar.

7. [Nancy's cousin] The board lent five thousand dollars.

8. [the university] The scholar sold his books.

9. [your neighbor] Have you given your special cranberry bread yet?

10. [Tom's brother] Why was the university mailing a notice?

Score _____

EXERCISE 7-4

NAME _____   DATE _____

Replace the underlined word with a pronoun and rearrange the sentence.

Example: The artist made the boy <u>a beautiful statue</u>.
                  The artist made <u>it</u> for the boy.

1. Mother bought the girls <u>tickets to the concert</u>.

2. My friend took the old man <u>fudge</u>.

3. Americans send their sweethearts <u>flowers or candy</u>.

4. The minister gave the newlyweds <u>his blessing</u>.

5. The school bought the English Department <u>a new computer</u>.

6. Tim lent Will <u>his book</u>.

7. The university mailed John <u>his diploma</u>.

8. The company shipped my office <u>the wrong forms</u>.

9. My sister left Bob <u>her address</u>.

10. The police officer threw her partner <u>a gun</u>.

Score_____

EXERCISE 7-5

NAME _____   DATE _____

Replace the underlined word with a pronoun and rearrange the sentence.

Example: The artist made <u>the boy</u> <u>a beautiful statue</u>.
The artist made <u>it</u> for <u>him</u>.

1. Mother bought <u>the girls</u> <u>tickets to the concert</u>.

2. My friend took <u>the old man</u> <u>fudge</u>.

3. Americans send <u>their sweethearts</u> <u>flowers or candy</u>.

4. The minister gave <u>the newlyweds</u> <u>his blessing</u>.

5. The school bought <u>the English Department</u> <u>a new computer</u>.

6. Tim lent <u>Will</u> <u>his book</u>.

7. The university mailed <u>John</u> <u>his diploma</u>.

8. The company shipped <u>my office</u> <u>the wrong forms</u>.

9. My sister left <u>Bob</u> <u>her address</u>.

10. The police officer threw <u>her partner</u> <u>a gun</u>.

Score _____

EXERCISE 7-6

NAME _____   DATE _____

With the formulas given in brackets, make English sentences that contain object complements.

Example:　　The medicine will make [he = sick]
　　　　　　　The medicine will make <u>him sick</u>.

1. The French consider [we = their allies]

2. The city must elect [Minors = mayor]

3. Universities consider [SAT = the most reliable test]

4. The president should appoint [she = chief justice]

5. They always call [I = clumsy]

6. The race steward declared [the race = official]

7. The prisoner kept [the knife = hidden]

8. The committee found [he = innocent]

9. Her music always makes [they = very happy]

10. The members designated [Judy = their representative]

Score_____

EXERCISE 7-7

NAME _____   DATE _____

Provide a synonym for the underlined verb or rewrite the sentence.

Example: The government <u>kept</u> the actual figures secret.
                 kept = <u>hid</u>

1. We <u>considered</u> buying that house.

    considered =

2. We always <u>considered</u> them close friends.

    considered =

3. At customs we <u>declared</u> the wine we bought in Portugal.

    declared =

4. The officials <u>declared</u> Sylvia the winner.

    declared =

5. The maid <u>made</u> the beds.

    made =

6. The maid <u>made</u> the beds dirtier.

    made =

7. The speaker could not <u>pronounce</u> my name.

    pronounce =

8. The minister <u>pronounced</u> us husband and wife.

   pronounced =

9. Did your group <u>find</u> him responsible?

   find =

10. Did your group <u>find</u> the missing dog?

    find =

Score_____

EXERCISE 7-8

NAME _____   **DATE** _____

Provide the appropriate form of the cued linking verb.

Example: [be] Yesterday, she had _____ weaker.
Yesterday, she had <u>been</u> weaker.

1.   [feel] It is difficult to _____ fine when you are sick.

2.   [grew] I am afraid they have _____ weary of our company.

3.   [taste] Revenge _____ sweet.

4.   [become] Afterward, you will have _____ bitter.

5.   [sound] It _____ horrible and it is.

6.   [be] Nonetheless, he really _____ a student.

7.   [be] Have you ever _____ gentle and forgiving?

8.   [remain] Children do not _____ children forever.

9.   [be] Are you sure that Mr. Lim _____ ill?

10.   [smell] Last summer, the flowers in the garden _____ very fragrant.

Score _____

EXERCISE 7-9

NAME _____   **DATE** _____

Decide whether an adjective (for a linking verb) or an adverb (for an intransitive verb) is needed.

Example: [bad] The flesh of the frog tastes _____ to me.
[bad] The flesh of the frog tastes <u>bad</u> to me. <u>adjective</u>

1. [good] Roses grow _____ and fast in this soil. _____

2. [quick] The ghost appeared _____ and disappeared just as

    _____. _____

3. [loud] My ears are sensitive. I guess that's why your horn sounds so_____.

    _____

4. [quick] The rabbit appears _____. But he is really rather slow.

5. [bad] If I don't shower every day, I will smell really _____.

    _____

6. [good] Because of my congested sinuses, I do not smell very _____.

    _____

7. [good] And your sister is quite _____ also? _____

8. [good] American children try very hard to be _____ around Christmas.

    _____

9. [good] Are you _____ at getting things done on time? _____

10. [bad] Dogs will turn _____ if you are mean to them. _____

                                                    Score_____

EXERCISE 7-10

NAME _____   DATE _____

Rewrite the possessive sentence given with a possessive subject complement.

Example: That vehicle belongs to the club.
That vehicle is <u>the club's</u>.

1. Those plans were their plans.

2. Carter does not own those planes.

3. He will be the owner of the house next year.

4. The necklace belonged to me.

5. Now the museum owns it.

6. That car will belong to the company.

7. Why does Maria own that boat?

8. How did Fred get to be the owner of the marina?

9. Those are Ned's horses.

10. That floppy disk belongs to the department.

Score _____

EXERCISE 7-11

NAME _____ DATE _____

Using the appropriate form of *be*, make these fragments complete sentences. Each of these fragments contains an adverb subject complement.

Example: The men in the house
    The men <u>are</u> in the house.

1. The meeting tomorrow

2. Test at 4:00

3. Yesterday, the class downstairs

4. She not outside as we agreed

5. My home in Memphis now

7. He always in a good mood

8. My family not in this country

9. But they here last year

10. Their plans on the table

Score _____

EXERCISE 7-12

NAME _____   **DATE** _____

Which relationship is each of these adverb clauses using? Underline the introductory word or words that express this relationship.

time, cause/effect, purpose, condition/result, contrast, comparison, place, manner

Example: _____ They ignored her just as if she were not there.
manner They ignored her just <u>as if</u> she were not there.

1. _____ There was nothing but pain where they had lived before.

2. _____ When they finally had enough money, they moved.

3. _____ So that no one would see them, they had left at night.

4. _____ Because their new home was far away, the trip was long and

dangerous.

5. _____ Although they were not sure their new lives would be better, they

were willing to risk everything.

6. _____ Whether or not they made it, they had to try.

7. _____ Before I moved to Memphis, I really disliked winter.

8. _____ In order that I could study cello, my family moved to a larger city.

9. _____ His book was read on the radio so that thousands could hear it.

10. _____ Until the yoghurt shop opened last year, there was no place to have

a nice dessert.

Score _____

EXERCISE 7-13

NAME _____ **DATE** _____

Using the cued relationship, make the second sentence an adverb clause of the first.

Example: [contrast] The river is safer. The woods are faster.
The river is safer <u>although</u> the woods are faster.

1. [comparison] American cars are well built. They last for years and years.

2. [cause/effect] The team would argue about the batting order. It was very important to win.

3. [purpose] Their parents each worked two jobs. The children had a chance to be educated.

4. [time] Their parents were so proud. Their children graduated from college.

5. [condition/result] You must work hard. You want to succeed.

6. [purpose] We visited the small village. We wanted to see Ortega's house.

7. [place] The family had just moved. There was room available.

8. [condition/result] You will pass. You complete your assignments.

9. [manner] She jumped up and down. She had won the lottery.

10. [contrast] Fast food is cheap. It is often tasteless.

Score_____

EXERCISE 7-14

NAME _____   DATE _____

Now reverse the order. Remember, we might need a comma.

Example: [contrast] The river is safer. The woods are faster.
Although the woods are faster, the river is safer.

1. [contrast] American cars are well built. They are not so expensive.

2. [purpose] The team would argue about the batting order. They could win.

3. [cause/effect] Their parents each worked two jobs. The children needed money to be educated.

4. [cause/effect] Their parents were so proud. Their children graduated from college.

5. [time] You must work hard. You want to succeed.

6. [purpose] We visited the small village. We wanted to see Ortega's house.

7. [place] The family had just moved. There was room available.

8. [condition/result] You will pass. You complete your assignments.

9. [manner] She jumped up and down. She had won the lottery.

10. [contrast] Fast food is cheap. It is often tasteless.

Score _____

EXERCISE 7-15

NAME _____   **DATE** _____

Make a noun clause from the first sentence given. If no other directions are given, use the underlined word as a guide for a wh- or -ever word. Use the noun clause as the subject of the second sentence.

Example: One might fly under one's own power <u>somehow</u>.
_____ has fascinated people for years.
<u>How one might fly under one's own power</u> has fascinated people for years.

1. They learned something at the party. _____ amazed

   the sisters greatly.

2. One of their friends was building a set of wings. _____ seemed

   unbelievable. [use *that*]

3. <u>Someone</u> is the inventor. _____ is not clear.

4. The secret trials of the wings will occur <u>sometime</u>. _____ is not known

   either.

5. <u>Something</u> happens. _____ doesn't matter.

6. <u>Someone</u> looks at the sky. _____ will want to touch the wind.

7. Someone will find a way to fly under our own power. [use *that*] _____ is

   unlikely.

8. Does he really think he can succeed? [use *whether*] _____ is still a central

    issue in the affair.

9. <u>Someone</u> dreams of things undiscovered. _____ has a chance to change

    the future.

10. We discover <u>something</u>. _____ will lead us to yet new discoveries.

                                              Score _____

EXERCISE 7-16

NAME _____   **DATE** _____

Decide whether you can delete the relative marker. If you can, delete it and, if necessary, the tensed verb. Otherwise, explain why you can't delete the relative marker.

Example: a. The neighbor <u>whom</u> I like lives upstairs.
b. The neighbor I like lives upstairs.

a. The neighbor <u>who</u> plays the drums is home.
b. We can't delete the relative marker because we would have to delete the tensed verb (<u>plays</u>).

1. a. Did you see the film <u>that</u> was playing at the Jewel?

    b.

2. a. Did you see that film, <u>which</u> won some prize at Cannes?

    b.

3. a. Have you seen the film <u>that</u> Newman made at home?

    b.

4. a. Do you know the film <u>that</u> those girls were talking about?

    b.

5. a. That woman <u>who</u> is running for president has my vote.

    b.

6. a. Our friends <u>that</u> we invited to visit us are arriving on Friday.

   b.

7. a. The people <u>who</u> are moving in next door once lived in Saudi Arabia.

   b.

8. a. Why have you not finished that work, <u>which</u> I gave you last week?

   b.

9. a. Are the painters <u>whom</u> we hired coming on Tuesday?

   b.

10. a. She preferred not to inquire about her past boyfriend, <u>who</u> was still living in town.

    b.

Score _____

EXERCISE 7-17

NAME _____   DATE _____

Delete as many of the underlined words as you can. If you end up with an isolated pronoun, add the correct form of the periphrastic *do*.

Example: a. She walks faster than Olive <u>walks fast</u>.
b. She walks faster than Olive.

a. Olive walked slower than she <u>walked slow</u>.
b. Olive walked slower than she <u>did</u>.

1. a. Who will go to the store for me? Bonnie <u>will go to the store for you</u>.

    b.

2. a. Kyle eats much less than they <u>eat</u>.

    b.

3. a. Kyle was eating much less than we were <u>eating</u>.

    b.

4. a. Who made this horrible mess in the kitchen? She <u>made this horrible mess in the kitchen</u>.

    b.

5. a. Who took my new pen from my desk? No one <u>took your new pen from your desk</u>.

    b.

6. a. Are you leaving for town now? No, but Tom <u>is leaving for town now</u>.

   b.

7. a. Have you been to see the exhibition at the gallery yet? No, we <u>haven't been to see the exhibition at the gallery yet</u>.

   b.

8. a. Did you want to leave at noon? Yes, we <u>wanted to leave at noon</u>.

   b.

9. a. Who watched the game last night? No one <u>watched the game last night</u>.

   b.

10. a. Did Kevin find the references he was looking for? Yes, he <u>found the references he was looking for</u>.

    b.

Score _____

EXERCISE 7-18

NAME _____   DATE _____

Delete what you can [delete] in the second sentence or clause. Explain what you can't [delete]. The number in brackets is the number of words your answer should have. You might need to add a periphrastic *do*.

Example: a. She hopes to go to Dakar. I <u>hope to go to Dakar</u> too.
b. [3] I <u>do</u> too.
c. [5] I hope to go too.
d. [4] I hope to too.

A.   She hopes to go to Paris for the summer. We <u>hope to go to Paris for the summer too</u>.

1. [3]

2. [5]

3. [8]

B.   You cannot explain the event. The academy can't <u>explain the event</u> either.

4. [4]

C.   You can fly to Rio for July, if you want to <u>fly to Rio for July</u>.

5. [4]

6. [5]

7. [7]

8. [3]

D.   She was able to pass her exams easily. But Fred <u>wasn't able to pass his exams easily</u>.

9. [3]

10. [5]

Score _____

EXERCISE 7-19

NAME _____   DATE _____

Explain why the following are not simple sentences. If they are, just write <u>simple sentence</u>.

Example: _____ She home.
<u>not</u>—this is a fragment

_____ Because she is here, I will call.
<u>not</u>—more than one subject-predicate

1. The man wanting the change.

2. Whenever you think of me, I'll be there.

3. The roses are once again in bloom.

4. Is a problem for us all.

5. I hope that the stamp will be issued soon.

6. Fritz at home.

7. Seeing the chance, Fred gained the lead.

8. Are you waiting for us?

9. Has it occurred to you that I might not want to be rich?

10. The man, eager to start, jumped the gun.

Score _____

EXERCISE 7-20

NAME _____   DATE _____

Break the compound sentences into simple ones or combine the simple sentences into compound ones. You may need to use the list of transitional expressions in the handbook "Glossary" to help you.

Example: He lives in the woods. He likes the city.
He lives in the woods, <u>but</u> he likes the city.

She knew the answer; she had written the test.
She knew the answer. She had written the test.

1. We are winners; we got here first.

2. The race was fair, but it was very long.

3. Fortunately, the rain is just starting. We have already finished the race.

4. Unfortunately, the prize is very small; this is a poor organization.

5. Nevertheless, I am happy, for I won something.

6. Having lost the race, he simply walked home. He would win another day.

7. Bill studied hard, but Edward never opened a book.

8. Jean was late. Lane was even later.

9. Are you leaving or are you staying for supper?

10. She needed the help, so I helped her.

Score_____

EXERCISE 7-21

NAME _____ **DATE** _____

Using your last composition, fill in the following chart. You need to do a little math here.

A. Number of sentences in text:

B. Number of simple sentences:

   Percentage of simple sentences:

[To find percentages, divide number of simple sentences by number of sentences in text.]

C. Number of compound sentences:

   Percentage of compound sentences:

D. Number of complex sentences:

   Percentage of complex sentences:

E. Number of compound-complex sentences:

   Percentage of compound-complex sentences:

F. Number of fragments [let's hope none]:

   Percentage of fragments:

Now, take a page from any book (preferably from your major) or magazine and fill in the same chart.

A. Number of sentences in text:

B. Number of simple sentences:

   Percentage of simple sentences:

C. Number of compound sentences:

   Percentage of compound sentences:

D. Number of complex sentences:

   Percentage of complex sentences:

E. Number of compound-complex sentences:

   Percentage of compound-complex sentences:

F. Number of fragments [let's hope none]:

   Percentage of fragments:

Were your percentages about the same as those in your sample? Try this exercise several times throughout the term. Are you using more sentence variety as you write more?

Part II

□ Revising Sentences:
Structural
and
Grammatical
Problems
□

8

Sentence Fragments

Remember that an English sentence must contain at least one independent clause. That independent clause must contain a subject and one tensed verb. If your "sentences" don't contain those elements, they are called *fragments*—just parts of sentences. Fragments really hinder communication and must be revised as you apply the editing process. Fortunately, it is very easy to make fragments complete sentences.

8a. Dependent Clause Fragments

If you try to treat a dependent clause as a sentence, you are producing a dependent clause fragment.

Fragment: Although he was on time.

A dependent clause *must* be joined to an independent clause.

Correct: Although he was on time, he still was the last to arrive.

If you can recognize subordinators [e.g., *although*], you will be able to avoid this error easily. If you still have trouble recognizing subordinators, review 7c.

Another source of these fragments is a faulty understanding of punctuation between clauses; review Chapter 21 and "Periods as End Punctuation" in Chapter 25 if you are not really sure of the roles of the comma and the period.

Be careful not to confuse *questions* with *dependent* clauses. If you forget to follow correct word order in questions, your product will look like a sentence fragment.

Correct question form: Which did he fail to finish?
Sentence fragment: Which he did fail to finish?

To correct a dependent clause fragment, just join the dependent clause to the clause it modifies. Make sure that there is at least one independent clause.

Fragment: Since I live in Memphis. Which is a major city.

Still a fragment: Since I live in Memphis which is a major city. [no independent clause]

Correct: Since I live in Memphis, which is a major city, there is much to do here.

Now try Exercise 8-1.

8b. Phrase Fragments

Phrases do not contain all of the elements of a clause; they are missing one or both of the two minimum elements: subject and tensed verb.

(1) Verbal phrases as fragments

Usually a verbal phrase fragment is lacking a *tensed verb* form. We must be certain that each clause has *one and only one* tensed verb. Remember the tensed form must be the first verb of the verb phrase. Often all that is missing is the *-s* of the third-person singular present. Review 11c if the *-s* is still causing you problems.

Fragment: Janet go to school every day. [base form alone]

Corrected: Janet goes to school every day. [tensed form]

If we use an irregular verb's *past participle* [*-en*] form in place of its *past -ed* form, we may end up with a fragment. In a clause the past participle *must* be preceded by a form of *have* or *be*; a participle cannot appear alone.

Fragment: The lion *eaten* the antelope. [past participle]

Revised with have: The lion *has* eaten the antelope.

Revised with past: The lion *ate* the antelope.

Very often the tensed form of *be* is forgotten when an adjective or predicate nominative is used. Likewise, the tensed *be* is forgotten when the passive [remember: *be* plus *-en* form] or the progressive forms [*be* plus *-ing* form] are used.

Fragment: Mr. Loomis an astronaut.

Revised with form of be: Mr. Loomis *is* an astronaut.

Fragment: Mr. Loomis picked by the government.

Revised with form of be: Mr. Loomis *was* picked by the government.

The auxiliary *do* is often forgotten in drafts. Without the auxiliary *do*, the sentence appears to be a fragment

Fragment: Why you not *visit* us more often?

Revised with do: Why *don't* you visit us more often?

Now try Exercise 8-2.

(2) Verb phrases as fragments

If we forget to include a subject, we usually end up with a verb phrase fragment. Remember that in English you must use a subject for all sentences except the imperative. Sometimes these fragments can be misinterpreted as imperatives.

In a sentence, we *must* have some kind of a *subject*. This necessary subject can be the dummy subject *it* or the expletive *there*. If these terms are not clear, review *expletives* (pp. 179-180, 211).

> *Fragment:* Do you know if *is* raining in Germantown?
> *Revised with dummy subject:* Do you know if *it* is raining in Germantown?

> *Fragment, misinterpreted as imperative:* Every day the girls meet us at the store. Wait for us in the parking lot. Let's go. [reads: *you* wait for us in the parking lot]
> *Correct with pronouns:* Every day the girls meet us in the store. They wait for us in the parking lot. Let's go.

It is also possible that the *that* of a dependent clause can be misinterpreted as the *subject* of the clause.

> *Fragment:* Our friends have not written lately, but we know *that* are doing well.
> *Revised with correct pronoun:* Our friends have not written lately, but we know that *they* are doing well.

Now do Exercise 8-3.

(3) Noun phrases as fragments

Sometimes writers forget to put in a predicate. Those fragments are called *noun phrase fragments.*

> *Fragment:* His taking the exam. [no verb]

A subject cannot stand by itself except as an answer to a question.

> *Question:* Who is going to write the report up?
> *Acceptable answer:* Murray.
> *Answer preferred by many:* Murray is.

Do Exercise 8-4.

(4) Avoiding fragments

Fragments are very disturbing. They are especially disturbing to most English instructors, who often consider fragments very serious errors. You must learn to find and revise fragments, since you will (just as native speakers do) produce them in your rough and first drafts.

When you are ready to check for fragments, make sure that each of your sentences and clauses has a subject and one and only one tensed verb.

EXERCISE 8-1

NAME _____ DATE_____

Join these clauses together with the appropriate use of commas. If the joined clauses still form a fragment, label it a *fragment*.

Example: She lives in Memphis. Where I also live.
She lives in Memphis, where I also live.

Because it's Memphis. Where she lives.
Fragment: Because it's Memphis where she lives.

1. Although I doubt it. Elvis is still said to visit Memphis.

2. No one knows. Why she did it.

3. He was an honor student at school. Which was in Michigan.

4. That is the very house. Which we wanted to buy.

5. While we were shopping. My mother bought me a new shirt.

6. She got the award. Because she was the best.

7. Whenever they visit Memphis. They must go to Mud Island.

8. Since we enjoy camping. We bought a tent.

9. Because he works at the mill. Which is very busy.

10. Although he is not from New Albany. He feels right at home there.

Score _____

EXERCISE 8-2

NAME _____ DATE _____

Determine if the following are fragments. If they are fragments, provide a tensed element by (a) adding the correct form of *have* or *be* if a participle is used or by (b) providing the correct form of the *-s* suffix or *do*.

Example: She been sick a long time.
a. fragment
b. She <u>has</u> been sick a long time.

1. We gone to find her checkbook.

    a.

    b.

2. They being stupid again.

    a.

    b.

3. She seem not interested in the affairs of the church.

    a.

    b.

4. He's not interested in what I have to say to him.

    a.

    b.

5. The lecture's point not forgotten by the class.

    a.

    b.

6. Where the boys live?

   a.

   b.

7. Without a doubt, Harold play the best game of chess in school.

   a.

   b.

8. It really hot today, but it not bother my family.

   a.

   b.

9. Did George visit his farm last week?

   a.

   b.

10. Why the auditors visiting our company again?

    a.

    b.

Score _____

EXERCISE 8-3

NAME _____ **DATE** _____

Decide if the following are fragments. If they are, supply a *subject*.

Example: Leave the bag under the table, Ellen.
a. correct, an imperative
b. [blank]

Really seems that is getting warmer every day.
a. fragment, dummy subjects missing
b. *It* really seems that *it* is getting warmer every day.

1. I saw Sam downstairs. Where is going now?

   a.

   b.

2. Where are you going? Can go with you?

   a.

   b.

3. Stay in the kitchen. Probably is cleaner in there.

   a.

   b.

4. Yesterday were six pears in this bag. Now they are gone.

   a.

   b.

5. Few Americans enjoy eating horse. They think is not good.

   a.

   b.

6. A new play is in town. See it today!

   a.

   b.

7. Why are you selling your businesses? Do you think that are not doing well?

   a.

   b.

8. Leave the driving to us.

   a.

   b.

9. Went to West Virginia over the holidays.

   a.

   b.

10. Did buy the camera last week, Sue?

    a.

    b.

Score _____

EXERCISE 8-4

NAME _____   **DATE** _____

Determine if the following are noun phrase fragments. If they are, supply an appropriate predicate. You will need to provide a tensed verb or combine the fragment with the main sentence.

Example: Vietnam. It is my country.
                  a. fragment
                  b. Vietnam is my country.

1. It is dangerous for your health. Smoking cigarettes.

    a.

    b.

2. Where do you come from? Louisville.

    a.

    b.

3. Last night I read a really good book. *Planet Earth*.

    a.

    b.

4. The problem with airlines. I think that is a serious issue.

    a.

    b.

5. Did you see Fred or Luis at the game yesterday? Luis.

    a.

    b.

6. The letter carrier at the door. She is knocking.

    a.

    b.

7. I saw the doctor. The doctor from Sri Lanka.

    a.

    b.

8. She asked a question. An intelligent question.

    a.

    b.

9. His real father. Has he ever seen him?

    a.

    b.

10. Do you enjoy it? The university.

    a.

    b.

Score _____

9

Comma Splices and Fused Sentences

It is an error to combine two independent clauses with just commas. We call that error a *comma splice*. Once you recognize comma splices, they are very easy to correct. The easiest way to correct comma splices is just to replace the comma with a period and capitalize the first letter of the second clause.

> *Comma splice:* She lives in the city, it is very large.
> *Revised:* She lives in the city. It is very large.

Unfortunately, that choppy style becomes tiresome very quickly, so you must have other means to solve this problem. You will learn some techniques in this chapter to get around this problem.

Slightly worse than the comma splice is the *fused sentence,* which uses no punctuation between independent clauses. Fused sentences are also very easy to correct. The easiest way to correct a fused sentence is just to put a period at the end of the first clause and capitalize the first letter of the second clause.

> *Fused sentence:* She lives in the city it is very large.
> *Revised:* She lives in the city. It is very large.

Unfortunately, when we encounter fused sentences in a student's work, we are afraid that the student does not really understand sentence boundaries. If that should be your case, you must review Chapter 7 of both the workbook and the handbook.

Let's look at some of the other ways you might revise comma splices and fused sentences.

9a. Revision with a Comma and a Coordinating Conjunction

If you do not remember the basic functions of the coordinating conjunctions (such as *and, but,* and *or*), review them in Chapter 6 before you attempt to do this section.

You could have revised each of our initial examples in this chapter with a comma and the appropriate coordinating conjunction, *and*.

> *Comma splice*: She lives in the city, it is very large.
> *Revised*: She lives in the city, and it is very large.
> *Fused sentence*: She lives in the city it is very large.
> *Revised*: She lives in the city, and it is very large.

Since each coordinating conjunction gives two clauses a special relationship, we must be careful not just to combine clauses with conjunctions for the sake of combining.

Now try Exercise 9-1.

9b. Revision with a Semicolon

Semicolons signal that two sentences have a close relationship; however, that relationship may not be close enough to use a coordinating conjunction. It is often best for ESL learners not to attempt to use the semicolon in this fashion. On the other hand, you must learn to use the semicolon with transitions, which are very important in American prose. We want relationships spelled out explicitly.

> *Without transition*: She asked me not to go. I went.
> *With transition:* She asked me not to go; nevertheless, I went.

Remember that coordinating conjunctions occur *between* clauses; their position cannot be changed.

> [clause] *coordinating conjunction* [clause]

Subordinators (such as *since, because,* or *that*) occur only at the beginning of the dependent clauses. Their position cannot be changed, but the position of the dependent clause can often be changed.

> [clause] [*subordinator* clause]
> He was sick *because* he ate too much.
>
> [*subordinator* clause], [clause]
> *Because* he ate too much, he was sick.

Transitions, however, can only be part of the second clause. Since transitions do not really unite two clauses, we must use the semicolon.

Try Exercise 9-2 before you read any farther.

Furthermore, most transitions can occur in three positions in the second clause.

> *Initial*: [clause]; [*transition*, clause]
> We like her; *after all*, she is my sister.
>
> *Final*: [clause]; [clause, *transition*]
> We like her; she is my sister, *after all*.
>
> *Medial*: [clause]; [clause, *transition*]
> We like her; she is, *after all*, my sister.

Generally speaking, the farther the transition is from the beginning of its clause, the weaker it is.

Now do Exercise 9-3.

9c. Revision with a Colon

Although you should read and understand the use of a colon to join independent clauses, do not attempt to use it unless your instructor wants you to try. Most native speakers do not ever use this rare device.

9d. Revision by Creating Two Sentences

The easiest way to revise fused sentences or comma splices is to make two sentences.

To correct comma splices or fused sentences, just change the comma (if there is one) to a period and capitalize the first letter of the second clause. This method is simple, if boring. Since you should be trying to write fairly straightforward sentences, you will need to use this technique frequently.

Now do Exercise 9-4.

9e. Revision with a Dependent Clause or Phrase

Whenever you change an independent clause to a dependent clause, you are making the relationships between clauses more explicit. Relationships in American prose should normally be as explicit as possible. Therefore, it is a good idea to try this revision technique occasionally.

We can use the explicit *subordinators* to create dependent clauses. Additionally, we can make one of the clauses a relative clause, which shows the interrelatedness of the two clauses.

Do Exercise 9-5.

EXERCISE 9-1

NAME_____ DATE _____

Put brackets around each of the clauses. Then, revise each of these sentences with a comma
and an *appropriate* coordinating conjunction.

Example: Sarah lives in a house, it is old and dirty.
a. [Sarah lives in a house,] [it is old and dirty.]
b. Sarah lives in a house, but it is old and dirty.

1. We don't like to eat out much we don't like to cook either.

    a.

    b.

2. Do the twins want to go to school, do they want to go to the playground?

    a.

    b.

3. Her attempts were very nice, I appreciated them.

    a.

    b.

4. The gentleman was most ashamed of his actions, we live in the South.

    a.

    b.

5. There are many car thieves in this city, don't worry if you don't have a car.

    a.

    b.

6. Are the boys spending the night at your house have they spent too much time there?

    a.

    b.

7. Well, she appears to have all the qualifications, does she really want the job?

    a.

    b.

8. Connect two independent clauses with just a comma, you have a comma splice.

    a.

    b.

9. Mary had found her glasses under the table they had fallen there during the earthquake.

    a.

    b.

10. Fortunately, the quake was not severe, it just knocked down a few power lines.

    a.

    b.

Score _____

EXERCISE 9-2

NAME_____ DATE _____

Revise these sentences with a semicolon and a transition from the handbook's "Glossary of Grammatical, Rhetorical and Literary Terms." Make sure that the transition is appropriate.

Example: I want to see the play, I have no money.
Revised: I want to see the play; *however*, I have no money.

1. You must buy a ticket before you can come in, go to the ticket window first.

2. The playwright couldn't expect me to do that, they don't pay me very much.

3. The play was a flop it was a disaster.

4. I'm sorry I must leave, I will not give you the loan.

5. Yesterday, I saw him with a new car, he must have gotten that nice raise he spoke of.

6. He was very motivated, he made great grades.

7. Those are the facts, it was all properly done.

8. The couple couldn't stand living in the dorms, they left.

9. You have won a million dollars, you are rich.

10. We could go to Bermuda, we could go to Hawaii.

Score _____

EXERCISE 9-3

NAME_____ DATE _____

Revise these sentences with a semicolon and a transition if one is not already supplied. Put the transition in the cued position.

Example: Jane works in the prison she is in favor of severe sentences. [medial *nonetheless*]
Revised: Jane works in the prison; she is, *nonetheless*, in favor of severe sentences.

1. The maids looked everywhere, *however*, they just couldn't find the missing shoe. [final]

2. The school's rules were extremely strict, many students were expelled, *accordingly*. [initial]

3. My little brother lost his job he wants me to lend him money. [medial *as a result*]

4. My dorm room isn't very big, *on the other hand*, it is mine. [final]

5. The child let out a frightened scream the mother ran to see if anything had happened. [initial *as a result*]

6. For years she had wanted to climb that slope, *finally*, she climbed it last summer. [medial]

7. She is simply perfect, she is hired, in other words. [initial]

8. I can't go tonight, I can't go tomorrow. [initial *furthermore*]

9. The school will pay for your tuition, you must pay for housing. [final *however*]

10. Southerners are usually very polite everyone says, "Excuse me." [initial for *example*]

Score _____

EXERCISE 9-4

NAME _____ DATE _____

Make two sentences from these incorrectly punctuated clauses.

Example: The students have done their homework again, the instructor will be
pleased.
Revised: The students have done their homework again. The
instructor will be pleased.

1. In 1940, the number of these associations increased these associations were originally
concerned with quality.

2. Edward Miller was a painter he was also a sculptor.

3. The associations disliked his work immensely, they refused to let him show his work.

4. The first stirrings of the newest movement had already been felt its major proponents
produced a thick manifesto.

5. Although they were able to sell their wares on the streets, the artists thought they
should have access to the salons the fashionable world bought only from the salons.

6. Her paintings hung in the homes of the rich, the paintings were very valuable.

7. Astronauts undergo rigorous training, many do not complete the course.

8. But for those who do, the prize is great, they fly to the stars.

9. The visiting scholar wanted to visit Oxford, Mississippi, he wanted to see the famous university there.

10. However, we didn't have time to go to Mississippi to visit Oxford, the scholar had to return to China.

Score _____

EXERCISE 9-5

NAME_____ DATE _____

Change the italicized words in each incorrect sentence to a dependent clause using the cued subordinator.

Example: *I am at school,* I love to slide down the stairs. [when]
            Revised: When I am at school, I love to slide down the stairs.

1. *She is my best friend* I must ask her first. [since]

2. We were unable to find the building, *my husband works in that building.* [relative clause]

3. The committee wanted the artist to bring his works *he was going to be in New York anyway.* [since]

4. *Betty is a really good artist* do you actually want to buy one of her works? [although]

5. Henry wouldn't stay *he wanted to go to the movies* with Jeanne. [because]

6. *The trip didn't start till Wednesday* Henry wanted to get there very early. [although]

7. Do we need to bring in the chairs, *it doesn't look like rain?* [since]

8. Their works were often displayed in museums, *museums specialize in modern artists' works*. [relative clause]

9. The committee *failed to find support in the company* they went elsewhere. [when]

10. *The episode was not serious* do not let it happen again. [although]

Score _____

10

Subject-Verb Agreement

It is fairly easy to make subjects agree with verbs in English. Basically, the only question is whether to add the *-s* suffix or not. Once you learn that fact, the rest is very simple.

You only need to worry about agreement in the present tense for all verbs and for *be* in the past in Modern English. Although many dialects of English have lost or are losing even this little bit of agreement, you must be careful to avoid agreement errors.

(1) Agreement with all verbs except *be*

Only two factors really matter, tense and number. Remember that each verb really only has two tenses: past and present. The other forms (base and the participles) are *non-tensed* forms. Additionally, each noun is either singular or plural. The only time you need to add the *-s* suffix is when you have a third-person, singular (*he, she*, and most importantly, *it*) present tense verb. Nothing else has the *-s* suffix.

> She *runs* the factory effectively.

Of course, if the verb's base ends in an *s-like* sound, you must add *-es* so that you can hear the *s* sound.

> *mess* plus *-es* equals *messes*: He messes up.
> *rush* plus *-es* equals *rushes*: He rushes around.

Go and *do* add *-es* even though they don't end in an *s* sound.
> *go* plus *-es* equals *goes*: Who goes there?
> *do* plus *-es* equals *does*: She does well.

Have is just a little irregular. The *-s* form is *has* and the past *had* is also the past participle.

Also remember that the *modals* are already tensed. As a result, you cannot *add* the *-s* tense suffix to the modals.

> *Incorrect:* He *musts* go now.
> *Correct:* He must go now.

Now do Exercise 10-1. Then, read (2) and do Exercise 10-2, which reviews the information in this section too.

(2) Agreement with the verb *be*

Be, which is quite irregular, does require a little more practice. Furthermore, it is the most commonly used verb since it is part of the *passive, progressive,* and *linking* constructions. As the forms are often contracted in speech, you may not hear them distinctly, but they're there.

The most important problem with *be* is remembering that *you* always uses the plural form even if there is only one you.

> *Singular:* Mr. Knowles, how *are* you?
> *Plural:* Mr. and Mrs. Knowles, how *are* you?

Some native speakers do not use the past plural forms. Although you may hear native speakers saying (and occasionally writing) *we was, they was,* and *you was,* use the plural forms (*we were, they were,* and *you were*) in the past in Standard English.

Do Exercise 10-2 now.

10a. Intervening Words between Subject and Verb

Many native speakers have problems finding the true subject when it is far away from the verb. We have a tendency to make the subject the first noun to the left of the verb.

> *Correct: The man* who had many friends among the conservative leaders *was* offered the position.
> *Common mistake: The man* who had many friends among the conservative *leaders were* offered the position.

Now do Exercise 10-3.

10b. Subjects Joined by *And*

Although the use of *each* appears to be an exception, it is really quite logical.

> *Apparent exception:* Each governor and attorney general *was* assigned a limousine.

But now look at the same sentence without *each.* How many limousines are going to be assigned in the following example?

> *Ambiguous:* The governor and the attorney general *were* assigned a limousine.

It's difficult to be sure. It could be just *one* that they must share, or it could be that *each* of them received one. When you use *each* in this way, you are really writing the following.

> *Non-ambiguous: Each* of the governors and the attorney generals *was* assigned a limousine.

However, one doesn't really know how many *governors* and *attorney generals* there are in this last example. Regardless of the number, *each* received a limo.

It is sometimes difficult to know when two items are considered a group. Often the verb signals the writer's real intentions.

> Pie and ice cream *was* served. [as a unit, no choice]
> Pie and ice cream *were* served. [which do you want?]

Now do Exercise 10-4. Don't forget that prepositional phrases (such as *along with*) don't have any influence on subject/verb agreement.

10c.   Subjects Joined by *Or/Nor*

If you need to join nouns with *or/nor*, try to make the plural subject last. It sounds more natural.

> *Awkward:* Either the roses or the garlic *is* smelling up the kitchen.
> *Better:* Either the garlic or the roses *are* smelling up the kitchen.

Do Exercise 10-5.

10d.   Indefinite Pronouns as Subjects

Before you can use indefinite pronouns correctly, you must be sure that you understand the count/mass distinction (see Chapter 1). In some cases, this distinction determines whether a singular or plural verb is used.

> *Mass [noncount]:* There is the rice; *some has* spilled on the floor.
> *Count:* There are the kids; *some are* just about ready to quit for the evening.

There are two groups of indefinite pronouns. The first consists of pronouns that *isolate one* member of a group from the others. Since they refer to only *one* member, we always need to use the *singular form*.

> *Only one: Each* one of you *needs* to bring this form tomorrow.

The other group consists of pronouns that refer to a *portion* of the group. As a result, we need to use the plural forms.

> *Portion of the group: Some* of her songs *were* really sad.

With mass nouns we cannot use the first group, since we cannot isolate one member of the mass.

> *Incorrect: Each of the rice* was burned.
> *Correct: Each grain* of the rice was burned.

With members of the second group, we always use the singular form, since there is only *one mass*.

> *Correct: Most* of the rice *was* burned.

Now try Exercises 10-6 and 10-7.

10e. Relative Pronouns as Subjects

You need to be careful that you make the verb of a relative clause agree with the *subject* of the relative clause. If the subject of the relative clause is a relative pronoun, you must step outside the relative clause to determine what the relative pronoun's antecedent is.

> Do you see the *men* [who *are* talking to Fred]?
> Do you see the *man* [who *is* talking to Fred]?

Do Exercise 10-8 now.

10f. Subjects of Linking Verbs

Native speakers have a tendency to make the verb agree with the complement. Don't do it; the verb agrees with the subject and not with the complement.

> *Incorrect:* His main problem *were* his three ex-wives. [*were* agrees with *ex-wives*]
> *Correct:* His main problem *was* his three ex-wives. [*was* agrees with *problem*]

10g. Subjects That Follow Verbs

For many native speakers, subject-verb agreement disappears when the tensed verb precedes the subject. Avoid this nonstandard practice.

> *Incorrect:* *Was* the boys going into town with you?
> *Correct:* *Were* the boys going into town with you?

Even normally careful native speakers often use singular *is/was* after *there*. Again, you should follow the conservative standard practice of making the verb agree with the subject. The exercise on this topic is combined with the next section.

> *Nonstandard:* There's the boys now!
> *Standard:* There *are* the boys now!

10h. Collective Nouns and Amounts as Subjects

The difference in form between *a number* and *the number* is easy if you remember that *a number* means *many* and *the number* is *one specific* number.

> A *number* of students *have* failed geometry.
> *Many* students *have* failed geometry.
> *The number* of students failing geometry *has* gone from 14 [a specific number] to 32 [a specific number].

Do Exercise 10-9 before you go on.

10i. Titles as Subjects

All country names are singular, even those that sound plural.

> The Netherlands *is* a quiet place to live.

10j. Foreign Nouns as Subjects

Remember that *data* and *criteria* are always plural. Nonetheless, many native speakers will use the singular forms with these words. *Data* is becoming acceptable as a mass noun, but still avoid it. *Criteria* will always remain plural in Standard English.

10k. Subjects Ending in *-ics*

Subjects that end in *-ics* are almost always singular. Learn them, since you will refer to them in school constantly.

> Physics *is* fun.

10l. "Words" as Subjects

Perhaps you wish to tell someone the word for *the seasons of the year* in your native language. Regardless of its form in English or your language, you will use a singular verb.

> *The seasons of the year* is not a term we use in my language. *The rainy days* is the most common form.

Review many of the problems in subject/verb agreement by doing Exercise 10-10.

EXERCISE 10-1

NAME_____ DATE _____

Give the person, number, and tense of the underlined word. Next add an *-s* or *-es* suffix if it should be there.

Example: She *walk* down the street
                third-person, singular, present
                She walks down the street.

                It seems to *have* its virtues.
                infinitive [non-tensed forms have no number or person]

1. It will <u>go</u> fine next year.

2. <u>Knowing</u> that, I will not return.

3. The man <u>hope</u> to visit the zoo while the panda is there.

4. He has thought about the subject every day now.

5. You are <u>planning</u> a trip to Mexico, aren't you?

6. <u>Do</u> the boy know the combination of the lock?

7. He <u>must</u> know it; I told it to him yesterday.

8. She <u>went</u> to the mountains every June.

9. Why <u>have</u> the doctor written out a prescription?

10. <u>Studying</u> French is not difficult.

Score _____

EXERCISE 10-2

NAME_____ DATE _____

Fill in the correct form of the cued verb.

Example: [past *be*] They _____ late.
                  They <u>were</u> late.

1. [present *do*] _____ he still live here?

2. [past *go*] As he _____, did he leave me anything?

3. [past *be*] We _____ sure if you _____ coming.

4. [present *be*] The sun _____ shining.

5. [past *do*] Why _____ she sell those shares?

6. [present *be*] Did you know that I _____ from a royal family?

7. [present *go*] And then the water _____ down the drain.

8. [present *do*] It _____n't seem quite fair, _____ it?

9. [present *have*] The woman _____ a right to be mad.

10. [past *be*] Strong words _____ flying left and right.

Score _____

EXERCISE 10-3

NAME_____ DATE _____

1. Underline the true subject. 2. Rewrite the sentence without the intervening words.
3. Provide the correct form of the cued verb. 4. Now go back to the original and fill in
the correct form of the cued verb.

Example: a. [past *be*] Our neighbor with all those funny dogs _____ over
to borrow some cat food.
b. Our neighbor <u>was</u> over to borrow some cat food.
a. <u>Our neighbor</u> with all those funny dogs <u>was</u> over to borrow some
cat food.

1. a. [past *be*] Two people from that really bizarre singing group "The Retreads,

 Dead" _____ signing autographs.

 b.

2. a. [present *be*] Two from the "Save the Snail Darter" committee

 _____ barred from entering the university's auditorium ever again.

 b.

3. a. [present *buy*] Every day that kid from the School for Drama and the Performing Arts

 _____ a fake hand.

 b.

4. a. [past *be*] Entire truckloads of the finest quality Basmati rice and Florida avocados

 _____ dumped on the freeway last night.

 b.

5. a. [present *seem*] The clumsy man with casts on both of his legs carrying a broken pair

    of skis _____ to be having some small difficulty with his balance.

    b.

6. a. [present *do*] That exhibition of valuable artifacts and enormous statues shown at the

    Convention Center's main ballrooms _____ not fail to draw a crowd.

    b.

7. a. [present *appear*] In spite of a very valiant attempt, the members of the executive

    board and the various visitor's bureaus _____ to be unsuccessful.

    b.

8. a. [past *be*] The artist, unable to afford the outrageous prices of Memphis studios and

    art materials, _____ forced to draw chalk pictures on the sidewalk.

    b.

9. a. [past *disappear*] Suddenly, the craftsmen who had worked through the night on

    finishing the royal barge _____ .

    b.

10. a. [present *suggest*] Administrators who have worked for years in city government

    _____ that the funds be approved.

    b.

Score _____

EXERCISE 10-4

NAME_____ DATE _____

Decide whether the subject(s) should be considered singular or plural. Provide the correct verb form.

Example.   a. [past *be*] She and I _____ only talking.
                   b. plural
                   a. [past *be*] She and I were only talking.

1. a. [present *get*] Each boy and each girl _____ to pick out a toy.

    b.

2. a. [present *be*] I'm afraid that cake and ice cream _____ the only dessert.

    b.

3. a. [present *have*] Memphis, along with West Memphis, _____ a population

    of almost one million.

    b.

4. a. [present *do*] _____ Dotty and Jean expect me to bring all the soda to

    the party?

    b.

5. a. [present *seem*] In addition to the United States, Canada _____ to be

    solving its economic problems quite well.

    b.

6. a. [present *be*] Without consulting the Islands, the prime minister _____

    appointing a new deputy.

    b.

7. a. [past *be*] Chili and beans _____ served at last night's party.

    b.

8. a. [present drive] When necessary, the mayor, along with the deputy mayor,

    _____ to the scene of a controversy.

    b.

9. a. [present *cut*] Together with the nurse's help, the surgeon

    _____ her first incision.

    b.

10. a. [present *rush*] The fire fighters, as well as the med tech people, _____ to

    the scene of any accident.

    b.

Score _____

EXERCISE 10-5

NAME_____ **DATE** _____

Provide the correct form of the cued verb.

Example: [past *be*] Either the maid or the dog _____ going.
                [past *be*] Either the maid or the dog <u>was</u> going.

1. [*can*] Neither the team nor the manager _____ be said to be at fault.

2. [past *be*] _____ Fred or the Brady boys who broke the window?

3. [present *do*] Which way do you want it? Either you or your sister _____ the

   dishes right now.

4. [present *be*] Who or what _____ that?

5. [present *appear*] Either the TV or I _____ to be out of focus. [awkward

   construction, avoid it]

Score _____

EXERCISE 10-6

NAME_____ DATE _____

Determine which of the underlined words refer to *only one* member of the group at a time and which refer to a *portion* of the group. Supply the correct verb form.

Example: [past *be*] <u>Anyone</u> _____ able to break in.
                 [past *be*] <u>Anyone was</u> able to break in.

1. [present *buy*] <u>Each</u> of the members _____ a book a year.

2. [past *be*] <u>Neither one</u> _____ able to remember telling the President

    anything.

3. [present *produce*] <u>All</u> of these factories _____ fumes.

4. [past *be*] <u>None</u> of his early works _____ destroyed in the fire.

5. [present *seem*] <u>Most</u> of the runners _____ to be in trouble.

6. [present *agree*] <u>Most</u> of the crowd _____ with her.

7. [present *do*] <u>Every one</u> of the women _____ work.

8. [past *be*] _____ <u>any</u> of the doughnuts missing?

9. [past *be*] _____ <u>any</u> of the milk missing?

10. [present *refer*] <u>All</u> of these pronouns _____ to something.

Score _____

EXERCISE 10-7

NAME_____ DATE _____

Decide whether the noun is count or mass. Use the appropriate verb form.

Example: [present *appear*] Some of the <u>information</u> _____ incorrect.

_____

[present *appear*] Some of the <u>information appears</u> incorrect. <u>mass</u>

1. [past *be*] Most of his <u>works</u> _____ destroyed in the fire.

_____

2. [past *be*] Much of his <u>work</u> _____ destroyed in the fire.

_____

3. [present *seem*] All of this <u>knowledge</u> _____ to be important.

_____

4. [past *be*] Some of the <u>sugar</u> _____ crawling with bugs.

_____

5. [present *sound*] None of the <u>news</u> _____ good.

_____

Score _____

EXERCISE 10-8

NAME_____ **DATE** _____

1.   List the subject of the relative clause. Be careful; the subject is not always the relative pronoun. 2.   Determine if the subject is singular or plural. 3.   Provide the correct verb form.

Example: a [past *tell*] That is the man [whom I _____ you about].
b. I
c. singular
a. That is the man [whom I <u>told</u> you about].

1.   a. [past <u>be</u>] The paintings [that _____ delivered by your men] were

damaged.

b.

c.

2.   a. [present *know*] Is that the boy [whom you _____ from school]?

b.

c.

3.   a. [past *be*] Why were you with that person [who _____ cruel to you]?

b.

c.

4. a. [present *seem*] Well, introduce me to that man [that you _____

remember meeting somewhere].

b.

c.

5. a. [past *be*] Where is that report [the secretary _____ to type up for you]?

b.

c.

6. a. [present *disappear*] Is that the gentleman [that _____ whenever we need

him]?

b.

c.

7. a. [past *be*] Where did the woman [who _____ sitting behind you] go?

b.

c.

8. a. [present *be*] When does the boat [on which you _____ going to France]

leave?

b.

c.

9. a. [present *rush*] Watch out! There's that person [who _____ around,

knocking over things].

b.

c.

10. a. [past *be*] When you get there, say hello to that family [to whom we

_____ sending cards].

b.

c.

Score _____

EXERCISE 10-9

NAME_____ DATE _____

Underline the grammatical subject and supply the appropriate verb form.

1. [past *be*] At last count, the number of pledges _____ the same.

2. [present *seem*] Ninety dollars _____ to be missing from the register.

3. [present *seem*] Ninety dollar bills _____ to be missing from the stack on the

   table.

4. [present *appear*] Five miles _____ to be his favorite distance to run in the

   heat.

5. [present *be*] The next five miles _____ going to be difficult, but you will

   survive them.

6. [past *be*] The most important benefit _____ the perks.

7. [present *seem*] There _____ to be six chimps in our living room.

8. [past *be*] One important consideration _____ his many friends.

9. [past *be*] His many friends _____ one important consideration.

10. [past *be*] At no time _____ there ever dangerous animals in this building.

Score _____

EXERCISE 10-10

NAME_____DATE _____

Give the reason why the underlined verb is singular or plural.

Example: <u>Physics</u> is not so difficult.
Words that end in *-ics* are almost always singular.

1. "The Years of our Life" *was* a very interesting article.

2. My grandmother makes little ceramic figures. Her ceramics <u>are</u> really hideous, but she likes them.

3. The criteria <u>were</u> changed suddenly.

4. Come quickly. The alumni <u>are</u> storming the administration building!

5. Sixteen hours <u>is</u> a long time to drive without stopping.

6. "Fajitas" <u>is</u> a new term for most Americans.

7. The United States <u>does</u> not permit dual citizenship in most cases.

8. Data <u>were</u> what he lived for.

9. *Wanting Freedoms* <u>is</u> a book I have meant to buy.

10. A number of professors <u>wish</u> to discuss the issue.

Score _____

11

Nonstandard Verb Forms

11a. Nonstandard Principal Parts

Incorrect verb forms disturb your reader. When you edit your papers, make sure that you remember which forms must follow which auxiliaries. Additionally, if you are unsure of an irregular verb's form, look it up. Practice your knowledge with Exercise 11-1, which asks you for rules. Then, do Exercise 11-2, which asks you to apply those rules.

11b. Dropped -s/-es and -d/-ed Verb Endings

By now you should know when to put the -s and -ed suffixes on verb, adjective, and noun forms in English. Forgetting to use the endings in a rough draft is not a problem. But as you prepare your subsequent drafts, you must make sure that these endings are correct.

Now practice your editing skills with Exercise 11-3.

11c. Verbs Confused with Similar Words

In addition to the commonly confused words given in the handbook, you will also need to distinguish words that sound alike to *you* because they sound alike in your native language. For example, for many speakers of Spanish, *sheep* and *ship* sound almost identical.

You should keep a list of words that you have been told you confuse. Review that list and practice them so that you can distinguish them in writing.

One area you might need to review is the difference between *it is interesting* and *I am interested in*. See p. 62 for more information on this common misunderstanding of forms.

Finally, you might confuse the many phrasal verbs [e.g., *get up, get over,* and *get to*] since they seem so similar. When you learn a new phrasal verb, try to learn a one-word synonym to help retain its meaning. For example, you might learn *go over the paper* and *review the paper* together.

Some common phrasal verbs are listed in Exercise 11-4. They should help you start your own list.

EXERCISE 11-1

NAME _____ DATE _____

You should be able to do the following exercise without much trouble. If you do have any problems, review Chapter 5.

1. Which verb form <u>must</u> follow the auxiliary <u>have</u>?

2. Which verb form <u>must</u> follow the auxiliary <u>be</u> in the passive?

3. Which verb form do we use with <u>be</u> to make the progressive?

4. Why does an infinitive follow <u>hope,</u> as in <u>She hopes to study medicine</u>?

5. What is wrong in the sentence: <u>He shoulds go to school</u>?

6. How is the past form of most verbs made?

7. What is wrong with the sentence: <u>We should have went to the other movie</u>?

8. Why is this sentence not possible: <u>The director has buys a new computer for the lab</u>?

9. What is wrong with the sentence: <u>Did you remembered to buy paper plates</u>? What verb form must follow the auxiliary <u>do</u>?

10. Which form must follow modals [<u>should, must,</u> etc.]?

Score _____

EXERCISE 11-2

NAME _____ DATE _____

Pretend you are editing someone's paper and correct these verb phrases. Then, explain why the initial form was incorrect.

Example: They have went to town.
                 Corrected: They have <u>gone</u> to town.
                 Reason: past participle [*-en* form] after <u>have</u>

1. The boy can goes with the other students.

2. The school board don't fire enough teachers.

3. We leaved our books at home.

4. They have talk really badly to the substitute.

5. Try to making them sit in their chairs.

6. The other teacher didn't mind went to the library with us.

7. However, he must could leave the school in a hurry.

8. I have was advised by the other teachers to watch out.

9. I have been advising by the other teacher to ignore you.

10. Does the class really thinks that it can act that way?

Score _____

EXERCISE 11-3

NAME _____ **DATE** _____

Edit this speech for errors in the *-s* and *-ed* suffixes. Some occur on verbs, some on nouns and adjectives. You might even need to delete some suffixes.

> *-s* and *-ed* suffixes
> Check verbs [he go _____ home]
> Check adjectives [the request _____ amount]
> Check after auxiliaries [he has say _____]

My company have spend years perfecting this much admire shoe. Now a major

breakthrough will allow us to makes our pressurize insert even better. When the feet

crashes into the ground, the insert provide the necessaried cushioning. It is hope that each

of you will bought our new shoe and tried it. Our company has wonned many prize for

these shoe and we are very prouds. You'll never regret buying a pair!

Score _____

EXERCISE 11-4

NAME _____ DATE _____

Here are some common phrasal verbs. Provide a near synonym for each of them.

Example: call out   <u>shout</u>

1. get up _____   10. put off _____

2. put up with _____   11. get out _____

3. run away _____   12. run off _____

4. turn off _____   13. look up _____

5. run into _____   14. stack up _____

6. go over _____   15. call up _____

7. pass out _____   16. pass out [papers] _____

8. get by _____   17. bring up _____

9. hand in _____   18. hand over _____

You might want to use these phrasal verbs in sentences and listen to the differences in style between these simple forms and the more formal one-word synonyms.

Score _____

12

Pronoun Reference

Since English structure requires many *dummy pronouns,* our prose could become very confusing if we fail to make explicit pronoun references.

Each pronoun (except for *dummy subject*) should have an explicit antecedent whenever possible.

Do Exercise 12-1 to review antecedents.

12a. Implied Reference

In Exercise 1 there is an example of *implied reference.* We said *it would have been horrible.* We aren't quite sure what the antecedent of it was, but we thought it was something like *the destruction of Cambodian dance.* To avoid confusion, we could have rewritten that sentence.

> *Revised:* For Cambodian dance to be destroyed would be horrible.

Do Exercise 12-2 now.

12b. Broad Reference

If the antecedent of a pronoun is a sentence or a paragraph, you must revise your writing so that there is a specific antecedent. Often you can summarize an entire paragraph with one phrase such as *this plan* or *this idea.*

Try *this idea* out in Exercise 12-3. Then use it on your own work in Exercise 12-4.

12c. Indefinite *You, They,* and *It*

Formal writing requires a specific antecedent for each pronoun. If you really need an indefinite pronoun, you can use *one*.

> *Formal:* Should *one* use the fish or the meat knife for squid?
> *Informal:* Should *you* use the fish or the meat knife for squid?

Some ESL speakers use *they say* to avoid saying *I think* or *I say*. However, in most cases, it is fine to use *I think* or *I say*.

Do Exercise 12-5 now.

12d. Ambiguous Reference

When sentences are not carefully constructed, pronouns often have two possible antecedents. This ambiguous situation can cause problems and confusion.

Try to resolve the ambiguities found in Exercise 12-6 now.

12e. Mixed Uses of *It*

We use *it* for many different reasons. For example, we can use it as an expletive.

> *It* seems safe to leave the house.

It can also just be a *dummy subject*.

> *It* is raining in New Zealand.

Of course, *it* can also be a predicate pronoun.

> He swims the channel daily.
> But I don't ever do *it*. [*it* stands for *swim the channel*]

Since it can be used for many different reasons, too many *its* can become confusing. Try to make sure that each *it* is clearly understood by the reader.

First try Exercise 12-8. Then, use Exercise 12-8 to explore your own work.

12f. Remote Reference

We need to make sure that a pronoun is close enough to its antecedent to prevent misunderstandings. If we repeat the antecedent occasionally, we can usually avoid remote reference problems.

Do Exercise 12-9.

12g. Titles and Headings as Antecedents

Modern English doesn't allow this. What was the antecedent of *this* in the last sentence? The antecedent was the title of this section. In standard usage, we do not allow titles to function as antecedents even though it would be clearly understood if the title were right above the pronoun.

Do Exercise 12-10.

EXERCISE 12-1

NAME _____ **DATE** _____

What is the antecedent of each underlined pronoun? If there is no explicit antecedent, try to describe what you think the antecedent is.

1. Cambodia's identity is evident in <u>its</u> dance.

2. When we see the Cambodian dancer, we gaze at <u>her</u> with wonder.

3. <u>It</u> is frightening to think that this dance form was almost destroyed by those who despised <u>it</u>.

4. <u>It</u> would have been horrible.

5. Fortunately, the Cambodians have been able to save <u>it</u>.

Score _____

EXERCISE 12-2

NAME _____ DATE _____

Rewrite these sentences so that there is an explicit antecedent for the underlined pronoun.

Example: At Fred's school, <u>he</u> always is polite.
                  At his school, Fred is always polite.

1. In Sara's story, <u>she</u> tells us about the life of Druin, who became king.

2. Being a king was difficult for <u>him</u>.

3. In the treacherous world of a king, <u>he</u> must always be careful.

4. Conducting meetings with the vizier was hard because he had never met <u>one</u> before he became king.

5. But Druin loved horseback riding because he had practically been born on <u>one</u>.

Score _____

EXERCISE 12-3

NAME _____ DATE _____

Think of a noun or noun phrase that will summarize the sentence. Replace the underlined pronoun with your new noun.

Example: You don't need much to make fudge in your kitchen. <u>It</u> is easy.
Revised: You don't need much to make fudge in your kitchen. Making fudge is easy.

1. The instructor taught us how to make stink bombs. <u>It</u> was not very complicated.

2. For many years I had to hide my true feelings about the new government in my country. <u>It</u> became second nature to me.

3. When you mow the grass, make sure that you rake up the leaves afterward. <u>That</u> is neater.

4. I had to study for the test for many hours while my friends were out having a good time. It was not easy, but I managed.

5. We were finally able to connect with a flight to Dallas, <u>which</u> meant we could attend the conference there.

Score _____

EXERCISE 12-4

NAME _____ **DATE** _____

Take the last rough draft you wrote and underline every pronoun. Now draw a line to each pronoun's antecedent. If you must draw a line to an entire sentence or clause, find a noun or noun phrase that can describe that unit.

Score _____

EXERCISE 12-5

NAME _____ DATE _____

Revise these sentences to eliminate the underlined indefinite pronouns .

Example: At some universities <u>you</u> need to take three literature classes to graduate.
At some universities <u>students</u> need to take three literature classes to graduate.

1. If <u>they</u> have so much money in Washington, why don't we ever see it here?

2. <u>It</u> says in my textbook that every citizen has certain inalienable rights.

3. <u>You</u> can really eat good pizza at that restaurant.

4. Let's go shopping. <u>They</u>'re open till midnight for the holiday rush.

5. At school <u>they</u> were all talking about the game.

Score _____

EXERCISE 12-6

NAME _____ DATE _____

Revise these ambiguous sentences so that the underlined pronoun can have only one possible antecedent.

Example: Since she needed to go, Martha spoke with Gina.
                 Revised: Since Martha needed to go, she spoke with Gina.
                 Revised: Since Gina needed to go, Martha spoke with her.

1. I promised to bring some new stories to my students, but I forgot <u>them</u>.

2. The mother told the father about the son's horrible report card, but <u>he</u> was not very upset.

3. You know, there is a new film in that theater that just opened. Have you seen <u>it</u> yet?

4. I think I left my wallet in the bag you took with you. Do you know where <u>it</u> is?

5. Lisa claims that her sister was lying about the burglary. Do you believe <u>her</u>?

Score _____

EXERCISE 12-7

NAME _____ DATE _____

Describe the use of each underlined <u>it</u>.

Example: It seems dangerous to walk down dark alleys alone.
       <u>expletive</u>
       <u>It</u> is snowing.
       <u>dummy subject</u>

1. If I ever want to buy something, I just do <u>it</u>.

2. When <u>it</u> rains, I can't stand <u>it</u>.

3. Did you know Fred has a new car? I really hope he doesn't wreck <u>it</u> as quickly as he did the last one.

4. <u>It</u> is never easy to say good-bye to old friends.

5. <u>It</u> was a clear and beautiful morning.

Score _____

EXERCISE 12-8

NAME _____ **DATE** _____

Underline every *it* in a portion of your last rough draft. Now write the use each *it* has. If you have any sentences or sequential sentences that have mixed uses of *it*, revise them.

Score _____

EXERCISE 12-9

NAME _____ **DATE** _____

Revise this passage to ensure that all pronoun references are clear.

Many teenagers refuse to eat dairy products. They are often stubborn about it. If you offer them cheese pizzas, they will eat all of them, which is good for them. They need the calcium from them so that they will be able to build strong bones and teeth, which helps them in later life.

Score _____

EXERCISE 12-10

NAME _____ DATE _____

Revise the opening lines of each of these books or articles if revision is needed.

Example: *Life in Antarctica*
              It is hard and dangerous.
              Revised: Life in Antarctica
              According to *Life in Antarctica*, life there is hard and dangerous.

1. *Birds of Tennessee*
   They are beautiful and ugly, gentle and cruel.

2. "Winter"
   It is hard to imagine that anyone really likes winter.

3. "Alone in the Crowd"
   We all are sometimes.

4. *History of Guam*
   It begins thousands of years ago.

5. *Grammar and Writing Made Very Easy*
   Our book will do it for you!

Score _____

13

Pronoun-Antecedent Agreement

Make sure you understand number [singular or plural] before you start this section. We can also use the same logic we used in the chapter on subject-verb agreement to help make pronouns agree with their antecedents. (See pp. 270-274.)

13a. Antecedents Joined by *And*

First, review subject-verb agreement of elements joined by *and*. (See pp. 271-272.) If you have determined that you would use a singular verb with the antecedent, you would use a singular pronoun also. The only slightly confusing problem is with elements joined by *every* or *each*. Just remember that *each* or *every* refers to a single event; therefore, you need a singular verb and a singular pronoun.

Every boy and faculty member *wants* to have *his* suggestion accepted by the committee.

Do Exercise 13-1 now.

13b. Antecedents Joined by *Or/Nor*

As in subject-verb agreement with *or/nor*, try to put the plural subject nearer to the pronoun to prevent awkward sentences. (See p. 272.)

Now do Exercise 13-2.

13c. Indefinite Pronouns and Sexist Language

Ask your instructors how they would suggest you avoid sexist language when using indefinite pronouns. Try the methods your instructor suggests in Example 13-3.

13d. Generic Nouns and Sexist Language

If a noun contains an explicit reference to gender, we may continue to use the appropriate pronoun.

The policeman dropped his gun.

However, we are in the process of developing new designations for the sexist forms. For example, we could change the last example to a non-sexist form.

The police officer's gun fell to the ground.

Practice non-sexist forms in Example 13-4. Then do Exercises 13-5 and 13-6, which are more open-ended.

13e. Collective Nouns as Antecedents

Try to avoid the plural use of a singular collective in American English; revise the sentence.

Avoid: The family are fighting for their favorite antiques.

When you revise, make sure that you do not accidentally introduce sexist usage.

Revised, but sexist: Each member of the family is fighting for *his* favorite antiques.
Better revision: The members of the family are fighting for *their* favorite antiques.

EXERCISE 13-1

NAME _____ DATE _____

Determine whether each pronoun agrees with its antecedent in number. Correct any that do not.

Example: Democrats and Republicans must give up *his* fight for this issue.
Revised: Democrats and Republicans must give up *their* fight for this issue.

1. Each boy and each girl must pick up his or her book.

2. Your closest friend and my husband sends you his greeting.

3. Both apples and pears have seeds in their cores.

4. Each day and each hour seemed to take their time passing.

5. The man and the woman turned in her entry.

Score _____

EXERCISE 13-2

NAME _____ DATE _____

If the pronoun does not agree with its antecedent, correct it. If the sentence is correct, but awkward, revise it.

Example: Either the students or the school must alter its position.
Correct, but awkward
Revised: Either the school or the students must alter their position.

1. Either the gophers or I am going to give up my share of tomatoes.

2. Neither the boy nor the men have given up so much of his time before.

3. Neither the Soviets nor the single Chinese representative has relayed his approval.

4. Either you or he will need to bring his book.

5. Either the parents or the child needs to have her position strengthened.

Score _____

EXERCISE 13-3

NAME _____ DATE _____

Revise these sentences to avoid sexist and colloquial forms. Try several methods.

Example: *Sexist:* Everybody needs to give the woman his name.
        Revised: Everybody needs to give the woman his or her name.

1. When someone offers you their hand, you must shake it.

2. Nobody seemed to want to be the first to explain his stance.

3. Everybody seems off their rocker in this room.

4. Every student was required to sign his name to the pledge.

5. We asked every one of the neighbors their opinions.

6. Each of the candidates was asked to explain his position on the controversial issue.

7. None of the candidates would explain how he reached that position.

8. Indeed, not one of the speakers was able to justify their thinking.

9. Are you sure that everyone has been told that they must provide their own transportation back to their homes?

10. Each of the women wishes to do their best to reach the top of the mountain.

Score _____

EXERCISE 13-4

NAME _____ DATE _____

Revise these sentences to avoid sexist references.

Example: A doctor must be responsible for his own actions.
Revised: Doctors must be responsible for their own actions.

1. The student must bring his cards to registration.

2. The chairman of the department should turn in his report by this afternoon.

3. The president of each club has to request his own office.

4. A physicist should be able to understand his own articles.

5. The next president of the United States will need to make his priorities very clear.

6. I doubt that the next mayor will be able to get his own way as easily.

7. A flight attendant must be concerned with his own safety first.

8. The professor who teaches this course must send us his book list today.

9. Do you know a pilot who has already finished his training?

10. Why does a jockey need to keep his weight down?

Score _____

EXERCISE 13-5

NAME _____ **DATE** _____

Check your last rough draft and make sure that all of your pronouns agree with their antecedents. Additionally, make sure that you have avoided sexist forms.

EXERCISE 13-6

Is Sexism an issue in your native language? Is it possible to avoid sexist forms in your language? If you are not sure, try to contact someone in your area who teaches or has studied your language. Report back to the class what you find.

Score _____

14

Case of
Nouns and
Pronouns

Case forms help identify the way a noun or pronoun is used in a sentence. By using the correct case forms of pronouns, we make sure that our audience can determine a noun's or pronoun's function.

In Modern English we have only two case forms for nouns.

> *Common:* the tiger, the tigers
> *Possessive:* the tiger's, the tigers'

We use the common form of nouns for both objects and subjects.

> [subject] *The tiger* was trained to eat only fish.
> [object] The keeper trained *the tiger* to eat only fish.

For nouns the most difficult case problem is remembering to add the possessive marker.

> [possessive] *The tiger's* food is not normally fish.

You must always be sure to edit for the possessive ending in your drafts.

As you know, many of the pronouns have a special *objective* form that must be used when the pronoun is used as any kind of an object [direct, indirect, or object of a preposition].

> [subject] *He* was trained to eat only fish.
> [object] The keeper trained *him* to eat only fish.

Thus, for these pronouns we need to talk about *subjective* [used as a subject] and *objective* [used as an object] forms.

As a result, you must be very careful in final drafts to use the correct case forms of pronouns.

Now do Exercise 14-1.

315

14a.   Case in Compound Constructions

Native speakers are beginning to have problems with case in compound constructions. For many native speakers, the incorrect versions sound "more elegant." These speakers are distancing themselves from the error of using the objective case (e.g., *me, him,* or *her*) where a subjective form should be used.

> *Error: Me* and *him* waited for you.
> *Error:* She waited for you and *I.*

You should try to avoid both types of errors. Just remember that compounding doesn't change the case of a pronoun.

> Fritz hired *me* to do the job.
> Fritz hired *you* to do the job.
> *Compounded:* Fritz hired *you* and *me* to do the job.
> *Incorrect:* Fritz hired you and *I* to do the job.

Now do Exercise 14-2.

14b.   Pronoun Case after *Be*

In conversational English, most Americans use the objective forms of pronouns after *be.*

> *Spoken, informal:* Oh no, it's *her* again!

Remember, however, that we would use the *subjective* forms in formal writing or formal speech.

> *Formal:* Madam, it is *she* again.

Do Exercise 14-3 now.

14c.   *Who/Whom* and *Who/Whomever*

Although the *whom* forms are rare in speech, they are normally used in writing. If you remember that whom is the same as *him,* you won't have many problems.

Some native speakers have problems with *who/whom* when a noun clause functions as an object of a preposition. This issue is also discussed in Chapter 7. Look at the following example.

> *Correct:* It really depends on *who shows up.*
> *Incorrect:* It really depends on *whom* shows up.

Notice that in the last example the whole noun clause is the object of the preposition *on* and the internal structure of the clause is not changed.

Try Exercise 14-4 now.

14d. Case in Elliptical Clauses

Speakers of American English want a subject pronoun [e.g., *he, she* or *I*] to be followed by a verb form. But in many formal elliptical constructions, there is just a subject pronoun, which is *not* followed by a verb form.

Formal: Fred is shorter than *she.* [subject pronoun—no verb form]

These forms sound awkward to most Americans, who prefer to leave the tensed verb form.

> *Correct and preferred:* Fred is shorter than she *is.*

In informal speech, many Americans use the objective form in order to avoid a subject pronoun without a verb. You should avoid that use.

> *Informal:* Fred is shorter than *her.*

In the preferred form, we repeat the auxiliary. Or if there is none, we supply the appropriate form of the periphrastic *do.*

> *Auxiliary:* She has been to more places than he *has.*
> *Periphrastic do:* I *ate* more than she *did.*

Now try Exercise 14-5.

14e. Possessive Case with Gerunds

In our discussion of *gerunds* in Chapter 5, we mentioned that the possessive form is needed for any nouns or pronouns acting as determiners in formal English.

> *Correct:* We shouldn't object to *his* piercing *his* ear.
> *Informal:* We shouldn't object to *him* piercing *his* ear.

When writing formal papers, make sure to edit for the possessive forms. Do Exercise 14-6 to practice the formal usage.

EXERCISE 14-1

NAME _____ DATE _____

Label each underlined element for case. Use the three case names given in the handbook [*subjective, objective,* and *possessive*] for all forms including nouns.

Example: *May* is a wonderful month.
subjective [or common in two-case system]

1. It was <u>I</u> who knocked.

2. Why are you hitting <u>your little brother</u>?

3. Why isn't <u>he</u> being punished for hitting <u>me</u>?

4. <u>His</u> loud laughter really disturbs <u>my baby's</u> sleeping.

5. On <u>the other hand,</u> <u>it</u> really doesn't bother my <u>sleeping</u>.

6. The winners, <u>Fred</u> and <u>you</u>, will fly to <u>New York</u>!

7. <u>What</u> did <u>Fred</u> do to win that <u>prize</u>?

8. <u>What</u> gave <u>him</u> the <u>idea</u> to enter the <u>contest</u>?

9. Well, at any <u>rate</u> your <u>father</u> is certainly a lucky <u>man</u>, isn't <u>he</u>?

10. <u>You're</u> going to give that new <u>car</u> <u>you</u> won a fancy <u>name</u>, right?

Score _____

EXERCISE 14-2

NAME _____ DATE _____

Use the given choices to fill in the correct pronoun in (a) and (b), the compounded version.

Example: I, me
a. Frank lives in the apartment above <u>me</u>.
b. Frank lives in the apartment above Shirley and <u>me</u>.

1. he, him

   a. All the reward for the capture should go to _____.

   b. All the reward for the capture should go to Sean and _____.

2. she, her

   a. At home _____ rarely watches television.

   b. At home Louise and _____ rarely watch television.

3. I, myself

   a. _____ often walk down to the barn to see the horses.

   b. Lucy and _____ often walk down to the barn to see the horses.

4. they, them

   a. Every time I come to New York, I enjoy seeing _____.

   b. Every time I come to New York, I enjoy seeing both you and _____.

5. me, myself

   a. The queen always asks for _____ to do that for her.

   b. The queen always asks for Alice and _____ to do that for her.

Score _____

EXERCISE 14-3

NAME _____ **DATE** _____

Decide which of the given forms you should use. Pay careful attention to vocabulary and tone to determine whether the situation is formal or informal.

Example: [he, him] Gosh, that was _____?
              [informal] Gosh, that was <u>him</u>?

1. [I, me] Mom, you know very well that it's _____. Now open that door!

2. [she, her] Please inform the President that the only candidate my government would

    accept would be _____.

3. [him, he] Lulu, do you think that could really be _____ sitting across from

    us in this dive?

4. [they, them] We are sorry to inform the Court that it was indeed _____

    who precipitated the violence under discussion.

5. [we, us] Don't hang up, Cindy. It's _____, Mommy and Daddy!

6. [she, her] She often wrote that it was _____ who successfully challenged

    the prime minister in cabinet meetings.

7. [me, I] Bobby, do you really think that crank call was _____?

8. [he, him] It is the opinion of this committee that as a result of the repeated successes of

    the mayor, it will be _____ who accompanies the President on her mission

    in May.

9. [they, them] It was thought to have been _____ who were able to avoid

the diplomatic crisis.

10. [we, us] It is _____ whom we must most fear.

Score _____

EXERCISE 14-4

NAME _____ DATE _____

Decide what the appropriate case should be. Explain your choice and fill in the correct form of the cued pronoun.

Example: [who] To _____ did she give it?
objective
[who] To <u>whom</u> did she give it?

1. [whoever] Hand it to _____ walks in first!

2. [whoever] Hand it to _____ you see first!

3. [whoever] _____ was that at the door?

4. [who] _____ did you say was the most important director in film's history?

5. [whoever] I have told you and _____ you brought with you last week that

   the farm will not be sold.

6. [who] _____ can we find to ask?

7. [whoever] Why would you say that _____ wants to buy this house must be

   crazy?

8. [whoever] The committee will be able to reject _____ you choose to

   appoint, sir.

9. [who] I'm sorry. You said I was to send this package to _____?

10. [whoever] Just send the package to _____ you most dislike!

Score _____

EXERCISE 14-5

NAME _____ DATE _____

Supply all the possible correct pronoun forms in these elliptical constructions. Sometimes two answers will be possible. If you need to use a subjective form, also supply the correct verb form.

Example: She annoys you as much as _____.
She annoys you as much as <u>me</u>. [as she annoys <u>me</u>]
She annoys you as much as <u>I do</u>.

1.   [I] You can write just as well as _____.

2.   [she] My sister is not older than _____.

3.   [he] She has been doing better than _____.

4.   [they] The cows were giving more milk than _____.

5.   [she] Her family disturbs me more than _____.

6.   [we] The district manager is friendlier to them than _____.

7.   [you] Liz is just as obnoxious as _____.

8.   [he] The trip to France relaxed Mary more than _____.

9.   [they] We really do see him much more than _____.

10. [I] Are you sure that he wanted to hire her more than _____?

Score _____

EXERCISE 14-6

NAME _____ DATE _____

Change all these sentences to formal usage.

Example: I was sickened by the band singing.
I was sickened by the <u>band's</u> singing.

1. Were you ever able to understand them wanting to go to New York for the weekend?

2. She never forgot him leaving her at the restaurant.

3. I misunderstand her wanting to chair the session.

4. They were really puzzled by us getting the award.

5. Do you have a solution for him arriving late every day?

6. The entire office is sick of him moaning about his salary.

7. Him wanting to win is hurting the team.

8. The researchers were astonished by you being able to remember all those grammatical terms.

9. Her winning the lottery in no way changed me wanting to marry her.

10. Would the boss mind us going on a trip around the world after we get married?

Score _____

15

Nonstandard
Adjective and
Adverb Forms

You may wish to review Chapter 3 to refresh your memory of the basic formation of adverbs and adjectives. If you understand the basic uses and formations of these elements, you will avoid many common errors.

15a. Confusion of Adjectives and Adverbs

If you are not sure whether you should have an adjective or adverb, ask yourself what the element modifies. If the element modifies anything but a noun, you must use an *adverb;* for nouns, you must use an adjective.

> The *government* was *strict.*
> The *government* was *strictly* run by business.

If you have trouble with the *smells good/smells well* pairs, do the exercise on p. 229 where this problem is discussed in detail.

Some native speakers may confuse *most* and *almost.* If you remember that *almost* is the same as *just about,* it will help.

> School was *almost* fun today.
> School was *just about* fun today.
> *Correct:* Just about *everybody* was there.
> *Correct:* Almost everybody was there.
> *Nonstandard: Most* everybody was there.

Now review adjectives and adverbs in Exercise 15-1.

15b.   Inappropriate Comparative and Superlative Forms

For ESL speakers, the main problem with these forms is being too eager and using *two* (or more) comparatives.

> *Correct:* That is the *fastest* car on the beach.
> *Overeager:* That is the *most* fast*est* car on the beach.

Using two comparatives does not make something even "more better." Practice editing for these forms in Exercise 15-2.

15c.   Inappropriate Demonstratives

If you forget to make the demonstratives agree with their related nouns in number, you will disturb many people, especially your instructor.

> *Incorrect: This* people are fun! [*this* is singular]
> *Corrected: These* people are fun! [everything agrees]

Now do Exercise 15-3.

EXERCISE 15-1

NAME _____ DATE _____

Decide whether you should use an adjective or adverb. Underline what the form modifies.

Example: [quick/quickly] The stream was running _____ .
                The stream was <u>running quickly</u>.

1. [good/well] She always does _____ on those tests.

2. [almost/most] The minister knew _____ all of the kids in that

   neighborhood.

3. [real/really] He can ride _____ fast on that new bike.

4. [good/well] The little girls were trying to be _____ .

5. [nice/nicely] That bunch of flowers will do _____ .

6. [real/really] I can't tell if this is a _____ old piece or if it is a good fake.

7. [awful/awfully] Don't you think that music is _____ loud?

8. [bad/badly] Very few people want to do _____ things.

9. [good/well] Were you able to smell _____ when you had the flu?

10. [most/almost] They brought in the _____ votes.

Score _____

EXERCISE 15-2

NAME _____ DATE _____

Correct any forms that may be wrong or even questionable. You should almost always avoid questionable constructions.

1. Most people buy the most cheap gas they can find.

2. Rarely, do they wonder whether that gas is as better as some other gas that might cost just a little much than the one they bought.

3. Some cars don't run as faster when they use the more cheap gas.

4. Fortunately, my eldest car still uses good old regular.

5. Regular is not as cheap than it used to be. But it is still a more good bargain than unleaded.

6. Of course, the newer cars do the most fine job of not polluting the air than my car does.

7. Next year, the new car will be even more perfect in not polluting.

8. Have you ever wondered what the most correct method for getting rid of all the pollution would be?

9. There are more easy questions.

10. But the mainest issue is to have the cleaner world possible for us and our children.

Score _____

EXERCISE 15-3

NAME _____ DATE _____

Make sure that the nouns match the demonstratives and the verbs. You may rewrite the
sentences as long as everything agrees.

1. Do you know those kind of neighbors who spy on your every single move?

2. When these type lives next door, they watch you all the time.

3. That people who do these activity are often a little lonely.

4. When you and your friend are going to have a party, you might invite this people over.

5. These gesture of goodwill might help make them feel they are a part of the
    neighborhood. Try these!

Score _____

16

Dangling and Misplaced Modifiers

Because language operates on the principle that related elements are put closely together, you need to try to keep modifiers and the words they modify together.

16a. Dangling Modifiers

You may need to review *verbal phrases* before you read this section of the handbook and this workbook.

(1) Dangling verbals: participles, infinitives, and gerunds

Since the "subject" of a verbal phrase is usually missing, the "subject" of the verbal must occur in the main sentence.

> *Clause:* I live in Memphis.
> *Verbal phrase, no subject:* living in Memphis
> *Subject in main clause:* Living in Memphis, *I* have learned to like grits.

Most often the *subject* of the verbal should be the same as the *subject* of the clause in which the verbal occurs.

Now try Exercise 16-1.

(2) Dangling elliptical clauses

The problems are the same as for dangling verbals; the subject of the elliptical clause should usually be the same as in the main clause.

Dangling: Living in fear, the police helped the victimized couple. [The *police* are not living in fear; the *couple* is living in fear.]
Corrected: The police helped the victimized couple living in fear.

Now do Exercise 16-2.

16b. Misplaced Modifiers

Pay careful attention to the placement of modifiers; a misplaced modifier can change the focus of your idea. A misplaced modifier can even change the meaning of your sentences.

Misplaced: The doctor studies sleep at the university.

In the last example, it seems that the doctor studies people who sleep in classes, but she really just studies sleep in general.

Corrected: At the university, she studies sleep.

Now do Exercise 16-3 to practice putting words in their correct place. After that, do Exercise 16-4 to practice on misplaced prepositional phrases as in the example above. Next, you can do Exercise 16-5 to work with misplaced clauses. Finally, Exercise 16-6 deals with *squinting* (misplaced) modifiers, which can cause sentences to be ambiguous.

Squinting modifier: The horses I ride *infrequently* are wild. [Does this mean that I ride wild horses infrequently or that normally the horses I ride aren't wild?]

EXERCISE 16-1

NAME _____ DATE _____

(a) Read the complete sentence.   (b) Look at the underlined verbal. Ask yourself who is doing the action. Then, make a complete (reconstructed) clause from the underlined verbal. (c) Compare the subjects in the two clauses. Are they the same?   (d) If the subjects are not the same, revise the sentence so that they are.

Example: a. <u>Leaving the room</u>, the door hit the man in the face.
   b. <u>Reconstructed clause</u>: As the <u>man</u> was leaving the room, the <u>door</u> hit the man in the face.
   c. The subjects of the two clauses are not the same. Therefore, the original is wrong.
   d. *Revised:* Leaving the room, the man was hit in the face by the door.

1.   a. <u>Saying goodbye to his wife</u>, a snowball fell on the man's head.

   b.

   c.

   d.

2.   a. <u>By giving you this good grade for a bad composition</u>, you are not learning a thing.

   b.

   c.

   d.

3.   a. <u>In freeing the prisoners</u>, important case law was established by the court.

   b.

   c.

   d.

4. a. <u>To aid in the fight against world hunger</u>, many people were asked to donate one day's lunch money by a group of dedicated volunteers.

    b.

    c.

    d.

5. a. <u>To tell the truth</u>, this assignment was a piece of cake.

    b.

    c.

    d.

Score _____

EXERCISE 16-2

NAME _____ DATE _____

Reconstruct the elliptical clause. Is the subject of the clause you have just made the same as the subject of the main clause in the original sentence? If they are not the same, revise the original so that they are the same.

Example: a. Although sure of the outcome, the votes were still counted by the committee.
b. Although the <u>committee</u> was sure of the outcome, the <u>votes</u> were still counted by the committee.
c. The subjects of the two clauses are not the same; the original is not correct.
d. Although sure of the outcome, the committee still counted the votes.

1. a. While visiting his parents, the police arrested him.

    b.

    c.

    d.

2. a. Although basically honest, a ticket had not been paid.

    b.

    c.

    d.

3. a. Although amused at first, the seriousness of the situation finally came to him.

    b.

    c.

    d.

4. a. Once booked, his lawyer paid his bill.

    b.

    c.

    d.

5. a. When telling the story later, the gang was greatly amused.

    b.

    c.

    d.

Score _____

EXERCISE 16-3

NAME _____ DATE _____

The underlined words are misplaced. Rewrite the sentences and put these underlined words in the correct position.

1. I was <u>nearly</u> paid six dollars an hour. I did get $5.85 an hour.

2. I was paid <u>nearly</u> two million dollars, but the computer caught the error before I got the check.

3. Monks must <u>simply</u> live.

4. Without a doubt, I must go <u>simply</u>!

5. <u>Even</u> Fred went to the beach, where he normally never goes.

6. Fred went <u>even</u> to the beach with the gang, and you know he never goes anywhere.

7. I want to send <u>just</u> Helen flowers, no candy.

8. I want to send Helen <u>just</u> flowers, not Gloria.

9. Make sure that Fred <u>politely</u> knows how to answer the phone.

10. Karen was able <u>almost</u> to finish on time, and she always takes at least fifteen extra minutes.

Score _____

EXERCISE 16-4

NAME _____ **DATE** _____

Move these misplaced, underlined prepositional phrases to their correct places.

1. <u>In a teacup</u>, she drank her tea.

2. The astronomers were unable to discover intelligent life <u>in Washington</u>.

3. She was unable to find <u>in a book</u> the information she had read in the library.

4. <u>With his sling</u>, Goliath was defeated by David.

5. <u>In a loud voice</u>, the attack dog was ordered to stop by its owner.

Score _____

EXERCISE 16-5

NAME _____ **DATE** _____

Move these misplaced, underlined clauses to their correct places. You may need to revise some of the sentences.

1. The government agents were unsuccessful in finding anyone alive <u>who were still working on the case</u>.

2. The man hates working in an office <u>that is retiring</u>.

3. The women often drove their cars down to the store <u>which were the most expensive models</u>.

4. He couldn't afford to eat his lunch in a fancy restaurant <u>which had to be cheap</u>.

5. The instructor told the few students to listen carefully to the visiting speaker <u>who attended the lecture</u>.

Score _____

EXERCISE 16-6

NAME _____ DATE _____

Move these underlined squinting (misplaced) modifiers so that the sentence is unambiguous.

1. The houses he sells <u>occasionally</u> are cheap.

2. She was instructed <u>the next day</u> to go to Mobile.

3. The books that we read <u>sometimes</u> are very good.

4. Those beautiful jewels that she wears <u>often</u> are stolen.

5. The lectures that I attend <u>rarely</u> are worthwhile.

Score _____

17

Shifts

Shifts are unnecessary changes in form. Try not to change forms if you don't have a good reason. Your reader will lose track of the most important element of your text, your ideas.

17a. Shifts in Verb Tenses

Reading is much easier if all the verbs are basically in the same time frame.

(1) Present and past tense

Normally, you should not mix these tenses in formal prose. Many ESL speakers think they are using consistent tenses, but if you forget the -ed endings on verbs, it looks as though the tenses are mixed.

> *Apparent mix:* She asked me for my opinion. I explain to her what I want, but she didn't believe me.
> *Correct with* -ed *endings:* She asked me for my opinion. I explained to her what I wanted, but she didn't believe me.

(2) Perfect tenses

While the past and the present belong to separate time frames, the *perfect* forms show time relationships between events. You might wish to review the interrelationships of the tenses to see how they work together (see Chapter 4).

> *Shift:* Ron *has visited* France and also *went* to Asia.
> *Corrected:* Ron *has visited* France and also *has gone* to Asia.

17b. Shifts with *Can/Could* or *Will/Would*

Can and *will* are for the real world; *could* and *would* are for a hypothetical [not real] or past world. Just as we should not mix the real with the hypothetical, we should not mix these forms. That mixture could pose problems.

> *Shift*: If we *could* get permission, you *can* go too!
> *Corrected*: If we *could* get permission, you *could* go too!

17c. Shifts in Mood

Often apparent shifts in mood are really the result of using the wrong forms. It is especially difficult to avoid shifts when using the subjunctive. Remember to use only subjunctive forms.

> *Shift*: If I *were* younger and he *was* richer, I would still stay in Memphis.
> *Corrected*: If I *were* younger and he *were* richer, I would still stay in Memphis.

17d. Shifts in Voice

Use the passive only when it is really needed to avoid shifts in voice.

Now do Exercise 17-1 to edit for shifts in mood or voice.

17e. Shifts in Number

If you forget to add plural *-s/-es* to nouns or third-person singular *-s/-ies* to verbs, it will appear that you have made many shifts in number. Watch that *-s*!

> *Apparent shift*: The students forgot to write their paper.
> *Corrected with* -s: The students forgot to write their papers.

Also remember that *each* and *every* are singular.

> *Apparent shift*: *Every* student forgot to write their papers.
> *Corrected*: *Every* student forgot to write her or his paper.

17f. Shifts in Person

Remember that we only use indefinite *you* in informal speech. If you avoid it in writing, you won't have many problems with shifts in person.

> *Shift*: All students must do their work if you want to go on the trip.
> *Revised*: All students must do their work if they want to go on the trip.

Now do Exercise 17-2 to practice finding shifts in number or person.

17g.   Shifts between Direct and Indirect Discourse

Either quote or paraphrase; don't try to do both in the same sentence.

17h.   Mixed Constructions and Faulty Predication

Try to avoid "The reason is that . . . " constructions in writing; they are fine in informal speech.

Do Exercise 17-3 to work on shifts in sentence structure and discourse. Finally, do Exercise 17-4, which concentrates on verb forms.

EXERCISE 17-1

NAME _____ DATE _____

Correct these shifts in mood or voice. Read the first five sentences as part of a recipe.

1. Get two eggs and you put them in a bowl. [Use imperative.]

2. Next, someone stirs the eggs. [Use imperative.]

3. The eggs are poured into a heated pan. [Use imperative.]

4. You must be careful not to burn these marvelous eggs. [Use imperative.]

5. Finally, everybody should eat and enjoy the scrambled eggs. [Use imperative.]

6. After Sheila spoke with the committee, her ideas were ripped to shreds by the committee.

7. The mixture was taken to the lab, where someone lost it.

8. Before I walked to the store, a grocery list with six kinds of cereals was given to me by my son.

9. You will be on time today and get out of bed! [Use imperative.]

10. If she were rich and he was not so stupid, the business might have a better chance of surviving.

Score _____

EXERCISE 17-2

NAME _____ DATE _____

Revise these sentences to avoid shifts of number or person.

1. All students must bring his paper to be graded today.

2. Everyone must be on time if you want to see the movie.

3. Each customer should feel they are special.

4. When one is insulted, you should not try to extract revenge.

5. Why should every one of the assignments be counted as tests?

6. Are you sure that many publishers will show his or her books at the fair?

7. Smart people fly to Maine if you want a nice vacation.

8. Many people experience grief in their life. [Careful!]

9. A professor who gives easy grades is not helping their students.

10. Leave your name at the door if anyone wants more information.

Score _____

EXERCISE 17-3

NAME _____ DATE _____

Rewrite these sentences to avoid shifts in sentence structure or between direct and indirect discourse.

Example: The reason I am going is that I am tired.
           Revised: I am going that I am tired.

1. Universities are where we learn to think and reason.

2. The lawyer said, "You will have to pay," and that I would probably be sued for millions.

3. Discussion is when no one yells.

4. The main reason why the team never wins is that they are lousy ball players.

5. She screamed, "I don't need to elect such fools as leaders!" and she would never sell her stocks.

6. The reason is because he has no money.

7. The reason why your eye is always black and blue is that when you open mouth, you say stupid, stupid things.

8. My father often told me, "Work hard, play hard," and I should study hard.

9. Students who don't study for classes were a topic at last week's meeting.

10. With the lack of agreement among the various factions, it brings about the weakening of the alliance.

Score _____

EXERCISE 17-4

NAME _____ **DATE** _____

Make these sentences consistent. Revise any shifts.

1. If you were to move to the new house, will you still belong to the country club?

2. I thought that I will just leave well enough alone.

3. She is a busy mother; she had five children.

4. When the farms were making money, we will buy new cars every year.

5. If the farms were making money, we can pay off the debts faster.

6. All of my travels have been recorded in a video that had been sold at the bookstore here in town.

7. In the past, my family gathered every year for Thanksgiving. We eat no turkey because we are vegetarians, but we had a big feast, nonetheless.

8. Unfortunately, we are now scattered all over. We spoke on the phone every year, but it is not as good as in the past.

9. I hope that we will be able to get together again. We could hope that it will be possible in a few years.

10. We had many good times together as we amuse each other with our stories of our own daily lives.

Score _____

18

Split Constructions

Keep related elements as close together as possible to avoid blurred meanings and awkward constructions.

18a.   Split Subjects and Verbs

In addition to blurring meaning, split subjects and verbs can make subject-verb agreement more difficult. Review Chapter 10a.

> *Blurred: John,* who lives with his grandmother, a nice woman even though she does think she's a witch, *wasn't* in school today.
> *Corrected:* John, who lives with his grandmother, wasn't in school today.

Now do Exercise 18-1.

18b.   Split Verbs and Complements

Keep the complement as close to the verb as possible.

> *Split:* The instructor *knew,* although he had not been there, *who had stolen the book.*
> *Corrected:* The instructor knew who had stolen the book, although he had not been there.

18c. Split Verbs

Unless a split is required by a grammatical structure, you should not split verb forms with lengthy modifiers. Look at examples in Exercise 18-2 to understand this issue.

18d. Split Infinitives

Split infinitives should be permitted only when the alternative is worse. Split infinitives really bother some instructors.

> *Split*: She expects *to* proudly *take* her place in history.
> *Corrected*: She expects *to take* her place proudly in history.

Now do Exercise 18-3.

EXERCISE 18-1

NAME _____ DATE _____

Rewrite these sentences so that the subjects and verbs are closer together.
Check subject-verb agreement.

Example: The *man*, whom you used to know when he was the director of the
          sports club at school, *was* involved in the accident.
          Revised: You used to know the man involved in the accident when he
          was the director of the sports club at school.

1. Various clubs, which all want a share of the meager funds the committee has to divide
    in a thousand ways, submitted grant proposals.

2. Unlike the others, the chef of that new French restaurant that received four stars in
    the city guide and was voted the most exciting restaurant in the state isn't French.

3. Our university with its hundred years of experience in helping young people become
    meaningful members of society and productive Americans in the old-fashioned sense
    of the word will close for Thanksgiving.

4. Because of the snow, the city, which is normally like an overactive beehive intent on
    producing more honey than a thousand hives could use in years, was as still as a fog-
    laden lake.

5. You, who have had every opportunity to study the great works of the Western world
    and to explore the mysteries of the mind with some of the greatest minds of the
    century, didn't know who Einstein was.

Score _____

EXERCISE 18-2

NAME _____ **DATE** _____

Revise these sentences so that the splits between verbs and complements are not disturbing.

Example: This study *will*, when completed by the committee next year after we have received additional funding, *show* that grammar exercises help students write better.
Revised: When this study is completed by the committee next year after we have received additional funding, it will show that grammar exercises help students write better.

1. Some students forget, during the rush of finals, to turn in their registration packets.

2. They were, by the guard at the front gate of the dorms, seen leaving at midnight.

3. Because the vacation is so short, we will, in the interest of fair play and our intrinsic sense of honor, postpone, at least for now until all sides have been heard, your finals till after you return.

4. We were forced, because of his obvious plagiarism in several courses, to expel him from the university.

5. At the end of the month, the auditors will, with great care and extreme caution, review your books, which seem to be slightly misleading.

Score _____

EXERCISE 18-3

NAME _____ DATE _____

Decide whether the split infinitives in these sentences are acceptable. If any are not, revise the sentences in which they occur.

Example: They agree to <u>quickly</u> determine their losses.
             Acceptable

1. The designers hope to with this new house stimulate trade in this town.

2. They allowed us to boldly go where no man had ever gone before.

3. And in front of my own eyes, he coolly proceeded to with great relish split a helpless infinitive.

4. Our factory had planned to never shut down.

5. The lost boys wanted to always remain young and wicked.

6. Several of their victims were found trying to hysterically escape from their prison cells.

7. Have you ever decided to more than triple your profits and done so?

8. Well, with our new guaranteed system, you will never need to at great interest borrow money from banks again.

9. In attempting to in cold blood steal the pensions of thousands of honest citizens, the auditors went beyond the law of the land.

10. Why were you unable to simply say no?

Score _____

19

Incomplete Constructions

Although you may normally use many types of incomplete constructions, you must revise any that cause ambiguity [two or more possible meanings] or create confusion.

> *Acceptable:* She admires you more than I. [only one possible meaning]
> *Ambiguous:* She admires me more than you.
> *Revised:* She admires me more than you do.
> *Revised:* She admires me more than she does you.

19a. Omissions in Compound Constructions

You should be very careful with phrasal verbs and verbs that require specific prepositions. It is easy to forget the particle or preposition in a compound construction.

> *Incorrect, preposition missing:* The scholar would often refer and explain her earlier works.
> *Revised:* The scholar would often refer *to* and explain her earlier works.

Now do Exercise 19-1.

19b. Omitted *That*

You may omit *that* when its omission does not cause a misreading.

> *Clear:* You said you would be on time!
> *Not clear:* The judge read the sentence was ambiguous.

If *that's* omission does cause confusion, reinsert it.

Clear: The judge read *that* the sentence was ambiguous.

19c. Incomplete Comparisons

See 14d for more information about and exercises on incomplete comparisons. In formal writing, we must be careful to include *other* when comparing one or many elements; otherwise, we seem to be comparing an element to itself.

> *Illogical but informally acceptable:* The greyhound runs faster than *any dog.* [but the greyhound is a dog]
> *Revised:* The greyhound runs faster than any *other* dog.

Also in formal writing, we must avoid using *so, such,* or *too* as simple intensifiers; these three words signal comparisons.

> *Informal:* The lyrics are *too* vulgar!
> *Revised:* The lyrics are *too* vulgar to print!
> *Revised:* The lyrics are *very* vulgar.

Try Exercise 19-3 now.

EXERCISE 19-1

NAME _____ DATE _____

Explain why the compound constructions in the following sentences are
incomplete. Next, revise the sentences to standard formal style.

Example: The school never has and will not discriminate against
international students.
a. *has* and *will* must be followed by different verb forms.
b. The school never has <u>discriminated</u> and will not <u>discriminate</u>
against international students.

1. Every day she refers and makes notes of various activities that happen in the class.

    a.

    b.

2. Because of the budget hearings, we must decide and plan for a definite
    course of action.

    a.

    b.

3. Few had heard of Memphis; soon, many.

    a.

    b.

4. The actor and playwright who were here last year will be on campus again. [notice
    verb forms]

    a.

    b.

5. Some companies have been making substandard parts; ours never will.

    a.

    b.

                                                        Score _____

EXERCISE 19-2

NAME _____ **DATE** _____

Insert *that* in any of the following sentences if it would improve the sentence's clarity.

Example: She often admitted her sins were minor.
            She often admitted <u>that</u> her sins were minor.

1. Vicki noted the amount was excessive for a business lunch.

2. Indeed, the auditor thought it was almost exorbitant.

3. Finally, the president of the corporation added no lunch could cost more than ten dollars.

4. In the company newsletter, the editor wrote the solution was in the hands of the auditing department.

5. Even Vicki knew the editor was not just a "yes" man.

Score _____

EXERCISE 19-3

NAME _____ DATE _____

Try to eliminate any confusion that results from incomplete or illogical comparisons. You may add anything you wish.

Example: She is so young!
She is so young to be so talented.

1. I really think that my efforts are just as successful, if not more so than, Alice's.

2. It's hard to believe that a cheetah, a cat-like animal, is faster than any dog.

3. Marvin, who is my best student, is also noisier than any student.

4. It is clear that she really is so intelligent.

5. The directors think that Claude is more important than you.

6. My advice to you is better than any other columnist.

7. That's the absolute best book!

8. Teresa insists that Dallas is richer than any American city.

9. Teresa insists that Rome is richer than any American city.

10. Mimi, you have created such a beautiful view of the Mississippi!

Score _____

20

Parallelism

20a. Parallelism in Compound Structures

When we use two or more elements in a list in writing, they must have the same grammatical structure. If we mix different grammatical structures, our writing will usually sound awkward.

> *Awkward, not parallel:* She enjoys *singing, dancing,* and *to twirl* batons.
> *Revised:* She enjoys singing, dancing, and twirling batons.

Try Exercise 20-1.

20b. Parallelism in Series, Lists, and Outlines

Since outlines are often lengthy, it is easy to forget to use parallel structures. Fortunately, you can easily catch these errors when you edit your work. Remember that in series, lists, and outlines the items must be the same structures.

> *Incorrect:* She agrees to the following:
> 1. *to leave* town quickly
> 2. *avoiding* the press
> 3. *will repay* the entire sum
> *Correct:* She agrees to the following:
> 1. *to* leave town quickly
> 2. *to* avoid the press
> 3. *to* repay the entire sum

Now do Exercise 20-2.

EXERCISE 20-1

NAME _____ **DATE** _____

Underline the word or words which should join two parallel structures. If necessary, revise the compound structures to avoid faulty parallelism.

Example: I must write to the president or the vice president.
I must write to the president <u>or</u> the vice president.
Revised for parallelism: I must write to the president or <u>to</u> the vice president.

1. Either to leave children at home or taking them with us will be about the same thing.

2. She asked not only if she could stay with us but also should she bring her own towels!

3. The hurricane is likely to cause both major power outages and to endanger both human and animal life.

4. The university should admit the students rather than allowing the federal funds to be withdrawn.

5. His attitude bothered me from the moment he walked through the door to leaving the next day, which was none too soon for me.

6. Of course, I discussed what I wanted to instead of the assignment.

7. Her agent insists that she can sing like a bird and dance like a feather as well as acting like Miss Streep.

8. It is not only the girls who want to stay an extra day but agreeing from the boys.

9. The actor was young yet acting well.

10. You should have driven along the side of the road or walk to the next station for help.

Score _____

EXERCISE 20-2

NAME _____ DATE _____

Correct the faulty parallelism in the following series, lists, and outlines.

Example: Before the conference, we must remember to buy notebooks, to supply water and coffee, get doughnuts, and had the speaker's reservation confirmed.
Revised: Before the conference, we must remember to buy notebooks, to supply water and coffee, <u>to</u> get doughnuts, and <u>to have</u> the speaker's reservation confirmed.

1. The committee must address these issues:
   a. Admitting more international students
   b. Provide meaningful educational experiences for international students
   c. Integrating international students into traditional composition classes

2. Why I should attend Memphis State University
   a. MSU is a respectable institution
   b. Its inexpensive nature
   c. There are not very many students from my country
   d. Dedicated faculty and staff

3. To register for classes, you must have the following:
   a. Signed adviser's slip
   b. You need to have filled out your section request form
   c. Library clearance form
   d. Bring a check or credit card

If you would like to succeed in this business, you must be willing to work long hours, being able to tolerate abuse from customers, remember stock numbers, and never left anything undone before you go home.

5. These are your duties in your new position:
    a. preparing the annual report
    b. to answer all customer correspondence
    c. filing media packets

Score _____

Part III

□ **Following Conventions: Punctuation and Mechanics** □

21

Commas

In English, no mark of punctuation can be the first element on a line.

> *Incorrect*: The gentleman had managed to steal the money, the car
>   , and the vase.
> *Standard*: The gentleman had managed to steal the money, the car,
>   and the vase.

Although there are many rules governing the use of a comma, remember that clarity is the first concern.

21a.   Commas between Independent Clauses Joined by Coordinating Conjunctions

You may want to review the use and purpose of coordinating conjunctions before you begin this section. (See p. 167.)

You *may* choose not to use commas between very short independent clauses joined by *and, but, or,* or *nor*. However, it would be more appropriate for you to continue to use commas even in those environments. You are always correct that way. Also remember that you must *always* use commas if the clauses are *joined* by *for, so,* or *yet*.

Be careful to distinguish between this use of *for, yet*, and *yet* as conjunctions from other uses of the same words.

> *Conjunction*: The swans returned, *for* their young were still in the nests.
> *Not a conjunction*: The swans returned *for* their young.

Actually we don't use *for* or *yet* as conjunctions very much in normal writing.

Again, it would be easier just always to use commas to join two independent clauses joined by any of the coordinating conjunctions.

Now try Exercise 21-1.

364

21b. Commas after Introductory Prepositional Phrases, Verbals, and Dependent Clauses

Make sure you know what *introductory prepositional phrases, verbals,* and *dependent clauses* are before you try this section in either the handbook or the workbook. See Chapter 5 and Chapter 7.

(1) Introductory prepositional phrases

Even if an introductory prepositional phrase is very short, it would be better for you to use a comma. You will always be right if you use one.

> *Acceptable*: By Friday have the report on my desk.
> *Safer*: By Friday, have the report on my desk.

Now use this rule to do Exercise 21.2.

(2) Introductory verbals and verbal phrases

You must always use a comma to separate introductory verbals and verbal phrases from the main clause even if the phrase is just one word long.

> Confused, the student forgot to put in a comma and failed!

(3) Introductory adverb clauses

Review the subordinate conjunctions in 7c if you have forgotten what they are. Always use a comma after an introductory adverb clause.

(4) Introductory noun clauses

If you do not remember what a noun clause is and how it functions, see 7c(3). If a noun clause is the subject of a sentence, you do not need a comma. However, if an introductory noun clause is really an object or a complement, you must use a comma.

Do Exercise 21-3 now.

21c. Commas to Set Off Nonrestrictive Elements

The distinction between *restrictive* and *nonrestrictive* is often very difficult to make. You must ask yourself if the information is *essential* to help your reader prevent mix-ups. If the information is essential, it is restrictive. If the information is not essential, it is nonrestrictive. Exercise 21-4 will help you learn the difference.

21d.   Commas between Items in a Series and between Coordinate Adjectives

(1) Items in a series

Although you *may* omit the comma before the last element in a series, you shouldn't. Occasionally, its omission can create ambiguity or messy structures.

> *Acceptable*: She has cats, dogs and children.
> *Preferred*: She has cats, dogs, and children.

(2) Coordinate adjectives

You might want to look at the section on adjective ordering again after you read this section and do its exercises. (See p. 60.) Coordinate adjectives can be rearranged. To show that they are coordinate adjectives, we separate them with commas.

> *Coordinate*: My family enjoys hot, spicy food.
> *Coordinate*: My family enjoys spicy, hot food.

Non-coordinate adjectives must follow the ordering we discussed in Chapter 3. We do not separate them with commas.

> *Non-coordinate*: My family enjoys spicy Hunan food.
> *Incorrect order*: My family enjoys Hunan spicy food.

Use this information to do Exercise 21-5.

21e.   Commas in Place of Omitted Words

The use of the comma in place of omitted words is not very common and should not occur frequently.

> Fred *enjoys* flying; Jean *enjoys* fishing.
> With commas in place of omitted words: Fred *enjoys* flying; Jean, fishing.

Now do Exercise 21-6.

21f.   Commas to Set Off Parenthetical, Transitional, and Contrastive Elements

Remember that we should avoid interrupting structures unless we have a good reason to do so. You might want to review the difference between subordinating conjunctions and transitional devices. Subordinating conjunctions can only occur at the beginning of a dependent clause; transitional expressions, however, can occur at the beginning, in the middle, and at the end of both dependent and independent clauses.

Subordinating conjunction, no comma: Although he was elected, he was unable to serve.
Initial transitional device, comma: He was elected; *however,* he was unable to serve.
Final transitional device, comma: He was elected; he was unable to serve, *however.*
Medial [in the middle] transitional device, two commas: He was elected; he was, *however,* unable to serve.

Do Exercise 21-7.

21g. Commas to Set Off Interjections, Words in Direct Address, and Tag Questions

Tag questions are often used by Americans in speech. You should practice them since the complex English form appears to be unique in all the world's languages.

English tag question: You brought the food, didn't you?
"Universal" tag question: You brought the food, isn't that right?

21h. Commas in Special Contexts

Some commas are simply required by tradition; you should just learn these special contexts and practice them. After you have read 21h (1-5), do Exercise 21-8.

(1) Dates, places, and addresses

When you copy an address from a letter or package you receive, make sure that you have copied it exactly as it was sent to you. Notice the commas and the periods in the first address, which are not used in the second one.

> 1245 Robin Lane, N.W., Atlanta, Georgia
> 1245 NW 19th Street, Gainesville, Florida

(2) Numbers

The American numbering system uses commas between groups of *three* digits.

> *American:* 110,000
> *Incorrect:* 11,0000

(3) Titles of individuals

If you use someone's title in a letter, make sure you have it exactly right. If you need to make sure, phone the company or look it up before you write that person.

(4) Direct quotations

When you use quotes to indicate the word is not to be read literally, you do not need commas.

> She wasn't really "late." She walked in just a second after the bell.

EXERCISE 21-1

NAME _____ **DATE** _____

Decide whether the underlined word is a coordinating conjunction joining two independent clauses. If it is, supply an appropriate comma.

Example: a. The girls returned <u>for</u> their books.
                  not a conjunction, no comma
                  b. The girls returned <u>for</u> they had forgotten their books.
                  conjunction: The girls returned, <u>for</u> they had forgotten their books.

1. She walked through the door <u>and</u> I never saw her again.

2. Fortunately, we had saved some money <u>but</u> it wasn't much.

3. The doctor hasn't returned <u>yet</u> <u>but</u> her nurse will speak with you now.

4. It was hard to determine what to do <u>so</u> I dropped the course.

5. The instructor was not very nice <u>yet</u> he did have some spark of genuine interest in students.

6. We spoke clearly <u>and</u> politely <u>for</u> we were afraid they would not listen to us if we were rude.

7. They were not only punctual <u>but</u> actually early.

8. Why would you like to live in Atlanta <u>or</u> would you rather not say?

9. You were gone <u>so</u> we left.

10. You weren't home <u>yet</u> <u>nor</u> was your husband.

Score _____

EXERCISE 21-2

NAME _____ **DATE** _____

Underline the introductory verbals, verbal phrases, or introductory prepositional phrases. Supply an appropriate comma.

Example: After Wednesday we won't meet here anymore.
<u>After Wednesday</u>, we won't meet here anymore.

1. They maintained that because of recent price hikes they would be forced to raise their own prices.

2. Founded in 1818 Memphis has grown to be an important city in the Mid-South.

3. He marched into the room; then without waiting for orders from the colonels he began to reveal the hidden plan.

4. In order to pay back my student loans I was forced to accept a job at a local fast-food restaurant.

5. Thrilled she marched up to claim her diploma.

6. To paint you need only paint, but to be an artist you need talent and dedication.

7. At dusk we often sat and watched the swallows swimming through the heavy evening air.

8. For the good of the community we have asked that during the next two weeks you discontinue watering your lawns.

9. Amused by the silly antics of the adults the child began to laugh.

10. As a professional clown I have encountered many crowds that seemed delighted with my activities. Of course at other times there were hostile crowds. But looking back there weren't many.

Score_____

EXERCISE 21-3

NAME _____ DATE _____

How is the underlined noun clause being used in the sentence? If it is not the subject, do you need to add a comma? If a comma is needed, add it in the appropriate place.

Example: Whatever the singer wants you are to get.
object; yes, because it is introductory
Whatever the singer wants, you are to get.

1. Whatever she said is not really important.

2. Whatever I said she must have misunderstood.

3. Wherever she goes is fine with this organization.

4. Don't forget that whomever we elect at the next meeting will be president during the conference here in March.

5. Every time we asked him a question he just told us whatever popped into his mind.

6. At no time did he discuss the issue with whoever was in his office.

7. Whatever the general was asking about I don't know.

8. Whomever she pushed down the stairs seems to be fine now.

9. Did you understand that whatever they decided last night was to be our final proposal?

10. She always said that whoever married Lucy her father would help.

Score_____

EXERCISE 21-4

NAME _____ DATE _____

Is the underlined information *restrictive* or *nonrestrictive?* First, remove the underlined section. Does this new sentence mean the same as the first sentence? If it does, the underlined element is nonrestrictive; use commas. If the sentence could be reinterpreted, the underlined element is restrictive, and you must not use commas.

Example: a. The phone always rings for Jim <u>who is always sleeping when I get home</u>. [base sentence]
b. The phone always rings for Jim. [remove underlined section]
c. The new sentence has the same basic meaning as the first sentence; the underlined information was nonrestrictive. Use commas.
d. The phone always rings for Jim, who is always sleeping when I get home.

1. a. I have two dogs. My mother says that I must get rid of the dog <u>that I found on the beach</u>.

   b.

   c.

   d.

2. a. During the school year <u>which is much too long</u>, I often wonder what summer will bring me.

   b.

   c.

   d.

3. a. Last night, I dreamt of a place <u>where summer never ends</u>.

   b.

   c.

   d.

4. a. I vote only for a man <u>whom I trust to tell the truth</u>.

    b.

    c.

    d.

5. a. That trick was first done by the magician <u>Kisma</u>.

    b.

    c.

    d.

6. a. In winter, I often drink hot chocolate <u>which should be sweet and steamy</u>.

    b.

    c.

    d.

7. a. In winter, I drink only hot chocolate <u>that is sweet and steamy</u>.

    b.

    c.

    d.

8. a. Susan always claimed to be a "telepath," <u>or a mind reader</u>.

    b.

    c.

    d.

9. a. My brother is often "short of funds," <u>broke, in other words</u>.

    b.

    c.

    d.

10. a. His present was the best of all, <u>a wind-up tin soldier who saluted</u>.

    b.

    c.

    d.

Score_____

EXERCISE 21-5

NAME _____ DATE _____

Decide whether these adjectives are coordinate or non-coordinate; insert commas in the appropriate places. You might also have to put commas between elements in a series.

Example: A new shiny British car pulled in.
A new, shiny British car pulled in.
British is not coordinate.

1. Each day was a hot brilliant trial of endurance.

2. Her friends were always elderly wealthy Italian nobles.

3. Because of his wet greasy black fur, the bear was not allowed in the house very often.

4. It's difficult to imagine that my beautiful tall graceful umbrella-shaped elm tree was just a small insignificant scrawny twig when Miss Rudy, my neighbor, planted it forty long hard exciting years ago.

5. Betty sent me to the store the cleaners and the bank.

6. I drove to the store I walked to the cleaners and I ran to the bank.

7. Have you ever seen a perfect round transparent crystal ball?

8. Many old-fashioned out-of-date grocery stores are better run than the brand-new ultra-modern one I must shop in.

9. Emmy was always a brash spirited pigeon.

10. My three favorite flowers are azaleas camellias and roses. But the gaudy dream-like magnolia will always have a special place in my garden.

Score _____

EXERCISE 21-6

NAME _____ DATE _____

Write out the omitted words represented by commas. Be careful to drop the commas that are no longer needed.

Example: a. Helen will study chemistry; Nellie, biology.
             b. Helen will study chemistry; Nellie <u>will study</u> biology.

1. a. Fred visited Turkey; Alex, Alexandria.

   b.

2. a. My paper route was in Memphis; my sister's, in Bartlett.

   b.

3. a. The young girl always ate pears, and the young man, avocados.

   b.

4. a. The students' notice was torn down, and the students' adviser, beaten.

   b.

5. a. Roberto reported on his trip to New Mexico; Sandra; on her trip to Wyoming.

   b.

Score_____

EXERCISE 21-7

NAME _____ DATE_____

Use commas to set off parenthetical, transitional, and contrastive elements.

Example: They insisted on going home nonetheless.
            They insisted on going home, nonetheless.

1. For example the director hopes to increase the number of students from Montana.

2. Gene according to the latest reports wasn't on that plane.

3. Lena believe it or not refuses to ask for a raise.

4. Strictly speaking I am not allowed to admit you without the correct form.

5. Since you have always been a good student I will make an exception

    however.

6. Fred on the other hand would not let his own mother in without the proper form.

7. International students as a general rule finish college faster than local

    students.

8. Then she asked for you're not going to believe this both Thanksgiving and New Year's

    Eve off!

9. The authorities were forced to cancel the concert as a result.

10. Therefore the concert committee lost its deposit which they had placed with the band's

    booking agent.

Score_____

EXERCISE 21-8

NAME _____ DATE _____

Put commas in the appropriate places; you might want to refer to 21i; in
the handbook first.

Example: 2 November 1987
no commas needed

November 2 1887
November 2, 1887

1. She lived in both Jackson MS and Jackson TN while she was in school.

2. The conference was being planned for March 1988.

3. There is no such address as 48 Larchmont Memphis Tennessee 38111.

4. The letters were all dated June 2 1943.

5. My favorite holiday happens on October 31 every year.

6. Dear Jane

7. Sincerely

8. Carl Halle Sr. chairman of the board is very conservative and insists on all the commas

   he has coming to him.

9. On the other hand, Carl Halle Jr. vice-president of consumer affairs doesn't use a

   comma before his "Junior."

10. The United States has around 220000000 people.

11. She rarely earns more than $1276 a month.

12. Our company employs over 1500 workers.

13. 11-1-87

14. We'll expect you 06 April 1988.

15. "Just sit a moment" said Bobbie "while I finish this letter."

16. The principal did not tolerate Jason's missing school for his so-called

     "alternative education days."

17. Frank screamed "Please, someone help me!"

18. "Your test scores are considerably above average" Professor Owens

     exclaimed.

19. "Where were you the night of June 30 1965?" the prosecutor asked.

Score_____

EXERCISE 21-9

NAME _____ DATE _____

Try to paraphrase each of the sentences.

Example: a. Fred thinks, Pat talks too much.
Fred thinks about things while Pat talks.
b. Fred thinks Pat talks too much.
Fred is of the opinion that Pat talks too much.

1. a. They cannot know, it is impossible!
b. They cannot know it is impossible!

2. a. The priests pray. The farmers are still hopeful.
b. The priests pray the farmers are still hopeful.

3. a. What kind of people are we looking for? Those who can dream.
b. Why are all the creative people so "spacy"? Those who can, dream.

4. a. The restaurant is full again. Who are those people? Those who must wait.
b. I don't really need to be here in this long line; however, those who must, wait.

5. a. Andrea thought Paul was very quiet. Normally, he is very loud and noisy.
b. Andrea thought, Paul was very quiet, and no one made a sound.

Score_____

EXERCISE 21-10

NAME _____ DATE _____

Rewrite these informal, topicalized sentences into formal, written versions.

1. Alex he is one amazing guy.

2. As for smoking, I don't do it.

3. Those people, they are sincerely lazy.

4. Gloria, you really hate her, don't you, Sue?

5. In the hospital, that is where I was yesterday.

6. My parents, they're coming home now.

7. Drugs, not for me!

8. Memphis, is a great town.

9. Sunday, boring.

10. Jets, I want to fly jets.

Score_____

22

Semicolons

In English, semicolons occur only between coordinate elements.

> *Incorrect*: While reading; I ran across the most amazing fact. [A phrase and an independent clause are not coordinate elements.]
> *Correct*: While reading, I ran across the most amazing fact.

Semicolons cannot begin a line; they are considered part of the last word of a line.

> *Incorrect*: She left
>   ;however, he stayed.
> *Correct*: She left;
>   however, he stayed.

Semicolons must be followed by something; they cannot act as terminal punctuation.

> *Incorrect*: She left;
> *Correct*: She left.

Since semicolons are not terminal punctuation, the word that follows a semicolon is not automatically capitalized.

> *Incorrect*: She left; He stayed.
> *Correct*: She left; he stayed.

Now do Exercise 22-1.

22a. Semicolons between Independent Clauses Not Joined by Coordinating Conjunctions

You might want to avoid using just a semicolon to connect two independent clauses. It is always appropriate to use a period, a conjunction, or a semicolon and a transition.

Acceptable: She ate; I just watched.
Preferred: She ate while I just watched.
Preferred: She ate; on the other hand, I just watched.

Do Exercise 22-2 now.

22b. Semicolons between Independent Clauses Joined by Transitional Expressions

Remember that transitional expressions are not grammatical connectors. As a result, we must treat the clauses they relate as separate independent clauses. See also 21g.

Separate independent clauses: John sings; he sings very badly.
No change with transition: John sings; *however*, he sings very badly.

Do Exercise 22-3 now.

22c. Semicolons between Independent Clauses Joined by Coordinating Conjunctions

When there are commas in the first of two independent clauses joined by coordinating conjunctions, we should use a semicolon between the two independent clauses; otherwise, it might be difficult to read the sentence correctly.

Messy: John was able to find a saw, a hammer, a nail, and a screw, and all I was able to find was an empty bottle of glue.
Better: John was able to find a saw, a hammer, a nail, and a screw; and all I was able to find was an empty bottle of glue.

22c. Semicolons between Items in a Series with Internal Punctuation

If the elements in a series already contain commas, we need to use semicolons to separate those elements.

Please send one to Springfield, TN; Hot Coffee, MS; and Little Rock, AR.

22e. Inappropriate Semicolons

If you have not seen an example of a specific use of a semicolon, that use is probably inappropriate. The semicolon is not very flexible.

Review all uses (and several misuses) of the semicolon in Exercise 22-4.

EXERCISE 22-1

NAME _____ DATE _____

Correct the following misuses of semicolons.

Example   Irene has gone;
            Irene has gone.

1. While you were at school; I stayed in the restaurant.

2. ; furthermore, I really don't think she wants the job.

3. I could go; However, if you went; it would be better.

4. The weather was fine; considering the time of year.

5. Jane was unable to go, on the other hand; Richard could.

Score_____

EXERCISE 22-2

NAME _____ DATE _____

Remove the underlined conjunction or punctuation mark and add a semicolon. Look carefully, because underlined periods look a great deal like regular ones.

Example: Yolanda went to the store, <u>and</u> Fred left for Dallas.
Yolanda went to the store; Fred left for Dallas.

1. William was not eager to study for the physics tests<u>.</u> In fact, he was trying to forget all about it.

2. Someone reported the crime<u>.</u> Fortunately, the police were already on their way.

3. At the ranch, I often ride the horses, <u>but</u> in the city, I never seem to have time.

4. Many years ago, this land was left for the citizens to enjoy<u>.</u> Today, it is a beautiful, scenic park.

5. Some settlers left their fortunes behind<u>.</u> Others brought vast sums of money with them into the wilderness.

Score _____

EXERCISE 22-3

NAME _____ DATE _____

Make the changes necessary to join each of the following pairs into a single sentence with a semicolon.

Example: She really likes Memphis. In fact, she wishes to move here.
She really likes Memphis; in fact, she wishes to move here.

1. New Albany has many tourist attractions. For example, there are several small, private museums.

2. You must register today. Therefore, you must hurry.

3. Most children dislike homework. Nonetheless, it must be done.

4. Some students would prefer the other method. For this reason, they should be given a choice.

5. We should file the application by tomorrow. Otherwise, it might not arrive on time.

6. Your opponent failed to file the necessary papers. Consequently, the issue will be dropped.

7. The court action would have been bad for my business. Additionally, it would have been costly.

8. The fine would have been steep. Moreover, the legal fees were going to be staggering.

9. Jane wants to go to law school. Eventually, she wants to specialize in civil rights cases.

10. The audience's actions were totally uncalled for. Eventually, the performer just left the stage.

Score_____

EXERCISE 22-4

NAME _____ DATE _____

Correct any misuses of the semicolon, insert semicolons where they are needed, and revise sentences in any way necessary.

Example: Dear Joy;
           Dear Joy,

1. My sisters' dates of birth are November 2, 1959, August 31, 1954, and September 16, 1951.

2. Although he arrived on time; he still missed the plane; which had left early.

3. She asked me to bring the following;
   a. paper plates
   b. paper napkins
   c. plastic flatware

4. Tiffany had lived in Clarkesville, however, she was transferred to Birmingham; Alabama.

5. Laura had already invited Olive, Paul, and Earl, and Tom was invited later.

6. Dear Sir;

7. Yours sincerely;

8. At first; we misunderstood his request, finally, it all made sense.

9. Be sure to be there at 10;50 a.m.; or earlier.

10. ;Fortunately, she was unable to accept the invitation.

Score_____

23

Colons

23a—e. Colons in Various Environments

Colons are easy to use correctly, because their use is very formal and specified. Of course, colons cannot begin a line.

> *Correct*: The colon after "correct" is correct.
> *Incorrect*: This is an example of an incorrect use of the
>   :colon

It is best for you to avoid the colon except for the very predictable uses that follow. You might want to read 23a-e in the handbook for information, however. After you have read 23a-e in the handbook, try Exercise 23-1.

23f. Colons in Correspondence

You might need to review the use of commas and periods in correspondence. Remember that the exclamation point cannot be used after a salutation in English.

> *Incorrect*: Dear Mr. Shaw!
> *Correct*: Dear Mr. Shaw:

23g. Colons with Numerical Elements

In other languages, other devices are used to separate the parts of numerical sequences of several types. However, in English, only the colon may be used for hours/minutes, chapters/verses and numbers in ratios to each other. Note, however, that we do not use colons for feet and inches.

Incorrect: She is 5:6 tall.
Correct: She is 5'6" tall.

Now do Exercise 23-2.

23h. Inappropriate Colons

If you haven't seen a colon in a specific way, that use is probably inappropriate.

EXERCISE 23-1

NAME _____ DATE _____

You should do this exercise only if you have read 23a-e in the handbook.
Correct any misuse of colons or supply one where one is needed. You might need to revise some of the material.

Example: <u>Holiday in Florida</u>; <u>Fun in the Sun</u>
                 <u>Holiday in Florida</u>: <u>Fun in the Sun</u>

1. Do the following before I get home;
   water the plants
   feed the dog

2. For dinner, we ate: watercress, tomatoes, carrots, and cabbage.

3. Finally, he had faced the most savage beast of all a man.

4. Read: pages 6-23, exercises on page 22, and review for the quiz.

5. Paul gave Linda his most valuable possession, He gave her his mother's ring.

6. <u>Light in the Darkness</u>, <u>Creative Visualization</u>

7. : do the following
   1. take out the trash
   2. wash the car

8. In an interview late in his life, he said; "Although I have tried to live life to its fullest, I have often felt as though something important were passing me by; a true sense of happiness."

9. To stay fit, you must: eat right, exercise regularly, see your health-care specialists, and maintain a good attitude.

10. "Getting: Information from the Periodicals"

Score_____

EXERCISE 23-2

NAME _____ DATE _____

These uses of the colon are fairly important.
Correct the misuse of colons or supply one if one is needed. You may need to revise some parts a bit.

Example: Dear Mr. President,
                Dear Mr. President:

1. Attention. Mr. Paul Rabin

2. CEH, rol [initials of writer and typist]

3. Re" Increases in salary

4. Example,

5. [Set up a memorandum with the following information:]
    All faculty members
    The department chair
    18 October 1987
    United Fund drive

6. 5,35 p:m:

7. Job 3;2

8. You need to take these at: 6;30, 4,15 and at midnight.

9. The train will arrive at 7'32".

10. My sister is taller than I am; she is 5:8.

Score_____

EXERCISE 23-3

NAME _____ DATE _____

Replace any inappropriate colons with the appropriate mark. You might also need to add some colons. Any colon use you haven't seen before is most likely inappropriate.

Example: The video stores hope to: increase sales, reduce overhead, and expand.
                 The video stores hope to increase sales, reduce overhead, and expand.

 1. The director insisted on knowing: his profits, your profits, and your salary.

 2. So far, we have received checks from: C. Church, R. Inez, and R. Young.

 3. Although she has succeeded in selling several houses: the real estate firm still doesn't want to hire her.

 4. Well: did you make $200:00 as you planned?

 5. Have you read: *Hope for Humanity Revolutions in Energy?*

 6. Harry received notification that: he must report to Dallas on Tuesday at 9;45 p:m: .

 7. There is only one person suited for that job; Mrs. Dorothy Massy.

8. Bring the following,
   a. towels
   b. swimsuit
   c. tanning lotion: coconut scented
   d. sunglasses

9. As I have stated, my reasons are:
   1. insufficient funds
   2. missing records
   3. excessive tardiness

10. Each morning at 6.50 am:, we do fifteen minutes of aerobics.

Score_____

24

Dashes,
Parentheses,
and Brackets

Dashes highlight information; parentheses de-emphasize information; brackets provide clarifying information. Unlike dashes or other internal punctuation, parentheses and brackets can begin both sentences and lines.

24a. Dashes to Set Off Appositives Containing Commas

Think of dashes as second-level commas; if there are already commas in an *appositive*, you must use dashes.

> She has three friends—Janice, Fred, and George.

24b. Dashes to Set Off Nonrestrictive Modifiers Containing Commas

Again, use dashes to set off modifiers only when the *nonrestrictive* modifiers already contain commas.

> My aunt—who has lived in Spain, Tunisia, and Turkey—is coming to visit next year.

24c. Dashes to Emphasize Sentence Elements

The use of dashes to emphasize sentence elements should be avoided or should occur very infrequently. A heavy use of dashes distracts the reader. There are other elements (e.g., the colon) that can signal emphasis just as well.

24d. Dashes with Interrupters

Dashes are used to set off interrupting elements. Again, dashes should occur infrequently. If used rarely, dashes retain a clear stylistic effect; otherwise, they are distracting.

Now review the uses of the dash in Exercise 24-1.

24e. Parentheses to Enclose Interrupters

Note the difference in punctuation when sentences in parentheses occur within or between sentences.

> Anne (she hated to be called by her real name) arrived late.
> Anne arrived late. (She hated to be called by her real name.)

Explanations in parentheses should be kept short and clear; otherwise, the sentence becomes difficult to read.

> *Awkward*: Alice (daughter of my first wife's second husband who had also been married to my elder sister) was here today.

Also notice that no commas are needed when parentheses are used.

> *Incorrect*: John, (Fred's elder brother), graduated at the top of his class.
> *Correct*: John (Fred's older brother) graduated at the top of his class.

Now do Exercise 24-2.

24f. Parentheses for References to Pages, Figures, Tables, and Chapters

Make sure you use the right punctuation for references. The correct form will depend on the specific style sheet you use in your classes and profession.

24g. Brackets around Insertions in Direct Quotations

If you need to explain or to correct something in someone else's words (a quotation), you should use brackets.

> Brian said, "Hilda [his sister] will be there."
> [his sister] is our explanation; Brian did not say it.

24h. Brackets for Parentheses inside Parentheses

If you need to use two levels of parentheses, you should first try to rewrite the sentence. If that is not possible, you must use brackets for the lower-level parentheses.

Incorrect: (See Delaney (1986) for further reference.)
Better: (See Delaney [1986] for further reference.)

EXERCISE 24-1

NAME _____ DATE _____

Remove inappropriate dashes, add them where they are needed, and revise any element that needs revising.

Example: At last (in October, mind you), she came knocking on my door.
At last—in October, mind you—she came knocking on my door.

1. Nadine really is a good person, in a strange way.

2. Roger, who already knows Hank, Jerry, and Uri, just met the last remaining star of the league, John Gibson, Jr.

3. Well, she said it was hers.

4. Politician, businessman, and naturalist, John Burgess has earned this award.

5. My best friend, a nervous, timid, shy gentleman, has just won the lottery for several million, lucky him!

6. The group was discussing, well arguing, how the money should be spent.

7. My aunt's bird sang, my aunt had once been a vocal coach, famous arias and popular tunes of long ago.

8. His grades, at Memphis State, at least, have been satisfactory.

9. The couple invited Harry, but not me, Mary, or Doc, to their party, the social event of the year.

10. Southern scholar, brilliant teller of stories, and reader of hidden talents, Professor Day was loved by her students.

Score_____

EXERCISE 24-2

Correct the punctuation of these sentences containing parentheses. There might be other errors involving parentheses also.

Example: William (Born in 1952) turned 35 today.
William (born in 1952) turned 35 today.

1. The artist (Who had been hired by the studio, walked off the job yesterday.

2. (see figure 5.2 for further information).

3. Donleavy, 1965, explores the nature of thought.

4. After the Hmong arrived, the refugee program began to expand. (see last year's financial report).

5. After the Hmong arrived, the funding (see last year's financial report.) for the refugee program was increased.

6. PgUp, Page up), is a fast way to scroll up.

7. Chatsworth Hall (To the left,) and Farnsdale Manor (on your right) were built by brothers. (See *Brother Builders*).

8. Mrs. Hinds (nee Williams.) held a luncheon for several friends yesterday at the Colonial Country Club, (Memphis).

9. Alex (He was the first to go by that name) was often seen riding along the river at dusk.

10. (Spoken quietly) "Leave now, please."

Score_____

25

Periods,
Question Marks,
and
Exclamation Points

Remember that periods, question marks, and exclamation points can occur only at the end of a sentence. Furthermore, they can never begin a line.

Incorrect: ?How are you?
Incorrect: .She was late again.

You will need to read through this short chapter before you begin the exercises. Don't forget to look back as you do them.

25a. Periods as End Punctuation

The period is the most common form of end punctuation. Unless there is a specific reason not to use the period [e.g., in a *direct* question], you should plan on using the period. In Modern English we even use the period after a polite demand that looks like a question.

Would you have the material sent to me.

25b. Periods in Outlines and Displayed Lists

To separate numbers and letters from the text of outlines and displayed lists, use periods.

Do the following:

1. Feed the dog
2. Wash the car

25c. Inappropriate Periods

A sentence cannot end in two periods.

> *Incorrect*: Send the letter to C. Hall, Jr..
> *Correct*: Send the letter to C. Hall, Jr.

Periods are not used in English to distinguish hours from minutes.

> *Incorrect*: She arrived at 6.15.

In many common abbreviations, do not use periods.

> *Correct*: CARE, FBI, NATO or even USA

For modern two-letter state abbreviations in the USA, do not use periods.

> *Correct*: Memphis, TN [Tennessee]

Some writers do not use periods after common forms of address. However, in the USA, you should continue to use periods there.

> *Encountered*: Mr, Mrs, Jr
> *Preferred*: Mr., Mrs., Jr.

25d. Question Marks as End Punctuation

Use question marks only with direct questions. For indirect questions, use the punctuation of the main clause.

> *Direct*: Are you going?
> *Indirect*: He is asking if you are going.
> *Indirect in a direct*: Is he asking if you are going?

Although the main clause of a tag question is not a question, use a question mark because the tag is a real question.

> *Main clause*: Wilma lives here.
> *With tag*: Wilma lives here, *doesn't she?*

In speech, many Americans express disbelief or surprise by using a non-question as a question. In those cases, a question mark can be used.

> A: Can you believe that John just landed at the airport?
> B: John dared to come back here? I don't believe it!

25e. Question Marks within Sentences

Using question marks within sentences is very unusual. If you use them in this way often, your reader will be distracted. It is usually best to change the direct question to an indirect one. [Watch word order when you change a direct question to an indirect one.]

Acceptable, but distracting direct question: Why would we go? has always bothered her.
Revised as indirect question: Why we would go has always bothered her.

25f.   Exclamation Points in Dialogue

Exclamation points are used only for very strong emotions. Avoid them in formal writing.

25g.   Exclamation Points with Interjections

Again, if the interjection is very strong, you may use exclamation points; otherwise, use commas.

25h.   Exclamation Points for Emphasis

To note danger, you may use exclamation points for warnings. However, even in these cases, Americans tend to use fewer exclamation points than other cultures do.

Don't try to use exclamation points to signal emotions; your words should do that.

If you haven't seen a specific example of the use of an exclamation point, that use is probably inappropriate. For example, never use exclamation points for salutations in either formal or informal letters.

> *Incorrect:* Dear Sandy!
> *Correct:* Dear Sandy,
> *Incorrect:* Dear Professor Bell!
> *Correct:* Dear Professor Bell:

Now do Exercise 25-1 through 25-3. Check back in the chapter frequently to make sure you understand what you are doing.

EXERCISE 25-1

NAME _____ DATE _____

Revise the following so that the periods are used in acceptable, standard ways.

Example: She was originally from Huntsville, AL..
                 She was originally from Huntsville, AL.

1   Did you find the error in this one?

2. My brother works for Ino, Inc..

3. Study the following.
    a; growing rice outside Little Rock, AR..
    b. raising pigs in Paducah, KY,.

4. Would you send me information on your festival?

5. No, I said .You cannot go to the dance,

6. October was mildly warmer than usual!

7. She wondered if we might borrow your car?

8. She wondered, "Might we borrow your car."

9. Check-out time is 1.00 p.m..

10. Don't leave. Until I have finished.

Score_____

EXERCISE 25-2

NAME _____ DATE _____

Revise these sentences so that question marks are used correctly.

Example: We asked to be excused?
                  We asked to be excused.

1. Tim has the tickets, doesn't he.

2. Why we should avoid an increase in taxes? was the first issue on the program.

3. ?How's it going?

4. The Battle of Memphis (?1863) did not do much damage to the city.

5. In what way can we decrease tensions must be our primary concern.

6. John asked if he could borrow my biology book?

7. Did John ask if he could borrow yours.

8. Just drop it, will you.

9. She didn't really know where her homework was?

10. A: The President just called!
    B: The President called me. I don't believe it!

Score_____

EXERCISE 25-3

NAME _____ **DATE** _____

Correct the improper use of exclamation points in the following sentences. You may need to supply exclamation points in some of the sentences.

Example: She went where??!!
                  She went where?

1. !Hold your hands up high!

2. Leave your name at the desk!

3. Well! I guess that seems fine.

4. Well, you nearly killed us back there!

5. "Please return to your seats!" the teacher said in a bored, tired voice.

6. Great! Here we are at school again!

7. Dear Sally!

8. I don't believe it!!!!!!

9. Your friend! [closing of an informal letter]

10. Overuse of exclamation points can be dangerous to your health and grade!

Score_____

26

Apostrophes

26a. Apostrophes to Indicate Possession

Using apostrophes with -s's is the most common way to signal possession.

> Joe's diner
> My uncle's car is broken.

Remember the basic rule is add 's to all singular nouns and to all plural nouns that don't already end in -s.

> Singular: John's boat   James's car
> Plural, but no -s: the children's song

For plural nouns that do end in -s, just add '.

> Plural with -s: the three boys' jokes

The handbook can help you with the exceptions.
One important exception involves the difference between *joint* and *individual* ownership.

> John and Jane's house needs painting [they both own *the same* house]
> John's and Jane's houses need painting [they each own a house]

Now do Exercise 26-1.

26b. Apostrophes to Create Contractions

Don't forget to put apostrophes in contractions. One important use of ' in contractions is with dates. When we write '89, we know it means 1989.

You should use only contractions that you have already seen; don't make up your own. Look at these two commonly confused pairs of words.

> *whose*—shows possession, not a contraction
> *who's*—doesn't show possession, means *who is* or *who has*
>
> *its*—shows possession, not a contraction
> *it's*—doesn't show possession, means *it is* or *it has*

Now do Exercise 26-2.

26c. Apostrophes to Indicate Plurals of Letters, Numbers, and Words Used as Words

When you are writing about a word or letter, not using it, you need to add *-'s* to show that.

> *Words used as words*: There were too many *his's* or *her's* in their writing.

26d. Inappropriate Apostrophes

If you have not seen a specific example of the use of an apostrophe, that use is most likely inappropriate.

Do Exercise 26-3 now.

EXERCISE 26-1

NAME _____ DATE _____

Add the appropriate signal of possession to the underlined word or words and explain why you chose that ending. You may need to refer to the handbook for some exceptional forms.

Example: <u>birds</u> voices
birds' [plural noun ending in -s]

1. the <u>problem</u> solution

2. several <u>students</u> books

3. The <u>boys</u> and <u>girls</u> team [joint possession]

4. The <u>boys</u> and <u>girls</u> team [individual possession]

5. my <u>sister-in-law</u> first husband

6. <u>someone</u> wallet

7. <u>farmers</u> hopes

8. <u>Laurel</u> and <u>Hardy</u> films [joint possession]

9. my <u>school</u> reputation

10. the <u>bosses</u> vacation plans

Score _____

EXERCISE 26-2

NAME _____ DATE _____

Correct the following misuses of apostrophes or contractions. You might also need to add some apostrophes or to do a little revising.

Example: Who's book is that?
                 Whose book is that?

1. Hed rather not go today.

2. I cant stay till 6 oclock.

3. Shell visit you next week.

4. Cant believe that record dates from 62, can you?

5. Theyre going to be there, arent they?

6. It's purpose's been forgotten.

7. Theres going to be a rock n roll museum in Cleveland, Ohio.

8. Whose there?

9. Normally, the chimps wouldn'tve been so angry.

10. His' boat's were always faster than Serges.

Score _____

EXERCISE 26-3

NAME _____ **DATE** _____

Correct any misuse of contractions or apostrophes. You may need to add some apostrophes or to revise the sentences somewhat. These issues are treated extensively in the handbook if you need any additional explanation.

Example: Shell stay 'till Tuesday.
                She'll stay till Tuesday.

1. Who's life is it anyway?

2. Have you see the Johnson's tree?

3. Is that car your's?

4. Hes going to be late again, isn't he?

5. In 40, my parents were still in Europe.

6. Have you ever heard anyone use so many <u>hences</u>?

7. The cellos owner could not be found.

8. Its hard to imagine its use.

9. Why're you going to leave they're book at home?

10. Every student hopes to make straight As.

Score _____

27

Quotation Marks and Ellipsis Marks

27a. Quotation Marks to Enclose Direct Quotations

Only the exact words of the source that you are quoting appear in quotation marks. If you wish to add or to explain anything, you must enclose the additional information in brackets. Make sure that you understand the use of single quotes within double quotes.

Double quotes: I hate having "fun."
Single quotes in double quotes: Larry said, "I hate having 'fun.'"

In English, we cannot use any other forms of punctuation to signal quotes.

Inappropriate: She said, <<Leave!>>
Inappropriate: She said, ,,Leave!"
Appropriate: She said, "Leave!"

27b. Quotation Marks with Other Punctuation Marks

We cannot have more than one end punctuation.

Incorrect: She asked me, "Which one do you want?".
Correct: She asked me, "Which one do you want?"

27c. Quotation Marks in Dialogue

If you remember that closing quotes indicate a change in speaker, you will find it easier to read material [such as novels or plays] with dialogue.

27d. Quotation Marks in Titles

Remember that works that could be part of larger works [such as articles in a magazine] are put in quotes. Works that can stand alone are underlined.

> Moby Dick [a novel]
> "How to Avoid Speeding Tickets" [an article]

27e. Quotation Marks around Words Used in Special Ways

When we put quotation marks around a single word or phrase, we are indicating that the word(s) in the quotes should be interpreted in a special sense. If we overuse this marking, our readers will not be able to follow our writing.

> My friend has a "special" problem. She cannot tolerate birds' singing.

27f. Inappropriate Quotation Marks

If you have not seen quotation marks used in a specific way, that use is most likely inappropriate.

Now do Exercise 27-1 and 27-2.

27g. Ellipsis Marks to Show Omissions

Remember that *three* spaced periods indicate an omission within one sentence, while four spaced periods indicate an omission involving more than one sentence.

> She asked me to bring . . . and her <u>gun.</u> [part of a sentence missing]
> She asked me to bring her gun. . . . The authorities were looking for her. [several *sentences* are missing]

Notice that the first of the four periods really belongs to the first sentence.

> She asked me to bring her gun.

27h. Ellipsis Mark to Show Interruption in Dialogue

If you need to indicate that a thought was unfinished or interrupted, you can use three spaced periods.

> *Incorrect*: "My friends won't be here..."
> *Correct*: "My friends won't be here . . ."

Now do Exercise 27-3.

EXERCISE 27-1

NAME _____ DATE _____

Correct any misuse of quotation marks or any other punctuation mark. You may need to revise the sentences a little or to add quotation marks.

Example: She said ", Where are you going?"
                 She said, "Where are you going?"

1. Then, they asked me "if I had read the story 'Alone.' "

2. They asked me, "Have you ever read "Alone?" "

3. She screamed, "You'll never work again"!

4. Why did you insist on discovering his "surprise?"

5. According to the article "Hope for Humanity", there will be just enough energy for the next twenty years.

6. We will sing the following lines from "Lost in Dreams:"

7. Martin once said, "They'll never understand my works in this century." (Marks 321)

8. "The first blow must be for freedom, Albert maintained."

9. Are you sure that he said, "How long have you owned that 'monstrosity?' "?

10. In his last "letter", the prisoner scribbled his confession on the walls of the cell.

Score _____

EXERCISE 27-2

NAME_____ **DATE** _____

Remove or alter any inappropriate quotation marks. You may need to revise the sentences. You may also need to consult the handbook for specific cases.

Example: "After all," we did get it done.
                 After all, we did get it done.

1. "Kevin said, Well, let's go."

2. We all just knew him as "Brother Bubba."

3. That man over there is George, "Prince Tango," Wilson.

4. "Hope for Humanity" [title on first page of a manuscript]

5. Finally, they replied, <<No way!>>

6. Then the salesperson offered us a "special deal.

7. Have you read his latest poem *Summers at Christmas?*

8. That poem appeared in the last issue of "*A.*"

9. *Summertime* is also from *Porgy and Bess.*

10. Did Elaine ask, "Did Marcy really ask, "Do you understand the use of the quotation mark now?""

                                             Score _____

EXERCISE 27-3

NAME _____ DATE _____

Follow the instructions in brackets. If there are none, correct any misuse of ellipsis marks.

1. " . . . . Furthermore, I will not leave," he insisted.

2. She started to speak, "Have you seen . . . ?"

3. Then, Robert insisted that " . . . the school is being ignored."

4. Harold wrote, "The marks that we have found on the side of the mountains in no way give support to the UFO theory. Furthermore, the hysteria provoked by those insensitive journalists is damaging the stability of this institution. When we have completed our report, we will release our complete files." [Omit everything from "by" to "journalists."]

5. Harold wrote, "The marks that we have found on the side of the mountains in no way give support to the UFO theory. Furthermore, the hysteria provoked by those insensitive journalists is damaging the stability of this institution. When we have completed our report, we will release our complete files." [Omit everything from "furthermore" to "institution."]

Score _____

28

Italics/ Underlining

For most purposes, italics and underlining are the same thing. However, as some word processors now allow both italics and underlining, we need to be careful in distinguishing them from each other.

28a. Italics/Underlining in Titles

Usually only works that can stand by themselves are underlined. (See 27d for information on quotation marks in titles.)

Moby Dick [a novel]

Remember that standard religious texts are *not* underlined.

The Bible   The Book of Mormon

Now do Exercise 28-1.

28b. Italics/Underlining for Words, Numbers, and Letters Used as Such

See 27e. Either italics or underlining is acceptable to indicate that we are using words as words.

28c. Italics/Underlining for Sound

Nonsense words are underlined.

I thought she said zmeheh.

28d. Italics/Underlining for Foreign Words

Even though we always use Latin names of animals and plants in scientific writing, those words are still signaled as foreign by being underlined.

If you were to give an example of a word from your native language in an essay or paper, you would need to underline it.

>   In Indonesia, we often eat <u>tempeh</u>.

28e. Italics/Underlining for Vehicles Designated by Proper Names

Sometimes proper names are given to vehicles [planes, boats, cars, trains, skateboards, etc.]. When those names are written, they must be underlined.

>   The <u>Titanic</u> sank quickly.

28f. Italics/Underlining for Emphasis

Do not overuse underlining for emphasis. It <u>quickly</u> loses its impact.

Now do Exercise 28-2.

EXERCISE 28-1

NAME _____ **DATE** _____

If underlining is incorrectly used, correct it. If underlining is needed, supply it. Explain why you did what you did. You might need to review the information in 27d before you do this exercise.

Example: The <u>Koran</u> has been translated into English.
The Koran has been translated into English.
[Standard religious books are not underlined.]

1. His most famous short story is <u>Owls at Noon</u>.

2. Sting's album "The Dream of Blue Turtles" was very haunting.

3. <u>Aida's</u> [an opera] appeal is its message of peace and hope within a frightful tragedy.

4. <u>Handbook of Tennessee Oaks</u> was the first report the publishing firm produced.

5. Almost every American house has the <u>Sears Catalog</u>.

6. This year Memphis will have three productions of the "Nutcracker," which is my son's favorite ballet.

7. We have yet to see the Mona Lisa.

8. Her first successful poem, "Thoughts of Stone, Thoughts of Sand," was over three hundred pages long.

9. Every week I read the "Nation," the <u>New</u> Republic, and the National Review. I really enjoy these magazines.

10. Would you say that the theme of <u>Man's Fate</u> is as universal as that of the movie <u>They Shoot Horses, Don't They</u>?

Score _____

EXERCISE 28-2

NAME _____ **DATE** _____

Some underlining is missing and some underlining is inappropriate. Correct both situations. Explain why you have made any alterations.

Example: "Pagans and Roses" is a book worth reading.
<u>Pagans and Roses</u> is a book worth reading.
[Books are underlined.]

1. All night I could hear the drip from the faucet—thunk, thunk, thunk.

2. Giselle is the most widely performed ballet in the South.

3. Can you believe that she "still" enjoys typing, after all those years?

4. Entre nous, the judge has no chance to win confirmation.

5. We hope to travel on the City of New Orleans when we take the train to <u>Chicago</u>.

6. The scientific name for <u>horse</u> is Equus caballus.

7. Why would anyone name a warship the <u>Flower of Peace</u>?

8. Nobody can see the 48 I painted on the side of my house.

9. When someone sneezes, many Americans say "Gesundheit!"

10. Some children confuse b with d.

Score _____

29

Hyphens
and
Slashes

Remember that hyphens and slashes are used inside sentences. They are used in words.

29a. Hyphens in Compound Nouns and Verbs

Compound nouns and verbs are either hyphenated, written together, or written separately. However, there is no way to predict which way will be used. Use a dictionary to help you do Exercise 29-1.

29b. Hyphens in Compound Modifiers

We use hyphens in compound modifiers to help the reader.

> *Unclear:* We use two letter codes. [We need to use two codes for a code that has two letters.]
> *Clear:* We use two-letter codes.

29c. Hyphens with Some Prefixes

Always use hyphens with *self-*, *ex-*, or *all-*. For the other prefixes, ease of reading is the determining factor.

> ex-wife
> self-denial
> all-knowing
> *Unclear:* reentry
> *Clear:* re-entry
> *Clear:* return

29d. Hyphens in Numbers

If you write out a number, remember to use hyphens for all numbers between twenty-one and ninety-nine. Now do Exercise 29-2.

29e. Hyphens for Word Divisions at the Ends of Lines

You must look up any word you wish to divide. Syllabication is often very confusing. Also, remember that you cannot leave one letter at the end or the beginning of a line.

> *Incorrect*: zinni-
> a
> *Better*: zin-
> nia

Now do Exercise 29-3.

29f. Slashes between Alternatives

Use slashes between alternatives only in informal papers.

> *Informal*: Choose—apples/oranges
> *Formal*: Choose either apples or oranges.

29g. Slashes for Making Combinations

When two or more words or numbers should be thought of as one, you can use slashes to accomplish that goal. They moved to the *Dallas/Ft. Worth* area.

You also use slashes to separate the month from the day and from the year. That order [month/day/year] must be followed in the USA; otherwise confusion can result.

> *Date*: May 6, 1984
> *USA*: 5/6/84
> *Many others*: 6/5/84

29h. Slashes between Lines of Poetry

If you must quote poetry in a paper, you can use slashes to separate the lines in prose form.

29i. Slashes for Fractions

For ratios, we use colons [3:4], but for fractions we use slashes [3/4].

Now do Exercise 29-4 as a review for all uses of slashes.

EXERCISE 29-1

NAME _____ **DATE**_____

Should the following be hyphenated, joined into one word, or left as two separate words? Use a dictionary to help you.

Example: shore bird
shorebird

1. shot gun _____

2. Mexican American _____

3. tape player _____

4. home grown _____

5. narrow minded _____

6. stomach ache _____

7. co editor _____

8. co owner _____

9. disco lounge _____

10. half life _____

Score _____

EXERCISE 29-2

NAME _____ DATE_____

Determine whether these hyphens are correctly placed. You might need a dictionary to complete this exercise.

Example: openended   <u>open-ended</u>

1. dead-end _____

2. nonamerican _____

3. fiftyseven bottles _____

4. during the years 1954 —1958 _____

5. One third pound of ground beef _____

6. a poorly-planned meeting _____

7. selfdenial _____

8. a-void _____

9. ten- or twenty-million people _____

10. semiinterested _____

Score _____

EXERCISE 29-3

NAME _____ DATE_____

Are the hyphens in the following words correctly placed for word division? If not, supply the correct word division.

Example: ment-hol   <u>men-thol</u>

1. di-ffi-cul-ty _____

2. doub-le _____

3. so-cial-ism _____

4. harm-o-ny _____

5. land-lady _____

6. ra-di-o _____

7. irr-a-tion-al _____

8. al-coh-ol _____

9. cash-i-er _____

10. hiber-nate _____

Score _____

EXERCISE 29-4

NAME _____ **DATE**_____

If you can, use slashes to show alternatives, combinations, dates, or fractions.

Example: April 7, 1845
                    4/7/45

1. We were able to increase sales only by one-third.

2. Date of birth: August 18,1943

3. This program is only for university or college students.

4. We flew into the Tampa and St. Petersburg airport.

5. Why did you insist on selling two-fifths of the stock?

6. You must purchase all train or bus tickets downtown.

7. This room category is single or double.

8. They're going to name their show <u>The Wayne and Wong Comedy Spectacular.</u>

9. Effective date 16 January 1968

10. Of course, he or she must sign this form.

Score _____

30

Abbreviations and Numbers

30a. Abbreviations vs. Full Words

You cannot abbreviate just any word. Be sure your abbreviations are acceptable for American audiences.

Time designations

If you wish to avoid using time designations that refer specifically to Christianity [*B.C.* means *before Christ* and *A.D.* means *in the year of our Lord*], you may use *C.E.*, which means *common era*, and *B.C.E.*, meaning *before common era*. Both these forms *follow* the date.

The Han dynasty lasted from 202 B.C.E. to 220 C.E.

30b. Punctuation and Capitalization in Abbreviations

Use a recent dictionary to be sure of correct punctuation and capitalization in abbreviations.

30c. Numbers Expressed in Numerals

You should consult the style sheet you will be using to determine when numbers should be expressed in numerals (e.g. 16).

You should always use numerals for standard dates.

Never begin a sentence with a number expressed in numerals. Rewrite the sentence if you must.

Incorrect: *17* students were given scholarships.
Better: Scholarships were given to *17* students.

30d. Numbers Expressed in Words

Only use numbers expressed in words (e.g. *twenty-one*) when the style sheet you are using requires you to.

30e. Mixed Numerals and Words

Sometimes two numbers occur next to each other in a paper. Try to make one a word (preferably the first); the other should remain a number.

Clear. She assigned four 5-page essays.

Now do Exercise 30-1, which reviews uses of abbreviations and numbers.

EXERCISE 30-1

NAME _____ **DATE** _____

In each sentence, there is a problem with an abbreviation. Correct that problem.

1. Last yr. I went to Austria.

2. While there, I met Dr. Fritz von Halle, Ph.D.

3. He has an outrageous I.Q., but he is really strange.

4. 1st, he mumbles to himself in rhymed verse.

5. He insists that he was born in 1854 B.C. [change to alternate system]

6. N.a.t.o. is an effective organization.

7. We can't remember if we were to send the 12 lb.s to Collierville, TN., or New York, N.Y.

8. She enjoys opera (eg, <u>Tosca</u> or <u>Aida</u>).

9. They were elected in 1452 A.D.

10. I will leave by 11.

Score _____

31

Capital Letters

Many ESL writers use different writing systems in their native languages. For some of them, just forming the English letters is a challenge at first. Some have never become accustomed to the importance we place on *capitalization.*

If the Latin alphabet is not the first writing system you learned, be careful that you do not use capital letters randomly.

Incorrect and disturbing: i Was the First chiLd in my fAmily to learn to Ski.

31a. Capitalization of First Words

Always capitalize the first letter of the first word of a sentence (see 24e for the only exception). We also usually capitalize the first word of a line of poetry.

31b. Capitalization of Proper Names and Proper Adjectives

In English, you must always capitalize proper nouns (see Chapter 1). Additionally, you must capitalize the names of different groups and the adjectives that describe them or their language.

Muslim	Christian
French	Coptic
Jew	Panamanian
Memphian	Swiss

You must capitalize those names even if you don't like those people.

31c. Capitalization of Titles of Honor or Rank

You should usually capitalize titles before names. Some people capitalize important titles that do not precede names. As long as you are consistent, it will be acceptable.

The Queen
a letter from the Secretary of Defense
Dear Madam:

31d.   Capitalization of Academic and Professional Degrees

Capitalize academic degrees only when they are abbreviated or follow a name.

> *Incorrect:* She is working on her ph.d.
> *Correct:* She is working on her Ph.D.

31e.   Capitalization in Titles of Written Material and Artistic Works

Although the rules given in the handbook are basically correct, there are some style sheets that have different rules for capitalization in titles. However, unless you are instructed to do otherwise, follow the rules in the handbook. Use them to do Exercise 31-1.

31f.   Capitalization in Some Abbreviations

Just follow whatever examples you find in the literature with which you deal most frequently.

31g.   Capitalization of *I*

In English, the pronoun *I* is always capitalized. This use is just a printing convention.

31h.   Inappropriate Capitals

If you have not seen a specific example of a possible use of capitals, that use is probably inappropriate. Areas of study are capitalized only in reference to a specific course.

> *Inappropriate:* Malaysian Literature
> *Appropriate:* She teaches Introduction to Malaysian Literature.

Don't capitalize the common noun in a compound with a proper noun.

> *Incorrect:* Alaskan Husky
> *Correct:* Alaskan husky

EXERCISE 31-1

NAME _____ **DATE** _____

Capitalize the following titles.

Example: the first snow
The First Snow

1. fires of heaven

2. "paradox: live without living"

3. i want to live!

4. conquering the fears within! live freely!

5. the rinehart esl workbook

6. How much? a guide to bargaining

7. co-owned clubs: fast money for fast people

8. cigarettes and holy smoke

9. "twenty-six north parkway"

10. reflections on a broken mirror

Score _____

EXERCISE 31-2

NAME _____ DATE _____

Decide which of the following words should be capitalized. Some may already be incorrectly capitalized. You may need to consult the handbook on some issues.

Example: she works on Tuesday.
She works on Tuesday.

1. "During the last shortage," Eva said, "There weren't even enough potatoes."

2. do you have the car keys?

3. Elizabeth has gone to Florida; Her mother has gone to Denver.

4. Capitalize the first letter of complete sentences (see 24e for the only exception).

5. She firmly believes that "The movement will triumph over darkness."

6. types of roses
I. hybrid tea
II. cabbage
III. damask
IV. Climbers
V. Ramblers

7. Dear sir:

8.   Yours Most Sincerely,

9.   We seek but one goal: freedom. [formal]

10.   he sent us another example of that horrible poetry of his:

     At last we walk the silent shores
     and listen to the distant oars.
     Our thoughts upon the lives we lost
     when first the path this way was crossed.

Score _____

EXERCISE 31-3

NAME _____ DATE _____

Decide which of these words should be capitalized. Some may be already incorrectly capitalized.

Example: the memphian character
                the Memphian character [adjective derived from proper noun]

1. central station in New York

2. the age of Reason

3. mayor Hackett

4. medal of valor

5. lithuanian

6. independence day

7. What is your sister's name?

8. xerox

9. cities beautiful Commission

10. english language

Score _____

EXERCISE 31-4

NAME _____ DATE _____

There are some problems with capitalization in the following sentences. Explain what is wrong and correct it.

Example: a. An english setter is a nice dog.
b. Proper adjectives are usually capitalized.
c. An English setter is a nice dog.

1. a. We really enjoy eating chinese food at juan Ching's.

   b.

   c.

2. a. but then, i always enjoy free food.

   b.

   c.

3. a. Our family met Juan when he was still majoring in Economics.

   b.

   c.

4. a. But after he took my Father's class in cornish literature, he became an english major.

   b.

   c.

5. a. Now mother and I visit juan mondays to learn to cook with the wildest combinations of cuban and taiwanese food.

   b.

   c.

6. a. My mother is from the north.

   b.

   c.

7. a. We prefer to go South for the Winter.

   b.

   c.

8. a. Her Sister is always bothering Grandma Bates.

   b.

   c.

9. a. Some planets have more than one Moon.

   b.

   c.

10. a. Algebra should be the most difficult course you take at any University.

    b.

    c.

Score _____

Part **IV**

☐ **Improving Prose: Style**
☐

32

Choosing Words

32a. Establishing the Formality

You will want to ask your instructor for help in determining the appropriate level of formality in your assignments. Usually, you should aim for a moderately formal tone in most of your work.

Often ESL students sound too formal because they use one-word verbs where native speakers of American English would use the less formal phrasal verbs or verbs with prepositions.

> *One-word verb:* The clients *castigated* the new owner.
> *Verb with preposition:* The clients *yelled at* the new owner.

Try to use the structure most appropriate to the level you are seeking.

32b. Controlling the Meaning

As a writer, you are in charge of determining what the reader understands. You must decide how specific or how general you wish to make your text.

(1) Denotation and connotation

In writing, we must pay careful attention to the *connotation* of words. For example, *cheap* and *thrifty* mean about the same thing; however, *cheap* is used only in negative contexts. *Thrifty*, on the other hand, is usually positive. As a result, we would stay in a motel called "Thrifty Suites," but we would not stay at a place named "Cheap Sheets."

Unfortunately, dictionaries are not much help in this area. Many times the dictionary (especially a small bilingual dictionary) will mislead you. You must observe how words are used before you can be sure that you are using them correctly.

Now try Exercise 32-1 and 32-2.

(2) General and specific words

In writing, we don't want too many general words, but we also don't want too many specific words. Usually, ESL students use too many general words because they lack the exact term they are looking for. As a result, they often write *around* the term.

> *Too general:* the man working in the hotel
> *Exact term:* the desk clerk

Do Exercise 32-3 to practice using specific and general terms.

(3) Abstract and concrete words

As with specific and general terms, you should try for a balance of abstract [impersonal] and concrete [personal or familiar] words. Exercise 32-4 will help you with these concepts.

32c.   Speaking with Vigor

Remember that in English we expect *you* to come up with something original when you write. We don't want you to repeat what someone else has already said. Thus, to speak with vigor, you must try new ideas and find new ways to express them.

(1) Clichés

Clichés are expressions that have been overused. In speech, we may use clichés such as *busy as a bee*. In writing, however, we should strive to avoid clichés. Avoiding clichés is often difficult, since in many cultures the use of clichés is normal and expected in writing.

(2) Euphemisms

Normally, we avoid euphemisms for people. But you should observe the local euphemisms for *toilets* and *bodily functions* (this term is itself a euphemism) and use them.

32d.   Clearing Out the Clutter

In American English, we normally want our writing to be very clear. Rid your work of unnecessary phrases, words, and dense noun phrases.

(1) Gobbledygook

Governments love "gobbledygook," which is just silliness in verbal form. You should probably never need to use gobbledygook. Exercises 32-5 and 32-6 will help you learn to recognize and correct gobbledygook.

(2) Surplus words

Some cultures enjoy and insist on redundancies [repetitions] in speech.

> Her life was *full and complete.*
> My very best *personal friend* was here today.

Indeed, some of the most beautiful verses in the Bible are crafted from poetic repetitions. However, in the USA, we are usually in a hurry. Accordingly, we avoid any redundancies.

(3) Dense noun phrases

Many languages allow noun phrases that can sometimes be interpreted in several ways. For example, *Tennessee History Commission* could be a commission on Tennessee history or a commission in Tennessee on all history. These noun phrases are called *dense* and should be rewritten when possible so that they will not be misinterpreted. Do Exercise 32-7 to practice rewriting dense noun phrases.

32e. Avoiding Sexist Language

In current usage, we must avoid sexist language: language that makes unnecessary reference to gender. We must also avoid making impolite reference to ethnic or racial issues. Try Exercise 32-8, which deals with avoiding sexist language.

EXERCISE 32-1

NAME _____ DATE _____

Supply a more appropriate word or phrase for the underlined one. You may also use negatives (e.g. <u>not very large</u>).

Example: Her feet were very puny.
Her feet were very small.

1. The <u>old</u> woman next door is always so pleasant.

2. One of my sisters is rather <u>fat</u>.

3. I'm afraid that Fritz is <u>stupid</u>.

4. You are entitled to your own <u>superstitions</u>.

5. The dogs had a <u>stench</u> about them.

6. Liza is a <u>fanatic</u> in a mild way.

7. My opponent is a <u>crook</u>.

8. His laugh was a little <u>sinister</u>.

9. The waitress was <u>slow</u>.

10. Your absence was <u>heinous</u>.

Score _____

EXERCISE 32-2

Replace the underlined informal words with more formal counterparts.

Example: The <u>guy</u> was punctual.
The man was punctual.

1. Where could we <u>buy</u> a television?

2. Are you forbidden to consume <u>booze</u> by your religion?

3. My family has sincerely enjoyed the <u>atmosphere</u> you have created in this exhibition.

4. <u>You gotta</u> be more careful.

5. Let's decide this in the <u>bar</u>.

6. Mrs. Brooks is always very <u>bouncy</u>.

7. We <u>shouldn't</u> have labored so long.

8. When might we <u>bank on</u> your compiled manuscript?

9. Unfortunately, the gentleman was somewhat <u>looped</u> when he returned our message.

10. <u>Beep in</u> when you want to talk.

Score _____

EXERCISE 32-3

NAME _____ DATE _____

Make the underlined word or words more general or specific according to the direction in brackets. You may be as creative as you wish.

Example: <u>A woman</u> spoke to me yesterday. [specific]
A ballerina spoke to me yesterday.

1. A woman <u>spoke</u> to me yesterday. [specific]

2. <u>Sometime</u> we must visit the Alps. [general]

3. <u>On Tuesday at eleven o'clock in the morning</u>, I expect to see you in court. [general]

4. I must do <u>some things</u> before dinner. [specific]

5. Do you enjoy <u>sushi</u>? [general]

6. The <u>person working on the plane</u> gave me a magazine. [specific]

7. The person working on the plane gave me <u>a magazine</u>. [general]

8. Why do you like <u>Wendy's</u>? [general]

9. Why do you like <u>Wendy's</u>? [specific]

10. The clerk <u>got</u> a shirt for me from another store. [specific]

Score _____

EXERCISE 32-4

Provide abstractions for the following concrete representations.

Example: weddings
hope for the future

1. dirty, run-down houses

2. fixing a flat tire

3. voting for an unpopular candidate

4. choosing your own major

5. failing your driving test

6. taking your driving test again

7. refusing to agree with a crowd when you think you're right

8. sitting on the banks of the Mississippi, watching the sun slowly set as you talk with two of your best friends

9. watching your baby brother graduate from high school

10. wanting to be the best

Score _____

EXERCISE 32-5

Take a paragraph from one of your more technical texts. Try to "translate" the paragraph into standard, non-technical English.

Score _____

EXERCISE 32-6

Go to the documents room of your library and find a government document about any subject. Try to "translate" one paragraph into standard, clear English.

Score _____

EXERCISE 32-7

NAME _____ **DATE** _____

Rewrite these dense noun phrases.

Example: committee chairman evaluation
evaluation of committee chairmen
evaluation for committee chairmen

1. recent arrivals assistance efforts

2. university health center

3. pension plan analysis form

4. new adjusters handbook

5. final paycheck assessment forms

Score _____

EXERCISE 32-8

NAME _____ DATE _____

Supply a non-sexist form for each of the following.

Example: chairman
            the chair

1. meter maid _____

2. policeman _____

3. stewardess _____

4. clergymen _____

5. newspaperman _____

6. newspaper boy _____

7. queen _____

8. actress _____

9. grantsman _____

10. a lady doctor _____

Score _____

33

Choosing Structures

When reading Chapter 33, you might need to review Chapter 5 and Chapter 7.

33a. Varying Sentence Lengths, Structures, and Beginnings

First, you should just write what you can. After you have gotten your rough draft under control, you can try the techniques given in the handbook for varying sentence elements. But first, you must be sure that your organization, content, and analysis are in fine order.

However, there are some easy techniques that allow you to combine two or more sentences to vary length. In Exercises 33-1 and 33-2 there are examples of these techniques, which you may try as you edit your drafts.

33b. Achieving Emphasis

Unless you are very advanced, you should not try too many "stylistic flourishes." You should concentrate on simple, clear structures. The only "flourish" you should consider attempting to produce in early compositions is the *cleft sentence*.

The cleft sentence really allows us to focus on a particular aspect of a sentence.

> *Base:* Sabina cooks German dishes.
> *Cleft to emphasize who:* It is Sabina who cooks German dishes.
> *Cleft to emphasize what:* It is German dishes that Sabina cooks.

It is Exercise 33-3 that works with cleft sentences.

33c. Streamlining Prose

Most Americans enjoy a quick, rapid style. If you practice streamlining your prose, your writing will come closer to that ideal.

(1) Empty verbs and nominalizations

As you revise your compositions, use your dictionary to determine whether there are action verbs that can replace any nouns you might have.

> *Weak:* She was having a discussion about the project with the clients.
> *Revised:* She was discussing the project with the clients.

Now do Exercise 33-4.

(2) Weak passives

Although you can use the passive effectively, you should try to use it only when necessary. Practice ridding sentences of weak passives in Exercise 33-5.

(3) Unnecessary *that, who,* and *which* clauses

When possible, use adjectives rather than adjective clauses.

> *Unnecessary:* His style, which is precise and neat, wins him many prizes.
> *Revised:* His style, precise and neat, wins him many prizes.

(4) Excessive verb forms

Try not to have too many possible main verbs in a sentence. Remember that each possible main verb is a new idea. Don't jam your ideas into one complex jungle.

(5) Making a clear connection between subject and verb

Keep the connection between subjects and verbs as clear as possible.

33d. Using Figures of Speech

Some cultures enjoy very "flowery" figurative language. However, figurative language should be rare in English prose. Especially in business correspondence, you should be careful to avoid creating flowery constructions; just stick to traditional forms.

> *Flowery:* Most honored and responsible sir:
> *Traditional:* Dear Sir:

33e. Working with Sound and Rhythm

When you have produced a well-organized rough draft, you can work on the sound and rhythm of your sentences.

EXERCISE 33-1

NAME _____ DATE _____

Combine these pairs of sentences with the technique suggested in brackets.

Example: The answers are in the back. Look at them after you have finished.
                  [;]
                  The answers are in the back; look at them after you have finished.

1. The family likes the city. The family also likes the school system. [not only but also]

2. His songs contain vague references to his past life. They also contain vague references, to his wife's past life. [and]

3. The lesson was poorly planned. It went just fine. [; transitional]

4. My novels are getting better. Or my taste is getting worse. [either, or]

5. Her music filled the park with beauty. Children stood hypnotized by the lush sound. [:]

6. The answers were not easily gotten. They were keys to greater knowledge. [, for]

7. The teachers failed to remember the test. And the administrators didn't either [Neither . . . nor]

8. The officials want to capture the spy. But they did not want to expose their plan. [combine infinitives]

9. Barry had always enjoyed working with animals. He became a veterinarian. [, so]

10. Paula left the basic plans to Peter. She left the detailed plans to us. [combine predicates]

Score _____

EXERCISE 33-2

NAME _____ DATE _____

Combine these pairs of sentences using the techniques of subordination suggested in brackets. You may need to review some of the terms used in this exercise.

Example: She lived in Memphis. She graduated from a local college. [when adverb clause from sentence 1]
 When she lived in Memphis, she graduated from a local college.

1. Judy graduated from a local college. The local college was not nationally recognized. [which adjective clause from sentence 2]

2. The team did not understand their opponents. They lost badly. [verbal phrase in sentence 1]

3. The Tiger Den is the only student club in the area. It is very well known. [appositive from sentence 1]

4. Many mistakes are made in entering the data. We have had no formal training. [since adverb clause in sentence 1]

5. The boys had lived in Amsterdam. They learned about diamonds there. [where adjective clause in sentence 2]

6. The crowd rushed the princess's carriage. They almost turned it over. [verbal **phrase in** sentence 2]

7. The registrar controls the actual process. The registrar is an extremely **patient,** considerate person. [appositive from sentence 2 inside sentence 1]

8. The chair had brought a good price at the auction. The auction was held **by the local** decorative arts group. [which adjective clause in sentence 2]

9. The issue had been dropped. She continued to dispute the findings. [although **adverb** clause in sentence 1]

10. The boy concentrated on only one issue. The one issue he concentrated **on was his** release. [: appositive at end of sentence 1]

Score _____

EXERCISE 33-3

NAME _____ **DATE** _____

From each of the following, make cleft sentences that emphasize the underlined word or
words.

Example: Marina studies <u>Spanish</u>.
                 It is Spanish that Marina studies.

1. Don lives in <u>Collierville</u>.

2. <u>Don</u> lives in Collierville.

3. <u>Yesterday afternoon</u>, Ellen stopped by for a quick chat.

4. Yesterday afternoon, <u>Ellen</u> stopped by for a quick chat.

5. Yesterday afternoon, Ellen stopped by <u>for a quick chat</u>.

6. <u>The administration</u> agreed to honor the contract.

7. My family used to know his <u>wife</u>.

8. <u>My family</u> used to know his wife.

9. <u>The directing, not the acting</u>, made that film good.

10. The founders were honored <u>for their good sense and foresight</u>.

Score _____

EXERCISE 33-4

NAME _____ DATE _____

Determine whether there are action verbs that can replace the underlined words. You may need to do some minor revisions in the sentences.

Example: She <u>made a nick</u> in the plate.
She <u>nicked</u> the plate.

1. The dentist <u>had to use a file</u> on my teeth.

2. The permit <u>has an expiration date of</u> May 23, 1999.

3. The army <u>moved to the flank</u> of the enemy.

4. The authorities <u>had hopes</u> that the strikers would give in.

5. The chef <u>made a mixture</u> of the ingredients on the table.

6. The model <u>held his posture</u> for the cameras.

7. The president <u>put her signature</u> on the treaty.

8. Each room should <u>make a note</u> of the votes.

9. Any member can <u>make a motion</u> to adjourn.

10. Of course, the chair <u>acted as chair</u> of the session.

Score _____

EXERCISE 33-5

NAME _____ DATE _____

Change these passives to actives. You may need to supply an agent.

Example: The car was wrecked.
                 Fritz wrecked the car.

1. You will be hurt by his promises.

2. The gift was really enjoyed by the children.

3. My son was promoted to lieutenant.

4. The change was stuck in his pocket.

5. The vote was recorded.

6. An analysis of his blood was made.

7. Have they been given a new assignment yet?

8. The group was banned in the US.

9. Their records were bought by millions.

10. Was it Claudia who was awarded a full scholarship to the university?

Score _____

Part V

□ The
Writing
Process
□

34

Getting
Ideas

It is a common saying that the best way to have a good idea is to have a lot of ideas. The first task of any writer is to generate ideas, many of them, before worrying about whether or not the ideas are any good. That decision comes later. This chapter contains exercises to set your mind free to create ideas.

Below is a list that matches each exercise with the appropriate section of the handbook. Remember that doing the exercises is much more important than just reading about techniques.

EXERCISE 34-1

NAME _____ **DATE** _____

There are two problems with keeping a journal. The first is deciding what to write. The second is building on what you have written. Below is a series of suggested journal entries that build on each other. Write for about ten minutes on each entry. Let at least one day, but not more than two, separate each entry.

Entry 1: Describe what you were like three years ago. Identify your attitudes toward what was going on around you. Pay particular attention to your emotions. How did you generally feel? How did you express those emotions? Who were your friends and what were they like? What were your major goals; that is, what did you hope to accomplish within the next year?

Entry 2: Describe what you are like today. Identify your attitudes toward what is going on around you today. Pay particular attention to your emotions. How do you generally feel? How do you express those emotions? Who are your friends and what are they like? What are your major goals; that is, what do you hope to accomplish within the next year?

Entry 3: Make two lists based on the first two entries. In the first list, jot down those aspects of your life and attitudes that are the same today as they were three years ago. In the second list, jot down those aspects of your life and attitudes that have changed. You do not need to write down complete sentences.

Entry 4: Look at one or two items from the list of aspects of your life that have changed. Try to explain to yourself why these aspects have changed. You don't need to begin the entry with an answer. Rather, you might begin with an observation such as, "I wonder why I seem to fight less with my parents than I did three years ago."

Score _____

EXERCISE 34-2

NAME _____ **DATE** _____

We all have "guilty pleasures," which we secretly enjoy but which we are ashamed to admit. For instance we may enjoy watching cheap horror movies or eating pints of chocolate ice cream. Think about some favorite guilty pleasure, why it gives you pleasure, and why you feel guilty about it. After you have meditated on your guilty pleasure for five minutes, describe the pleasure briefly and explain why you feel guilty about it.

Score _____

EXERCISE 34-3

NAME _____ DATE _____

In the spaces provided, write down twenty ideas about the topic listed below. Spend no more than three minutes on this assignment.

Topic: You have just been called on to explain your culture or way of life to a group of people totally unfamiliar with you or your culture. QUICK—what do you mention or describe?

1. _____

2. _____

3. _____

4. _____

5. _____

6. _____

7. _____

8. _____

9. _____

10. _____

11. _____

12. _____

13. _____

14. _____

15. _____

16. _____

17. _____

18. _____

19. _____

20. _____

Score _____

EXERCISE 34-4

NAME _____ **DATE** _____

Review 34d on clustering in the handbook and use this page to draw appropriate lines and balloons out from the topic given in the middle of the page. You might wish to think about such issues as physical appearance, an anecdote (short story), how others see the relative, and how the relative sees you and other members of your family.

My Favorite Relative

Name _____

Score _____

EXERCISE 34-5

NAME _____ **DATE** _____

A. Complete the sentence below and then use it as the lead sentence for your freewriting. Write for exactly five minutes. Then go on to part B of this exercise. Do not worry if you wander from the original topic. The point of freewriting is to discover a topic, not merely to write about one. You will need to use your own notebook paper for the first part of this exercise.

I always have trouble when it comes to _____ (list your most difficult

subject). Whenever I think about _____ , I . . . (continue writing for five

minutes).

B. Go over what you have just written. Select the <u>best</u> <u>sentence</u> from what you wrote above and copy it below. Use that sentence as your lead sentence and continue writing for five minutes. Again, use your own paper.

C. Underline the <u>best</u> <u>sentence</u> from the freewriting in B. Explain briefly whether or not the sentence you just underlined could form the basis for an effective essay.

Score_____

EXERCISE 34-6

NAME _____ DATE _____

Ladders are ways of learning to become more specific and concrete. For each of the terms below supply three or four increasingly specific terms.

Example: Food
Ethnic food
Chinese food
Szechuan beef

1. Temperature

    _____

    _____

    _____

    _____

2. The future

    _____

    _____

    _____

    _____

3. Television

    _____

    _____

    _____

    _____

4. Jobs

_____

_____

_____

_____

5. Racism

_____

_____

_____

_____

Score_____

EXERCISE 34-7

NAME _____ DATE _____

List ten questions on <u>one</u> of the topics below.

A. Government support for poor people

B. Immigration quotas

C. Equal rights for women

D. Requiring all residents of the United States to learn English

1.

2.

3.

4.

5.

6.

7.

8.

9.

10.

Score_____

EXERCISE 34-8

NAME _____ DATE _____

Answer the following questions about the day you graduated from high school. [If you did not go through high school graduation, pick some other public event that marked a turning point in your life—for instance, your twenty-first birthday or a close relative's funeral. Answer the equivalent questions.]

1. Who were the most important people present?

2. What people significant to you were *not* present?

3. What did you think about during the graduation ceremony?

4. When did you realize that your life was somehow going to be different after high school?

5. Where did the graduation take place? What did the place look like?

6. How did you feel, and why did you feel the way you did during graduation?

7. How did others feel during graduation?

Score_____

EXERCISE 34-9

NAME _____ DATE _____

Ask ten logical questions about *one* of the following topics.

A. Preparing for an examination

B. My best friend before coming to college

C. My last birthday

D. Being really rich

1.

2.

3.

4.

5.

6.

7.

8.

9.

10.

Score_____

EXERCISE 34-10

NAME _____ **DATE** _____

The classical topics are definition, comparison, relationship, circumstance, and testimony. Which classical topic most closely fits each statement below?

1. We always hurt those we love. _____

2. If grades were abolished, we would all be better students. _____

3. Preparing for an examination is like getting ready for a race. _____

4. Holiday depression results from the pressure to appear to be happier than we feel.

   _____

5. English composition is more difficult than chemistry. _____

Score _____

EXERCISE 34-11

NAME _____ DATE _____

Read through a recent issue of *Time, Newsweek*, or other weekly news magazine. List five facts that you found out from your reading and that you could develop into short essays. Draw each fact from a different article in the magazine.

Name of magazine _____ Date of issue _____

1.

2.

3.

4.

5.

Score _____

35

Making Decisions

The key to effective writing lies in identifying an appropriate audience, establishing a purpose for writing, and creating an appropriate voice or tone.

EXERCISE 35-1

NAME _____ DATE _____

Identify a possible purpose for each of the following topics.

Example: Topic: How to buy a good used car.
Purpose: To explain the three main points in buying a used car—talking to the previous owner; having the car checked by a mechanic; looking at overall condition.

1. Topic: Mandatory drug testing in high schools
   Purpose:

2. Topic: How to change a flat tire
   Purpose:

3. Topic: Which is better—Wendy's or McDonald's?
   Purpose:

4. Topic: How I lost my best friend
   Purpose:

5. Topic: How to avoid getting a speeding ticket
   Purpose:

6. Topic: The role of women in today's society
   Purpose:

Score _____

EXERCISE 35-2

NAME _____   **DATE** _____

Identify a possible *audience* for each of the following topics.

Example: Topic: How to buy a good used car
Audience: People under thirty with little knowledge of cars and less than $2,000 to spend.

1. Topic: Mandatory drug testing in high schools
    Audience:

2. Topic: How to change a flat tire
    Audience:

3. Topic: Which is better—Wendy's or McDonald's?

4. Topic: How I lost my best friend
    Audience

5. Topic: How to avoid getting a speeding ticket
    Audience

6. Topic: The role of women in today's society
    Audience:

Score _____

EXERCISE 35-3

Write two letters. In the first letter, ask your parents, or another appropriate person, for money to help with your education. In the second letter, write to a friend explaining how you have gone about persuading your parents to give you some money. You may wish to give your friend advice on how to ask for money. Note which letter was easier to write. Note major differences in word choice. Which letter sounds more like you?

Letter to parents:

Letter to friend:

Score _____

EXERCISE 35-4

NAME _____ DATE _____

Each of the following thesis statements is too broad. In the space provided, write a *narrowed* thesis.

1. Broad: Young people should show old people more respect.
   Narrowed:

2. Broad: (Your city/town) is a nice place to live.
   Narrowed:

3. Broad: Everybody expects something for nothing.
   Narrowed:

4. Broad: Criminals ought to be punished more severely.
   Narrowed.

5. Broad: My room reveals my personality.
   Narrowed:

Score _____

36

Ensuring a Logical Composition

36a. Gathering Evidence

In many composition assignments, you will not have time to do library research. Instead, you must depend on your own knowledge and experience to give substance to your paper. Exercise 36-1 deals with using common knowledge to start the evidence-gathering process. Exercise 36-2 involves logical fallacies.

EXERCISE 36-1

NAME _____ **DATE** _____

For each of the topics below, cite a specific experience or fact that you already know and that you can use in support of a paper on that topic.

1. Learning responsibility

2. Successful interviewing for a job

3. Discrimination on the basis of age, gender, or race

4. Learning a second language

5. Accepting limitations

Score _____

EXERCISE 36-2

NAME _____ DATE _____

Each of the following statements involves one or more of the logical fallacies listed below. Beside each statement, place the letter of the most appropriate term that identifies the fallacy in the statement.

A. Appeal to tradition

B. Irrelevant testimonial

C. *Ad hominem* attacks

D. *Post hoc* reasoning

E. Hasty generalization

1. People who speak with an accent are not as bright as those who speak without an

    accent. _____

2. Nixon's China policy was a disaster because Nixon was a crook. _____

3. English speakers must never end a sentence in a preposition. _____

4. Use Glow Toothpaste. Madonna, the famous rock star, uses it every day.

    _____

5. It must have been the crab salad. I was sick as a dog all night after eating the sandwich.

    _____

6. These apples are terrible. I just bit into one and it was sour. _____

7. We must have turkey at Thanksgiving. We've always had turkey at Thanksgiving.

    _____

8. The anti-drug laws must be good. After all, they are attacked by drug addicts.

    _____

9. Friday the thirteenth is an unlucky day. On the last Friday the thirteenth I lost my

    girlfriend and broke my foot. _____

10. Aerobics exercise must be good for you. Jane Fonda has promoted aerobics for years.

    _____

Score _____

37

Structuring the Composition

37a. Considering a Structure

It is important to determine the most appropriate structure for a composition as early in the composition process as possible. The handbook describes ten different structures: *description, narration, enumeration, comparison/contrast, classification, illustration, definition, analysis, problem/solution,* and *cause/effect.*

Exercise 37-1 gives you practice in finding appropriate structures.

37b. Drafting a Working Outline

You should try to work out a rough working outline to guide you during the writing. The rough working outline can be very informal.

EXERCISE 37-1

NAME _____ DATE _____

Which of the structures listed earlier might be most appropriate for each of the following ideas? Two or more answers might be correct.

Example: An honest man is more than someone who doesn't lie.
definition

1. The beauty of my hometown

2. More computers should be installed in the student labs to make it easier for all students to have access to a computer.

3. Ways to succeed in business

4. My first day in the USA

5. Malaysian and American school systems

6. Career opportunities for linguists

7. Required subjects according to their purpose

8. Madonna shows the power a pop star has

9. Why Homeless, Heartless is not a good book

10. Strategies for winning at badminton

See Chapter 34 for additional work in considering a structure or strategy.

EXERCISE 37-2

NAME _____ **DATE** _____

Make a rough working outline from these ideas about American television.

stereotypes   dull   commercial   mindless   informative

"what life should be"   "ignores real problems"

"misleads people"   "insufficient variety"

"information is predigested"   "people want to be entertained"

Score_____

EXERCISE 37-3

NAME _____ **DATE** _____

From the rough working outline you did for Exercise 3, make a more formal outline using either of the two systems [decimal or traditional].

Score _____

38

Drafting Paragraphs

First, write and then write some more. Don't worry about spelling, grammar, or punctuation. Just write. When you revise your composition, you can worry about those "details."

38a. Drafting Body Paragraphs

After you have worked up a rough outline, you might want to begin to draft body paragraphs. Many people waste time on getting the introduction "just right" before they begin the body paragraphs. Most of the time, it is easier to begin in the middle.

Constructing Paragraphs with Topic Sentences

Try always to have a clear topic sentence for each paragraph. Furthermore, you should try to put the topic sentence at the beginning of the paragraph.

A topic sentence should have a topic and a *controlling idea*. The controlling idea states the writer's thoughts, views, or ideas about the topic.

> *Topic sentence:* An enormous problem for doctors is the stress of making life-and-death decisions.
> *Topic:* an enormous problem for doctors
> *Controlling idea:* stress of making life-and-death decisions

Do Exercise 38-1 now.

38b. Drafting Introductory Paragraphs

Introductions must *hook* your reader. The introduction must convince your readers that they should continue and read the rest of your work.

As you saw in the handbook, there are many techniques for introducing a composition. Try different techniques for every paper you write.

Now do Exercise 36-2.

38c.   Drafting Concluding Paragraphs

Often compositions just stop. Sometimes one can almost see the countdown—"498, 499, 500 words, done!" And when that word is done, the paper is, too.

Perhaps the most traditional way to conclude a paper is to restate the thesis. This method is usually very effective. It is this method that you should use most often.

However, there are other effective means to conclude a composition.

First do Exercise 38-3. Then you will need to do Exercise 38-4. Conclude with Exercise 38-5, which is more general as a review.

EXERCISE 38-1

NAME _____ **DATE** _____

For each of the following topic sentences, write out the topic and the controlling idea.

1. The most important advantage the Democratic Party has in my city is the well-organized block leaders.

    Topic:

    Controlling idea:

2. The diversity of housing design in Memphis reminds us of the city's economic history.

    Topic:

    Controlling idea:

3. Aerobics is a safe way to reduce stress and tension.

    Topic:

    Controlling idea:

4. Driving after drinking can lead to death and destruction.

    Topic:

    Controlling idea:

5. The PerfectionPlus word processing program is powerful, yet flexible.

    Topic:

    Controlling idea:

6. We might increase our foreign trade if we produce better products.

    Topic:

    Controlling idea:

7. Randy's presence was unforgettable.

   Topic:

   Controlling idea:

8. Reducing the drinking age to eighteen would mean increased traffic deaths.

   Topic:

   Controlling idea:

9. Permitting smokers to smoke in public buildings is hazardous to non-smokers' health.

   Topic:

   Controlling idea:

10. A topic sentence must be clear and focused.

    Topic:

    Controlling idea:

Score _____

EXERCISE 38-2

NAME _____ DATE _____

Use two different techniques to write introductions for the last composition you did. Which technique was more effective? Why?

Score _____

EXERCISE 38-3

NAME _____   DATE _____

Taking the two introductions you have from Exercise 2, write two concluding paragraphs.

Score _____

EXERCISE 38-4

NAME _____ **DATE** _____

Take one of the conclusions you wrote in Exercise 3 and change it to another appropriate technique.

Score _____

EXERCISE 38-5

NAME _____ **DATE** _____

What technique might be appropriate for each of the following topics? Using the techniques in the handbook, suggest one or two techniques that might work.

Example: pollution
            making a recommendation

1. benefits of nuclear power

2. an interview with the last inhabitant of a dying town

3. the effects of increased drug activity

4. the inconclusive results of a program to help illiterate Americans learn to read

5. investigation of a new process for reducing stress

6. the benefits of increased literacy

7. rights of adopted children

8. newly discovered sources of energy

9. apathy toward stricter gun-control laws

10. interview with a famous playwright

Score _____

39

Revising

Revising is the most important step in the composition. You have important, good ideas to communicate; it is up to you, however, to ensure that those ideas can be understood as *you* want them to be.

39a. Checking Unity

Before you sit down to revise a paper, ask yourself what you have written about. Now, as you sit down, write down what you just thought. You can even write it in your native language if you want. First, compare that idea with your thesis statement. Are they similar? Let's look first at your thesis statement. Is it a complete sentence that expresses *one* opinion? If not, you must revise it. Now do Exercise 39-1.

With your revised thesis statement in mind, read your composition through and ask yourself whether your reader would easily and clearly understand what you wanted to communicate. Ask yourself whether each paragraph in your composition relates directly to your thesis statement. Do Exercises 39-2 and 39-3.

39b. Checking Development

When people write in a second language, they are often worried about using too many words. They are afraid that, with every new word or idea, they will make new and frightening mistakes. Don't worry. It is good and, in fact, essential to make mistakes if you wish to improve your writing abilities.

Because of the "fear of words," ESL writers tend not to use sufficient supporting information. When you write, add more details even if you think you have already added enough. Remember that it is better to add too many details than to have too few. Although it is unlikely that you will have too many details, you can just cross them out later if you do. Try adding details in Exercise 39-4.

39c. Achieving Coherence

To help your composition flow smoothly, be sure that you have adequate connections between sentences and paragraphs. Use many transitional expressions and subordinating conjunctions. In many cultures, a writer doesn't need to be explicit in stating the obvious relationships among elements. In English, however, we want connections to be as explicit as possible. Do Exercise 39-5.

Each pronoun should remind the readers of someone or some idea to which they have been introduced at an earlier point in the text. If, on the other hand, you use vague or broad pronouns, the readers will be confused and wonder whether they have forgotten or misunderstood something. Each pronoun should have a clear purpose. Try Exercise 39-6.

Conjunctions and transitional expressions are stage directions for the readers. If you use these devices, you can direct your readers' thoughts to your analysis of the issues. Otherwise, the readers must attempt to formulate their own ideas about the relationship you have implied.

39d. Improving Style

Often you are glad that you are able to express an idea at all. Then, you are asked to "improve" on that hard-won text. It is not always easy to make your composition more appropriate; at first, you should read writings that do what you want to do in your own composition. If you want to write technical articles, read technical journals. If you want to write an informal essay about your life, ask the librarian for other informal autobiographies. Before you can write appropriate compositions, you must have read many appropriate writings.

39e. Editing Grammar, Punctuation, and Mechanics

Editing your composition for errors in grammar, punctuation, and mechanics is the easiest part of the editing process. It is very simple to change *recieve* [sic] to *receive*, especially with a word processor. Of course, you must spend time looking for and ironing out these problems. Even a word processor wills not catch the grammatical error in this sentence. Did you? Use the following checklist *in addition* to the checklist in the handbook. This list deals mainly with situations that an ESL writer might encounter.

1. ***Fragments***: Does every sentence have at least one tensed verb form? Is there a subject in every sentence except imperatives?
    Test: Can you circle a tense marker?
    Example: The gentlemen running home. He opened the door. There is no tense marker in the first sentence. Remember *-ing* is not a tense marker. In the second sentence, *opened* has the *-ed* tense marker.

2. ***Fused sentences and comma splices:*** Can you make two yes/no questions for one sentence? If you can, is there a comma and a coordinating conjunction [*but, and, or,* and less frequently used *so* and *for*] OR a semicolon *between* each independent clause? If there isn't, you have a comma splice or a fused sentence.
    Test: Draw circles around each independent clause. Is there a semicolon or a comma and a coordinating conjunction between each pair of circles?
    Example: The shoppers ran madly out of the store a man was threatening to turn the pet alligators loose.
    Test: Draw circles around each independent clause. [The shoppers ran madly out of the store] [a man was threatening to turn the pet alligators loose]. There is nothing between the clauses; it is a *fused* sentence.